W9-DHL-654

DATE DUE

Sex,
Pornography,
and Justice

SEX, PORNOGRAPHY, and JUSTICE

By
ALBERT B. GERBER

LYLE
STUART
INC.
NEW
YORK

Published by Lyle Stuart, Inc.
239 Park Avenue South
New York, N.Y., 10003
© Copyright 1965 by Albert B. Gerber
Library of Congress Catalog Card Number: 65-20566
Designed by Peter Bergman
Manufactured in the United States of America

To

RHONA,

CHARLOT,

and

ONYA

CONTENTS

TABLE OF ILLUSTRATIONS

Sex,
Pornography,
and Justice

I

Clarification

WHAT AND WHY

In the Middle Ages debating monks were fond of topics such as "How many angels can dance on the head of a pin?" In discussing such a subject, the debater can demonstrate erudition, semantic skills, and imagination. There is little need for, and practically no room for, intellectual honesty. Much of the discussion of "obscenity" resembles a pre-Renaissance debate. Even the conclusions are similar.

In the late 1920's the League of Nations sponsored an international conference on "The Suppression of International Traffic in Obscene Materials." The agenda called for a definition of terms. Consequently, the first task of the participants was to define the term "obscenity." For two and a half days the learned representatives of some thirty-five countries discussed, debated, and wrangled. Finally they reached almost unanimous agreement that the term "obscenity" could not be defined. Thereupon, having decided that they did not really know what they were talking about, they began to advocate ways and means of suppressing *IT*—whatever *IT* was!

For purpose of clarification, then—and not for purpose of definition—the term *obscenity* as used in this book will refer to material in its relationship to the law. In other words *obscenity* will be employed as a legal term. The laws of almost every state of the United States and of most nations have specific written statutes, ordinances, or codes which prohibit the sale or distribution of material which the law regards as *obscene*. Do not be misled! This is not a definition; it is a legal conclusion. Once the judge, the court, the Post Office Department, or any other

15

body with jurisdiction decides that a particular item is *obscene*, then that object becomes obscene. In some cases the material may bear no relevance to what the reader or observer regards as obscene. However, as a legal conclusion, the item is obscene. For example, in a test case involving John H. Griffin's *The Devil Rides Outside*, the Recorder's Court of Detroit made the initial decision, categorizing the book as obscene. When the Michigan Supreme Court refused to hear an appeal, this book for a time became legally obscene in Michigan. Eventually, the United States Supreme Court unanimously reversed the decision and thereafter the book was no longer obscene any place in the United States. (Full discussion of the case will appear later in the section dealing with the History of Obscenity.)

Griffin wrote his book in 1952 and the case was decided in 1957. It is possible to state with complete confidence that neither at the time the book was written, nor at the time the Supreme Court heard the case, nor today, would anyone with the slightest objectivity call *The Devil Rides Outside* "obscene" or apply to it any of the synonyms such as *lewd, lascivious, pornographic, filthy, indecent,* or *disgusting.* The book is a poignant, simple, and tender story of a young musician and his experiences in a monastery. It contains no *graffiti,* no significant sexual passages, practically no sex, and yet it must be discussed as *obscene* because this was the legal conclusion of duly constituted authority and respectable courts.

Tropic of Cancer rounds out the other view of this picture. It contains all the *graffiti* and the candid details of sex that one could possible imagine, yet it is not *obscene* today because the Supreme Court of the United States decided that it was not obscene.[1] However, that useful word *pornographic* can be applied to this material because it is simply a descriptive adjective and not a legal conclusion. Of course, describing *Tropic of Cancer* or any other book as pornographic depends entirely upon the apperceptive background of the reader. The major

16

purpose here is to agree on semantics in order to achieve communication.

Going back to the basic meanings of the words gives little assistance. The word *obscene* comes from the Latin *obscenus,* which meant *inauspicious* in the sense that, after taking the various tests for omens and asking the oracles, the conclusion was negative. From this came the meaning *adverse,* and subsequently *obscene* began to be used as a synonym for not decent, then filthy, disgusting, and the like. The word *pornography* comes from two Greek words: *porne* (a prostitute), and *graphos* (writing about); thus, the word originally referred to writings concerning prostitutes and later came to refer to writings or pictures concerning sexual matters. Today, the term is employed even to describe a radio broadcast, a song, or a nightclub act. This produces quite a strain on a word that originally meant written material. However, many of the words in this field have little precise meaning any more. Inasmuch as it is impossible to use terminology without the existence of scientific terms, the dimensions of this problem are apparent.

In any case, the term *obscene* is used wherever possible to refer to the legal contention that an item so described has run or may run afoul of some legal prohibition. The term *pornographic* is used to describe material which many people would regard as sexy, usually candid with respect to sex items, and material relating to or descriptive of nudism, homosexuality, and similiar topics.

A third term occasionally employed in this book is *scatological.* This comes from the Greek *skatos,* which was the word for dung, and *ology* which refers to the study of. Here is a word that deals with the study of excrement and, when placed in an adjectival sense to describe an item, connotes overly candid description or depiction of human or animal excrement.

Some writers and judges lump all of these materials together and call them *pornographic.* However, this is erroneous, because the basic element of pornography is that it will arouse sexual interest in a normal adult, and scatological items tend to destroy sexual interest.

Legislatures and courts use a lexicon of additional words, in this field, including: lewd, lascivious, indecent, filthy, dirty, licentious, lustful, prurient, and scurrilous. However, these synonyms add nothing to the picture and, except where reference is required by the context, will be omitted from this book as terms of description or analysis.

THE SHIFTING, CHANGING SCENE

The entire field of *obscenity* and *pornography* is constantly changing. The alterations occur so rapidly that it would take a congress of sociologists, psychologists, and lawyers to give any accurate descriptions of the status of either field at a given moment. This fluidity was not always so apparent. Twenty-five years ago decisions were comparatively simple, but there was little freedom. The Catholics had just formed the National Legion of Decency, which was succeeded by the National Organization for Decent Literature in 1938. These organizations listed as indecent any items of fact or fiction to which any mid-Victorian spinster or minister might object. A partial list of the objectional books over the years includes[2] Nelson Algren *The Man with the Golden Arm,* Niven Busch *Duel in the Sun,* C. S. Forester *The African Queen,* Ernest Hemingway *A Farwell to Arms,* James A. Michener *Tales of the South Pacific,* Christopher Morley *Kitty Foyle,* John Dos Passos *The 42nd Parallel.* Nor was the list restricted to fiction. It also included *The Sexual Side of Marriage* by M. J. Exner, M.D., *How Shall I Tell My Child* by Belle S. Mooney, M.D., and *The Story of My Psychoanalysis* by John Knight.

The trial courts submitted the matters to the juries, and the juries convicted. The appellate courts were loath to take jurisdiction on appeals. Where an absolute right to appeal existed, the upper courts generally affirmed.

A wave of fresh air had come from the Federal courts when a brilliant Federal judge cleared *Ulysses* in 1933, but by and large lawyers knew that any offbeat sexual material could get their clients into trouble. An examination of hundreds of books and magazines had to be made for clients to endeavor to insure them against criminal prosecution. Arbitrary rules had to be set up on the basis of fragmentary dicta enunciated by judges and holdings in various courts throughout the country. Decolletage was all right provided it went no further than the nipple. The nipple of a woman's breast was taboo. Only an outside view of the thigh was permissible. The inside of the thigh raised questions. (This came from the movie censorship by the Hays office.)

All four-letter words were taboo unless used in a dictionary or similar scholarly work relating to semantics. Descriptions of sex had to be circumspect. If the writer was overly candid the book was certainly going to cause difficulty. Finally, lawyers had to make decisions with respect to "extrasensory taboos." For example, sex could never be mixed with patriotism. The girl in the bikini might be all right alone, but she became taboo if her bra or panties were red, white, and blue or if she held an American flag or other patriotic symbol. This type of portrayal infuriated the superpatriots and the veterans' groups. (There appears to be a strong affinity between right-wing groups and anti-pornography groups. On October 17, 1964, outside Philadelphia, a group held a meeting to devise ways and means of fighting pornography locally. Tickets were sold for $1.00 each and could be obtained only from a box number—the same box number used by the local John Birch Society to sell its literature.)

Much of this confusion and need for individual decision has

now changed. With the United States Supreme Court taking jurisdiction in more cases than ever, much that was formerly taboo is now permissible. A current story illustrates the point.

A young woman, unable to stop her car in time, ploughed into the rear of a truck. The truck driver clambered down from his cab bellowing four-letter words at whoever was responsible for the mishap. The girl listened in rapt wonderment, and finally exclaimed enthusiastically, "That's marvelous! I thought those words were only used in books!"

Volumes could be written about that little bit of humor. To-day, as more and more people acquire or are subjected to edu-cation, the four-letter words are falling into disuse. (In the Armed Forces though the situation is probably still un-changed.) In the late twenties and most of the thirties four-letter words spiced a locker room conversation like salt on food. In the sixties these words have all but disappeared. They emerge now primarily from the lips of teenagers who use them as attention-getters, simulating maturity, etc. Scholars have recognized that a person with a rich vocabulary does not require profanity to express himself. Obviously, people today are in-creasing the wealth of their vocabularies. Engage in conver-sation with elevator operators, taxi drivers, porters, and bell-hops and behold a richness of language that does not need profanity. If television—the wonder and the drug of this age—has accomplished nothing else, it has made its contribution to a more diversified vocabulary for the less well-educated seg-ments of the population who in past decades kept the four-letter words alive.

This may partially explain why the use of the profane four-letter words is now permitted in literature. The words cease to be shocking and start to sound archaic. No one would today get excited at the use of the word *drit* to describe excrement. How-ever, it was the original Anglo-Saxon term and from it we got the word *dirty*.

THE OTHER SIDE OF THE COIN OF TIME

As society today retreats from the high-water mark of mid-Victorian morality, the theories of what constitutes legal obscenity change to meet the ever-changing needs and thoughts of the people. However, among the cast of characters involved in this drama a fatigue factor may be setting in. People go along to one point or another and then drop off or switch their views. Some few—but very few—remain consistent to principle throughout; that is, either to the principle that practically all is obscene or to the principle that freedom is more important than restriction. Here are two brief, recent, significant examples:

The modern theory of legal obscenity began to evolve with the United States Supreme Court opinions of 1957. In these the Chief Justice was a stalwart exponent of freedom. In the *Kingsley Books*[3] case the New York City Corporation counsel brought an action under a statute[4] to prevent booksellers from selling a series of books entitled *Nights of Horror*. The New York courts, including the highest court (Court of Appeals), affirmed the obscenity of the books and prohibited their sale. Since it was a new and novel statute, the case was appealed to the United States Supreme Court, which in a five-to-four decision, sustained the statute. The most important part of the case was a vigorous dissent by Chief Justice Earl Warren:

> This is not a criminal obscenity case. Nor is it a case ordering the destruction of materials disseminated by a person who has been convicted of an offense for doing so, as would be authorized under provisions in the laws of New York and other states. It is a case wherein the New York police, under a different state law, located books which, in their opinion, were unfit for public use because of obscenity and then obtained a court order for their condemnation and destruction.
>
> The majority opinion sanctions this proceeding. I would not. This New York law places the *book* on trial. There is

21

totally lacking any standard in the statute for judging the book in context. The personal element basic to the criminal laws is entirely absent. In my judgment, the same object may have wholly different impact depending upon the setting in which it is placed. Under this statute, the setting is irrelevant.

It is the manner of use that should determine obscenity. It is the conduct of the individual that should be judged, not the quality of art or literature. To do otherwise is to impose a prior restraint and hence to violate the Constitution. Certainly in the absence of a prior judicial determination of illegal use, books, pictures and other objects of expression should not be destroyed. It savors too much of book burning.

I would reverse.

Throughout the following seven years, the Chief Justice remained firmly on the side of freedom. True, he did not adopt Justice Black's theory that the Constitution prohibited *any* form of censorship, including the censorship of obscenity. Also, he did not follow Justice Douglas in his theory that unless the material in question created danger of a criminal act it should not be censored. But he did have a theory of his own that the conduct of the defendant, and not material in the abstract, is what should be punished.

In his dissent in the *Times Film*[5] case (which contains that rarity—the Chief Justice writing for Justices Black, Douglas, and Brennan), he wrote an opinion which has been aptly described as "long, impassioned, and brilliant."[6] In part, the Chief Justice said:

> I cannot agree either with the conclusion reached by the Court or with the reasons advanced for its support. To me this case clearly presents the question of our approval of unlimited censorship of motion pictures *before* exhibition through a system of administrative licensing. Moreover, the decision presents a real danger of eventual censorship for every form of communication, be it newspapers, journals, books, magazines, television, radio or public speeches. The Court purports to leave these questions for another day, but I am aware of no

constitutional principle which permits us to hold that the communication of ideas through one medium may be censored while other media are immune.

* * * * *

It would seem idle to suppose that the Court today is unaware of the evils of the censor's basic authority, of the mischief of the system against which so many great men have waged stubborn and often precarious warfare for centuries, of the scheme that impedes all communication by hanging threateningly over creative thought.

* * * * *

There is no sign that Milton's fear of the censor would be dispelled in twentieth century America. The censor is beholden to those who sponsored the creation of his office, to those who are most radically preoccupied with the suppression of communication. The censor's function is to restrict and to restrain; his decisions are insulated from the pressures that might be brought to bear by public sentiment if the public were given an opportunity to see that which the censor has curbed.

* * * * *

A revelation of the extent to which censorship has recently been used in this country is indeed astonishing. The Chicago licensors have banned newsreel films of Chicago policemen shooting at labor pickets and have ordered the deletion of a scene depicting the birth of a buffalo in Walt Disney's *Vanishing Prairie*. Before World War II, the Chicago censor denied licenses to a number of films portraying and criticizing life in Nazi Germany, including the March of Time's *Inside Nazi Germany*. Recently, Chicago refused to issue a permit for the exhibition of the motion picture *Anatomy of a Murder* based upon the best-selling novel of the same title, because it found the use of the words "rape" and "contraceptive" to be objectionable. The Chicago censor bureau excised a scene in *Street With No Name* in which a girl was slapped because this was thought to be a "too violent" episode. *It Happened in Europe* was severely cut by the Ohio censors who deleted scenes of war orphans resorting to violence. The moral theme of the picture was that such children could even then be saved by love, affection and satisfaction of their basic needs for food.

The Memphis censors banned *The Southerner* which dealt with poverty among tenant farmers because "it reflects on the south." *Brewster's Millions,* an innocuous comedy of fifty years ago, was recently forbidden in Memphis because the radio and film character Rochester, a Negro, was deemed "too familiar." Maryland censors restricted a Polish documentary film on the basis that it failed to present a true picture of modern Poland. *No Way Out,* the story of a Negro doctor's struggle against race prejudice, was banned by the Chicago censor on the ground that "there's a possibility it could cause trouble." The principal objection to the film was that the conclusion showed no reconciliation between blacks and whites. The ban was lifted after a storm of protest and later deletion of a scene showing Negroes and whites arming for a gang fight.

Memphis banned *Curley* because it contained scenes of white and Negro children in school together. Atlanta barred *Lost Boundaries,* the story of a Negro physician and his family who "passed" for white, on the ground that the exhibition of said picture "will adversely affect the peace, morals and good order" in the city. *Witchcraft,* a study of superstition through the ages, was suppressed for years because it depicted the devil as a genial rake with amorous leanings, and because it was feared that certain historical scenes, portraying the excesses of religious fanatics, might offend religion. *Scarface,* thought by some as the best of the gangster films, was held up for months; then it was so badly mutilated that retakes costing a hundred thousand dollars were required to preserve continuity. The New York censors banned *Damaged Lives,* a film dealing with venereal disease, although it treated a difficult theme with dignity and had the sponsorship of the American Social Hygiene Society. The picture of Lenin's tomb bearing the inscription "Religion is the opiate of the people" was excised from *Potemkin.* From *Joan of Arc* the Maryland Board eliminated Joan's exclamation as she stood at the stake: "Oh, God,

24

why hast thou forsaken me?" and from *Idiot's Delight,* the sentence: "We, the workers of the world, will take care of that." *Professor Mamlock* was produced in Russia and portrayed the persecution of the Jews by Nazis. The Ohio censors condemned it as "harmful" and calculated to "stir up hatred and ill will and gain nothing." It was released only after substantial deletions were made. The police refused to permit its showing in Providence, Rhode Island, on the ground that it was communistic propaganda. *Millions of Us,* a strong union propaganda film, encountered trouble in a number of jurisdictions. *Spanish Earth,* a pro-Loyalist documentary picture, was banned by the Board in Pennsylvania.

During the year ending June 30, 1938, the New York Board censored, in one way or another, over five percent of the moving pictures it reviewed. Charlie Chaplin's satire on Hitler, *The Great Dictator,* was banned in Chicago, apparently out of deference to Chicago's large German population. Ohio and Kansas banned newsreels considered pro labor. Kansas ordered a speech by Senator Wheeler opposing the bill for enlarging the Supreme Court to be cut from the March of Time as "partisan and biased." An early version of *Carmen* was condemned on several different grounds. The Ohio censor objected because cigarette-girls smoked cigarettes in public. The Pennsylvania censor disapproved the duration of a kiss. The New York censors forbade the discussion in films of pregnancy, venereal disease, eugenics, birth control, abortion, illegitimacy, prostitution, miscegenation, and divorce.

A member of the Chicago censor board explained that she rejected a film because "it was immoral, corrupt, indecent, against my . . . religious principles." A police sergeant attached to the censor board explained, "Coarse language or anything that would be derogatory to the government—propaganda—is ruled out of foreign films." "Nothing pink or red is allowed," he added. The police sergeant in charge of the censor unit has said, "Children should be allowed to see any movie that plays in Chicago. If a picture is objectionable for a child, it is objectionable period." And this is but a smattering produced from limited research. Perhaps the most powerful indictment of Chicago's licensing device is found in the fact that between the Court's decision in 1952 in *Joseph Burstyn, Inc. v. Wilson,* and the present case, not once have the state courts upheld the censor when the exhibitor elected to appeal.

This is the regimen to which the Court holds that all films must be submitted. It officially unleashes the censor and permits him to roam at will, limited only by an ordinance which contains some standards that, although concededly not before us in this case, are patently imprecise. The Chicago ordinance commands the censor to reject films that are "immoral," or those that portray "depravity, criminality, or lack of virtue of a class of citizens of any race, color, creed, or religion and (expose) them to contempt, derision, or obloquy, or (tend) to produce a breach of the peace or riots, or (purport) to represent any hanging, lynching, or burning of a human being." May it not be said that almost every censored motion picture that was cited above could also be rejected, under the ordinance, by the Chicago censors? It does not require an active imagination to conceive of the quantum of ideas that will surely be suppressed.

These are the words of a fighter. This is a man, a student, a scholar, a judge, who will not, in the name of morality, expediency, or otherwise, permit censorship. Inevitably time creates change. In 1964 (six years and many cases later), in a case of no particular significance involving the criminal prosecution of the manager of a small Ohio theater for showing a movie called *Les Amants* [The Lovers], the Chief Justice is ready to uphold the conviction of the theater manager who was fined $2,500 for his action and sentenced to the workhouse if the fine was not paid.[7] Anyone who has seen this movie must agree that it contained little to censor. But the Supreme Court had been bombarded with cases from all the states and neither the Chief Justice nor the Supreme Court wanted this state of affairs to continue, so the Chief Justice said:

> . . . protection of society's right to maintain its moral fiber and the effective administration of justice require that this Court not establish itself as an ultimate censor, in each case reading the entire record, viewing the accused material, and making

an independent *de novo* judgment on the question of obscenity.

This theory holds that once a proper test had been made and a respectable court had found obscenity, the existence of reasonable evidence to support the finding should end the matter. He concludes: "This is the only reasonable way I can see to obviate the necessity of this Court's sitting as the Super Censor of all the obscenity purveyed throughout the Nation." A careful reading of these words suggests that the Chief Justice has grown weary of his responsibilities in the field of censorship and would grant the Court a respite from the multitude of cases clamoring for a final definition.

Fortunately for those who are proponents of freedom four justices remain adamant against inroads on liberty. This grouping consists of Justices Black, Douglas, Brennan, and Stewart. Justice Byron White is in the middle, and Justices Clark and Harlan, now joined by the Chief Justice, form the militant minority who are proponents of a tight rein on judicial interference. Judge Abe Fortas is an unknown.

ARE *LIFE'S* ARTERIES HARDENING?

Just as individuals fall by the wayside, giving up the battle against censorship, institutions switch allegiance. *Life Magazine* presents an excellent illustration of this type of change.

In 1938 *Life,* combined with *Life Magazine,* under the stewardship of Roy Larsen, a courageous editor and publisher, ran an article, profusely illustrated with photographs, on the subject of how a baby is born. The report contained diagrams of anatomy and stills from a motion picture entitled *The Birth of a Baby.* In spite of the fact that the story was in good taste, accurate, and scientific in tone and content, it set off a storm among the Comstocks and precipitated an attack by an important Catholic organization. In many states street corner newsstand proprietors were arrested for offering that particular issue of the magazine for sale, and in New York the District Attorney arrested the publisher. The main case came before a three-judge criminal court in Bronx County. Justice Nathan D. Perlman wrote the unanimous opinion[8] of the court in its acquittal of Editor Larsen:

> Conceptions of what is decent or indecent are not constant. The early attitude of the Courts upon this subject is not reflected in the recent cases. The trends to be observed in the cases have mirrored changing popular attitudes. Recent cases illustrate the caution with which Courts have proceeded in this branch of the law to avoid interference with a justifiable freedom of expression.

> * * * * *

> The Court is aware of the fact that the prosecution might well have produced honest and responsible individuals who may differ widely as to the expediency of presenting this type of picture story. This honest difference of opinion, however, demonstrates the necessity of avoiding arbitrary censorship by a Court.

> My own conclusion is that the picture story, because of the manner in which it was presented, does not fall within the forbidden class. The picture story was directly based on a film produced under the auspices of a responsible medical group. There is no nudity or unnecessary disclosure. The subject has been treated with delicacy.

That was in 1938. In 1963 Judge J. Irwin Shapiro of the Supreme Court, Queens County, had before him a series of *Nightstand Books* (these books are discussed in more detail in another section) and the judge dismissed the indictment in an outstanding opinion:[9]

The books contain a great number of descriptions of sexual activity which, in many cases, are only tenuously associated with the plot and story line. They thus, no doubt, provide erotic reading material, but no more so than many works of literature which have received acclaim as classics. In that connection it should be remembered that the fact "that adulterous or other sexually immoral relationships are portrayed approvingly cannot serve as a reason for declaring a work obscene without running afoul of the First Amendment" . . . because the constitution protects "advocacy of the opinion that adultery may sometimes be proper, no less than advocacy of socialism or the single tax. . . ."

Writings which have received favorable recognition in all types of civilizations, in all ages, have delineated societies' cultures and the relationship of the individual to them. Throughout the annals of recorded history, these have been writers who failed to achieve the higher plateaus of literature and art. Their failure to achieve literary recognition does not thereby make their works more objectionable, legally or morally, than that of the writer who merits, or receives, the high acclaim of the critical community for his literary style and grace. . . .

The civilizations of the past provide the basis for our modern culture and society. Literature,—good, bad and indifferent,— has been the tissue which formed the umbilical cord nurturing all societies from Homeric Greece to the present. The passage of time has seen honors bestowed upon authors whose writings are replete with words and incidents that were deemed lurid and pornographic contemporaneously with their appearance. Aristophanes, Plautus, Shakespeare, Brinsley, Swift, Boccaccio, Rabelais and Balzac, to name just a few, are *now* noted and recognized for the vigor of their writings and for the artful way in which they delineated and portrayed the ethical and moral conditions of their times. They were not always so regarded, however. and many of their works were attacked and ridiculed by those of tender sensibilities upon the same basis that the finger of accusation is pointed at the books here under scrutiny.

Nothing is truer than that with the passage of time we constantly see a reshuffling of the gods in the world's literary pantheon. We should therefore proceed with the utmost caution before determining, *as a matter of constitutional judgment* that those who write about the serpent in Eden, in their own way, should have their writings banned and that they themselves should be denominated criminals.

Words which are not in use (supposedly) in polite society and are denoted as "four letter" words do not in and of themselves make for obscenity. If they did "The Arabian Nights," just to cite one accepted classic, would require suppression. Many readers may be disgusted or revolted by the use of foul language but the scenes that are depicted thereby are not, in context, necessarily pornographic. . . .

Most books which have been heretofore attacked as obscene and pornographic, and which have been defended as having over-all literary merit, have presented a problem in research which usually consisted of a detailed search for "four letter" words, phrases and descriptions which could be lifted from the text to provide a basis for their indictment as pornographic. The books here offer no such problem for they contain no "four letter" words. So far as the purity of the language used is concerned the books could well be made required reading for fourth year elementary students. Fully 90% of each book, however, is filled with lurid descriptions of sexual activities, both hetero and homosexual, in sufficient detail to act as an erotic stimulus to those so inclined. However, in all their erotic descriptions they maintain a clever, and apparently deliberate, avoidance of socially unacceptable language, and the descriptions of erotic activity are so similar, in language and action, as to appear to be written by one author using one outline for all the books. Even those books which have a stronger plot and story line reflect this outline in the description of the sexual scene. Page after page contains details and descriptions of similar erotic behavior. In that respect they remind one of the similiarity of all the Horatio Alger stories of this Court's youthful days except that the latter dealt with the rise from "Rags to Riches" and these books deal with the march from "Puberty to Prostitution."

In the opinion of the Court (compelled by statute to act as a literary critic) these books are plain unvarnished trash, but novels and stories of no literary merit have a place in our society. There are those who, because of lack of education, the meanness of their social existence, or mental insufficiency, cannot cope with anything better. Slick paper confessions, pulp adventure and "comic book" type of magazines provide them with an escape from reality. However, the fringes of society are not the only cover for those neurotics unable to satisfy their sexual needs through acceptable outlets. Events of the past and present tell us that. So called pillars of society number among them men and women whose sexual outlet is the eroticism of literature and pictures designed to relieve their libidinous repressions. . . . Many of these people provide a ready, although, no doubt, clandestine market for the pornographic. As Sigmund Freud, the contentious founder of psycho-analysis and one whose own writings many no doubt would like to see suppressed, said in his "Wit and Its Relation to the Unconscious," . . . "common people so thoroughly enjoy such smutty talk, . . . that it is a never lacking activity of cheerful humor. . . ."

In a pluralistic society, such as ours, censorship is neither truly possible nor, in the opinion of many, either desirable or legal. . . . If the flow of what is considered offensive literature is to be dammed it should be done by the exercise of censorship in the home and not by judicial fiat. Undue legal restraint must be guarded against since the exercise of censorship tends to feed upon itself and to extend into, and encroach upon, areas of personal liberties which are the very foundation of a free society. We should not attempt to suppress writings dealing with those sorrier aspects of human behavior in our national life that most of us, had we the choice, would change.

G. Rattray Taylor in "Sex in History" discusses the medieval style of nakedness. In his chapter on "Medieval Sexual Behavior," he describes a scene, in conformity with the practice of those days when outstanding personalities were being honored, in which ". . . the Queen of Ulster and all the ladies of the Court, to the number of 610, came to meet Cuchulainn, naked above the waist and raising their skirts so as to expose their private parts, by which they showed how greatly they honored him."

Just as the pendulum of public taste and manners has swung far away from such presently considered crude behavior, it has also swung far past the repressions of prurient and prudish Victoria. Today, skirts are shorter and the outlined erogenous areas of women are taken matter-of-factly. The undergarment model has dropped the mask from her eyes and looks at you slyly as she displays the advantage of any-brand's bra and girdle in advertisements published by ladies' magazines and our most respected newspapers, and in telecasts coming into the home. These media reflect the trends of the times. In addition, many children are dressed in suggestive clothing, the boys in skin tight trousers and the girls in revealing bodily outlines; the adolescent drives the family car, with his girl friend, to a drive-in-movie where they see sex comedies which make light of pre-marital and extra-marital sexual relations. Sex and sophistication surround them. A single page of one of our metropolitan newspapers contains reviews or advertisements of a number of motion pictures variously described as follows: "a romp of bawdy tales completely in the Gallic tradition that sex dalliance is the funniest topic on earth"; "loaded with burlesque seductions, orgies" and a description of the actress "who plays the mistress"; "a bold, sexy, disquieting film."

Such, whether we approve or disapprove, is the temper of our times and it is in that light that one must determine whether the books here are obscene for "the community cannot where liability of speech and press are at issue, condemn that which it generally tolerates. . . ."

It is of the utmost importance in this field that judges be not motivated to assume the guise of censors by reason of personal predilections, and that decisions be not dictated by their personal whims with little consideration given to the fact that liberty is not divisible and that when we deny its privileges to others we place our own in jeopardy, or by pressure *sub-consciously* exerted by groups of well-meaning vigilante guardians of the public morals who often refuse to recognize that free societies are dynamic and that literature and art, *and badly written books too,* are merely the mirror reflections of some phase of existing life. Truth, so evidenced, is often bitter and distasteful, but so are many facets of our existence for there is a "huge and disproportionate abundance of evil" on earth. . . .

Totalitarian-dictated monotonous conformity in the use of the written word is too great a price to pay to receive the approbation of the ultra sensitive or the easily psychically devastated. Writing can reflect the changes which are taking place in a culture or they may lead a society to change. What is good or bad in the past or present, or may be in the future, is described by perceptive writers in various ways and many dialects.

If any of these eight books truthfully picture any considerable segment of our society, we may be doomed to the same destruction which befell the hedonistic, voulpturian civilizations of Greece and Rome, and Hamlet's disillusionment and disgust with the world as being "no other thing than a foul and pestilent congregation of vapors" could find little dissent.

However, whether the word portraits painted in these eight books are an accurate recital of existing conditions or are pure fantasy, to attempt to blot out the portrayal by judicial censorship would be completely unavailing just as the book burners of old did not by the flames of their fires succeed in consuming the truth contained in those books. Any such attempted prohibition of books, in the long run, will be no more effective than our last noble experiment, the liquor prohibition amendment.

After this opinion appeared, *Life Magazine*[10] made unfavorable comment in an editorial, stating:

Is Any Book
Legally Obscene
Any More?

A first-class book critic, Stanley Edgar Hyman, recently gave his readers in *The New Leader* a systematic "Defense of Pornography." [11] Reviewing a couple of books which he found obscene, worthless, and "suppressible under the Law," he added that "the law is wrong. Neither book should be banned. In fact, no publication should be banned." He went on to defend pornography for the reason usually held against it—that it induces lascivious thoughts and (possible) behavior. Even books without literary merit are either "harmless or beneficial" to a society which, said Hyman, suffers from too much guilt about sex.

That's the unorthodox view of a literary man. But a few days later a New York Supreme Court justice, J. Erwin Shapiro, said almost the same thing in an official decision. He had before him a batch of books which he called "profane, offensive, disgusting and plain unvarnished trash," but he refused to call them legally obscene. The judge's reasoning should be of interest to parents as well as lawyers and publishers.

In the Roth and Alberts cases (1957) the U.S. Supreme Court gave its first official definition of obscenity. It extended the protection of the First Amendment to "all ideas having even the slightest redeeming social importance," the lack of which is one test of obscenity. The other is whether "to the average person, applying contemporary community standards, the dominant theme of the material taken as a whole appeals to prurient interest." On this test the Supreme Court declared the material then before it obscene, although Black and Douglas dissented on the ground that "the test that suppresses a cheap tract today can suppress a literary gem tomorrow." The Shapiro decision turns their apprehension upside down.

Reluctantly, Shapiro felt obliged to read some twenty-five pieces of lewd trash (*Sex Kitten, Hill-billy, Nympho, etc.*) and to be their critic "because the law in its present state requires just that." The books all had the same plot (which Shapiro described as "from puberty to prostitution") and no pretense of literary merit. In that respect they differed from Henry Miller's *Tropic of Cancer,* which has litigated its way to freedom in several states because critics have persuaded the judges of Miller's "serious purpose." Indeed the trend of obscenity decisions is such that no work of recognizable literary merit, whatever its lingo or subject, is in much danger of suppression if its publisher is willing to fight for it in court. Now, if the Shapiro view holds, works of no merit are equally safe.

Is obscenity, then, an obsolete concept? Not quite. Even Shapiro made a point of the absence of four-letter words in his "bundle of trash" (another difference from Miller) and said the books were not "hard-core pornography." But he rejected the "literary merit" argument on the democratic ground that the mean and uneducated who "cannot cope with anything better" than trash are entitled to their "escape from reality." He met the "contemporary community standards" test by deciding that these are pretty low. His decision, obviously, is not going to make them any higher.

The history of literary censorship is not a pretty one. Percy Bysshe Shelley, Walt Whitman, George Bernard Shaw, Theodore Dreiser, D. H. Lawrence, James Joyce, are just a few of the great writers who have been pronounced unprintable by one official bluenose or another. But Anthony Comstock has been dead since 1915, and the United States, thanks largely to the Supreme Court, is now almost censor-free by civilized standards. This widening of freedom has been good for art, letters and our cultural level.

An ideal society would let anything be printed. But so long as professional pornographers exist, no state is likely to repeal its obscenity statutes. And there is danger that if our courts become too permissive, a public reaction will bring Comstock roaring back from his grave.

Definitions of obscenity—even of "hard-core pronography"—are inherently imprecise and changeable. But besides the lack of "redeeming social importance" there is another test which Warren relied on in the Roth case. It is the motive of the purveyor—what Frankfurter once called "dirt for dirt's sake, or more exactly for money's sake." Although reputable publishers and authors are doubtless guilty of this motive in isolated passages, a discriminating judge should be able to recognize pure dirt from its total lack of other values or motives, and acknowledge that the public has a right to keep it off the street. The Shapiro doctrine is too permissive and should not survive.

Thus, as it has always been, the oppressed become the oppressors and those who were once victims of the censor's knife begin to wield it.

THE FORMAT AND *RAISON D'ETRE*

Unlike such topics as nuclear fission, finding a cure or preventive for cancer, or the elimination of poverty throughout the world, *obscenity* is not really a major international problem. Certainly early legal doctrine on the subject acted as a drag on the wheels of intellectual and artistic progress; nevertheless men of letters and the arts achieved success to the extent that they ignored the doctrine. Although obscenity is not at the top of the list of pressing issues of the day, probably as much has been written about this problem as about many more urgent dilemmas of society at the moment. This is primarily because most people with any leaning toward literary expression who investigate this problem are fascinated by its labyrinthian maze. While libraries have been filled with discussions of the problem of obscenity, it has become mandatory for any new book to have a *raison d'etre* to merit publication, circulation, and reading. It is respectfully submitted that, since this is the first time that the legal case analysis has been combined with an actual sample of the subject matter under discussion, there is sufficient significance to merit the attention of all those interested in this field.

The stimulus which gave rise to this book may best illustrate its need. Not long ago I was arguing a case before a three-judge court and the question arose as to whether certain magazines could be regarded as obscene under applicable constitutional standards. One judge, obviously no expert in the field, leaned forward with some asperity: "I have looked at the nudist magazines involved in this case and I don't think such magazines have ever been held entitled to constitutional protection. These magazines actually show male and female together, completely nude, with genitals and pubic hair clearly evident!"

The judge obviously expected me to fold under that attack, but I answered as factually as possible, "Your honor, if you will look at the case of *Sunshine & Health vs. Summerfield*,[12] you will find that the United States Supreme Court granted constitutional protection to a nudist magazine which had photographs of both male and female in the same picture with genitals and pubic hair showing."

The judge, surprised momentarily, quickly recovered, and asked, "Counselor, do you have a copy of the magazine involved in that case?"

I was reluctantly forced to reply in the negative.

The judge firmly pressed his advantage. "Does the United States Supreme Court mention the exhibition of genitalia and pubic hair?"

Again, I had to reply in the negative. "The United States Supreme Court simply reversed the District of Columbia Court of Appeals without opinion. However," I added hastily, "the opinions in the lower courts make it abundantly clear that there were photographs of men and women in the same picture and that the genitals and pubic hair were not blocked out."

The judge, as judges from time immemorial have done, disregarded this statement. "As far as I'm concerned," he stated triumphantly, "the case is clear. You can't show me the magazine involved in the opinion, and the Supreme Court doesn't mention it, and that's as far as I'll go. I don't believe the case is a precedent."

My inability to produce the magazine lost that round for me. Eventually the case was won, but fifty additional hours of legal work and thousands of dollars of fees and costs were expended needlessly. Then and there I determined to gather together the materials so that next time I, or any other lawyer, became involved in a similar problem the item needed in the case could be produced.

Many attorneys have decried the unavailability of this type of material. A recent book, *Censorship,* written by the dean in this field, Morris L. Ernst, and his associate Alan U. Schwartz, points up this need. The first case discussed in that book is the Pennsylvania case of *Commonwealth vs Sharpless*[13] in which Jesse Sharpless was convicted of exhibiting a "lewd, wicked, scandalous, infamous and obscene painting." The only thing known about the painting is what the judge says: "I hold it to be sufficient to state, that it represented a man in an obscene, impudent, and indecent posture with a woman. . . ." After setting forth the facts, the authors, Ernst and Schwartz, lament, "If only we could now look at the picture for which Sharpless took money and was punished! How would it compare with the "Girly" magazines or with any of the great masterpieces at our most important art museums? Time goes on—attitudes change. Only a few decades ago a woman at a public bathing beach would have been arrested if she were not attired in full-length black stockings and long sleeves to her wrists. Nowadays a woman bathing with stockings and sleeves might well gather a crowd and be arrested for interfering with the dignity and peace of the community."

In order to fill the need, to preserve the evidence, and to give attorneys a long-needed tool in the handling of obscenity cases, many of the more significant items involved in these cases have been gathered together for presentation in the pages which follow.

NATURE OF THE ITEMS PRESENTED

There was little problem in selecting the material in certain cases, because a single picture was involved or the opinion made it clear which item had caused the material to be held obscene. However, in a case like *Doubleday & Co. vs. New York*,[14] in which Edmund Wilson's *Memoirs of Hecate County* was held obscene by the New York Court of Appeals, and the United States Supreme Court divided equally without rendering any opinion, a problem existed. The book contains six stories in 447 pages. "The Princess with the Golden Hair," which appears to be the culprit, runs over 200 pages. Obviously, both book and story are too long to include in anything short of an encyclopedia.

The problem was solved in the following manner: The book was read by a series of people ranging in age from seventeen to fifty, and each received the following directions: "This book was held obscene or accused of obscenity. Read it carefully and select those pages which you regard as most likely to have aroused the censors."

Interestingly enough, most readers agreed on the same page or pages. For example, in the illustration just given (*Memoirs of Hecate County*) everyone selected as the only likely episode the vignette of the sexual intercourse scene between the author and Imogen Loomis. This, of course, is the section found in this book.

In the case of photographs or selections from magazines, the most extreme pictures or items were chosen. In pictures, only the faces were changed, to avoid any accusation of invading the subject's right of privacy. No other retouching was done.

THE POSITION OF THE UNITED STATES TODAY

From time to time the careful reader will detect in this book a note of disappointment where the censor was permitted to interfere with the communication of ideas. Unquestionably, my views lie in the direction of freedom, and I do not like any form of censorship. Therefore, it is only fair to point out that the United States today probably has greater freedom for the communication of ideas than any other country in the world. It is not uncommon to hear that certain countries have a great deal of freedom and that the absence of restraint is superior to that accorded by the courts of the United States. Usually investigation reveals this to be erroneous. As an example, it appears superficially that Australia grants great freedom, but Australia has two significant forms of censorship. One involves the Customs Department, which decides what may or may not be imported according to its interpretation of what is obscene. It is a hindering form of censorship and can be exercised by the authorities so as to make a legal appeal almost impossible. Some of the novels now banned in Australia and permitted in the United States are D. H. Lawrence's *Lady Chatterley's Lover,* John O'Hara's *Butterfield 8,* Gore Vidal's *The City and the Pillar,* and of course, Henry Miller's *Tropic of Cancer.* In addition, for those who feel that Australia may be a Utopia of free thought, it should be mentioned that not only is *obscenity* a ground for censorship in Australia but so also are *blasphemy* and *sedition.*[15] Generally, the United States does not censor either blasphemy or sedition.

France, once the citadel of freedom, is now an extremely restricted area. Much of the censorship in France relates not so much to obscenity as it does to politics. In 1959, for instance, a French publisher issued a book entitled *The Gangrene.* Four days later the French police physically smashed the printer's plates so that no further printings could be made. Subsequently, Lyle Stuart published the book in the United States. *The Gangrene* is basically the story of the tortures used by the deGaulle government to obtain information from those engaged in the Algerian fight for freedom.

Censorship in France now runs the gamut of all forms of the creative arts. For example, in 1945 in the movie field, the Commission of Control was established as a subdivision of the Ministry of Information. Not only does this commission review all completed motion pictures but it insists upon *seeing scripts before shooting has begun,* thus perpetrating a complete system of pre-censorship which causes considerable difficulty for the French producers. When Roger Vadim, first husband of Brigitte Bardot, produced *Liaisons Dangereuses,* he applied for an export permit. The story is a French classic of a husband and wife who agree to take lovers but promise to avoid becoming emotionally involved with them. The film contains nude shots and details of sexual intercourse. The commission, before granting the permit, required a series of changes including the following: In the film the husband held a diplomatic post in the United Nations. The commission insisted on a change in employment for the husband because it reflected on the UN!

A nudist movie entitled *Nudist Paradise* presented a challenge to the nations of the world. On the theory that nudity is obscenity, the film was banned in Mexico, Cyprus, West Germany, France, Australia, Malaysia, Hong Kong, and Ireland. However, the Scandinavian countries, The Netherlands, Belgium, and Great Britain found the film acceptable.

Great Britain, while generally liberal, has reactionary moments. In the movie field England's major problem is the classification system, which has been opposed by producers throughout the world. The British Board of Film Censors grants every film a category under which it is classified either (a) for adults only, (u) universal (can be shown to all), or (x) for adults only, with the warning that the film may be distasteful to many. Interestingly enough, the (x) category is generally applied to films with a considerable amount of criminal conduct and violence rather than those that portray sex misconduct. The British have not been averse to sexual themes in their movies, but their censors oppose violence and criminality.

Even plays are censored in advance in England, primarily to prevent unflattering reflections upon the Royal Family or upon any of the British taboos. The over-all British system of censorship, while not particularly efficacious in limiting the content of books, plays, or movies, does constitute one of the worst examples of pre-censorship.

41

Japan is an excellent example of uneven and ragged censorship. Nudity is an accepted part of the Japanese way of life. Men and women bathe together in public baths. Women attendants supervise the men's rooms. In rural areas the only separation between male and female toilets is a slatted grid-type screen with only the semblance of privacy. Nude shows are common-place. Nevertheless *Tropic of Cancer* was banned for obscenity by the Japanese Supreme Court.[16]

The Soviet Union represents the quintessence of pre-censorship and the suppression of sexual material. When, on his visit to the United States, Nikita Khrushchev took offense at Hollywood's version of *Can-Can,* he was reflecting several decades of indoctrination designed to convince all true Communists of the bourgeois evils of public nudity and sex symbols.

Immediately after the revolution the Reds carried on a brief flirtation with "free love," easy divorce, and *laissez faire* in sex matters, but this did not last long. Joseph Stalin's rise to power brought an official attitude of Puritanism and stern morality in dress and behavior. Thereafter, the depiction of sex, the novels of love, even suggestions of sin, were equated with capitalism and became taboo. One writer recently said, "Never in the history of man's misrule of man have prudery and politics been so successfully combined in the interests of the ruling party as in the Soviet Union."[17] For a time not only were nudity and sex *verboten* but also jazz, rock and roll, abstract art, American-style dancing, and almost any form of modern artistic expression.

Khrushchev, himself a product of this sterile life, brought about a relaxation of the rules. Today, American music and dancing, hot dogs and cokes, and even some painting and sculpture, have been introduced into the major cities—with especial emphasis on youth—to keep the young from becoming stolid, phlegmatic, vodka-drinking prudes, as so many Russians in their late thirties and forties are.

All of this is done under the censor's watchful eye. There is no spontaneity, and the entire atmosphere is artificial. Some predict that the day is not too far distant when the government of the Soviet Union will have sufficient confidence in the people to grant them complete intellectual and artistic freedom. That day is not here yet. Today, every book, every magazine, and every film is either government approved or government permitted. An occasional novel critical of the government may be published, but neither *Playboy* nor *Lady Chatterley's Lover* could circulate behind the Iron Curtain.

In sharp contrast, the United States has made notable progress in freedom of communication of sex matters. At one time almost any four-letter word, scatological reference, or candid sex description was cause for censorship of a book, magazine, or movie. Today, assuming the item is in reasonably good taste, there is little danger of censorship at the highest level. The problems of the overzealous district attorney, the biased lower court judge or magistrate, and the adamant intermediate courts still exist, but these must go with time. It is actually difficult to define the position of the United States today.

Every state in the United States (except New Mexico) has a specific statute making it a crime to exhibit, show, sell (even sometimes possess) an item which can be categorized as obscene. (Even New Mexico has a statute which gives cities, towns, and villages specific statutory power to prohibit the sale or exhibition of obscene or immoral publications, prints, pictures, and the like.)

The statutes of the various states do not differ significantly from each other. A typical statute is found in Penal Law, Section 1141, of the State of New York. This law provides:

> A person who sells, lends, gives away, distributes, shows or transmutes, or offers to sell, lend, give away, distribute, show or transmute, or has in his possession with intent to sell, lend, distribute, give away, show or transmute, or advertise in any manner, or who otherwise offers for loan, gift, sale or distribu-

tion, any obscene, lewd, lascivious, filthy, indecent, sadistic, masochistic or disgusting book, magazine, pamphlet, newspaper, story paper, writing, paper, card, phonograph record, picture, drawing, photograph, motion picture film, figure, image, phonograph record or wire or tape recording, or any written, printed or recorded matter of an indecent character which may or may not require mechanical or other means to be transmitted into auditory, visual, or sensory representations of such character; or any article or instrument of indecent or immoral use, or purporting to be for indecent or immoral use or purpose, *. . . is guilty of a misdemeanor. . . .

Basically the law means that a person who has in his possession any item which the law could regard as obscene becomes guilty of a crime if he intends to let others see that item. The crime becomes obvious if he actually does let others see it. It should be pointed out, in passing, that possession of an item which the law otherwise regards as obscene, but which the possessor does not intend to show to any other person, is not a crime in most states. As has been stated, all of this is simple, so where is the problem? It exists in the inability to agree on the definition of "obscene."

Obviously the words of the statute which describe the forbidden matter would give anyone difficulty. The laws of New York State and of many other states, refer to items which are "obscene, lewd, lascivious, filthy, indecent or disgusting." Unfortunately for the interpreters of the laws, these terms are not legal. They are factual descriptions and, like beauty, depend entirely on the eyes of the beholder. One man's beauty is another man's lewdness. It is easy to analyze these points in the abstract and to conclude that laws prohibiting so-called obscenity or indecency should never have been passed. Both the law and the objective it endeavors to attain are meaningless. However, the courts have enforced them, and the results have approached the ludicrous.

The law tackles an idiot's task in the obscenity field because it endeavors to set forth an objective criterion to test a subjective

44

phenomenon. To elaborate: Suppose it were constitutionally permissible to set up degrees of aesthetics. Perhaps it would not be a bad idea to have some form of aesthetic standards for billboards. Such a law might say that it shall be unlawful for anyone to set forth on a public highway an *ugly* billboard. Now, *ugly* could be defined as repulsive, unaesthetic, inartistic, etc. Visualize a court or commission characterizing as *ugly* a billboard prepared by some advertising agency. What now? Most analysts would conclude that ugliness is in the eyes of the beholder and cannot be legislated against because no two people can agree on what is ugly.

This is, if approached from an intellectually honest viewpoint, precisely the situation with respect to obscenity. Whether an item is obscene or not depends entirely on the education, background, and exposure of an individual to the item and similar materials in question. To a child who regularly visits a nudist camp with his parents, nudity will never be obscene. This is a part of his accepted way of life, his apperceptive background, and it is no more obscene than a loaf of bread. To a child raised in an Amish or hardshell Baptist household where exposure of a female calf or thigh is cause for a lecture, nudity equals obscenity.

The subjective nature of obscenity explains why, when the same item goes before ten courts, ten different shades of opinion may result. Since each judge has a different apperceptive background and came out of a different environment, he responds to the stimulus of the item with a different and varying reaction. This is natural, normal, and expected. The only problem arises from not facing it with intellectual honesty.

Accordingly, a major problem in the field of obscenity is emotionalism. The electricity of passionate feelings charges the entire subject. True, a large segment of the population shrugs its collective shoulders at this topic. Another large body of opinion regards each example of nudity, candid sexual word pictures, and the like as a direct and personal insult to their integrity and modesty. At the other end of the spectrum is an equally large body of opinion which regards every upholding of censorship as a blow to freedom of speech, press, and the communication of ideas. Eventually the freedom side will probably win. In the interim, however, some accommodation must be made with those who are offended by the unclad body, the words of sex, and the verbal pictorialization of physical love. Some suggestion of how to achieve this accommodation is made in a later section of this book.

THE CASE OF THE *TROPIC OF CANCER*

The absurdity of the law is probably best illustrated by the cases which tried to decide whether the adults of the United States could be trusted to read *Tropic of Cancer* without ill effect. The book was and is widely-known both to students of English literature and of eroticism. First published in Paris in 1934, for two decades it was regarded as beyond the bounds of decency in the United States. At regular intervals literary scholars and collectors of pornography brought copies into this country from France and other places. The book is a series of episodes in the life of an American in Paris in the early 1930's. In the late 1950's, as a result of a series of decisions by the United States Supreme Court, the Grove Press, Inc., decided that the law had reached the point where no book of reasonably serious purpose would be ruled out of bounds by the courts.[18] Grove obtained the rights from the author, Henry Miller, published and distributed a hard-cover edition of *Tropic of Cancer,* and found itself enmeshed in litigation.

In the lower courts the book collected a mixed bag of results. Philadelphia[19] and Los Angeles[20] held the book obscene; Chicago cleared it.[21] It then went to the appellate courts, where it was cleared by Massachusetts,[22] Wisconsin,[23] and California.[24] A considerable body of thought began to build among attorneys and other experts in this field that, at last, in the United States no book of serious intent and purpose could be regarded as obscene.

Then came the case of the *People of New York State vs. Marguerite Fritch.*[25] The sellers of the Miller book were arrested and tried by jury for the violation of Penal Laws, Section 1141, previously discussed, because they sold someone a copy of *Tropic of Cancer*. On appeal, the next court reversed the conviction under the theory that the sale of a book of this nature was constitutionally privileged and could not be a crime. The case was appealed to the highest court of New York, which reversed the intermediate court, found the book obscene, and sent the case back for a new trial on the definitive theory that the book was obscene.

The following selections from the original opinion of the highest court of New York furnish an insight into the thinking of the majority of the court:

> In order to render more meaningful our duty to make an independent constitutional appraisal we feel compelled, though loath to do so, to refer to certain words and passages contained in the book, with all due respect for the dignity of this court and the judicial system. We do so to bring to the attention of the the bar the factual basis for our conclusion that the book is obscene, as well as to demonstrate that this conclusion is not predicated upon any preconceived notions or predilections on our part.
>
> Throughout its pages, "4 and 5 letter" vile and filthy words and derivatives thereof, by conservative estimate, are used more than 300 times. We are mindful that the use of these words, standing alone, may not necessarily render the book obscene by legal standards. We therefore are constrained to set forth some excerpts which typify the manner in which this language is used throughout the book.
>
> On page 5 [page references are to pages in the hardback edition] of the book the central character describes his desires for Sylvester's wife Tania:

47

Where now is that warm cunt of yours, those fat, heavy garters, those soft, bulging thighs? There is a bone in my prick six inches long. I will ream out every wrinkle in your cunt, Tania, big with seed. I will send you home to your Sylvester with an ache in your belly and your womb turned inside out. Your Sylvester! Yes, he knows how to build a fire, but I know how to inflame a cunt. I shoot hot bolts into you, Tania, I make your ovaries incandescent. Your Sylvester is a little jealous now? He feels something, does he? He feels the remnants of my big prick. I have set the shores a little wider, I have ironed out the wrinkles. After me you can take on stallions, bulls, rams, drakes, St. Bernards. You can stuff toads, bats, lizards up your rectum. You can shit arpeggios if you like, or string a zither across your navel. I am fucking you, Tania, so that you'll stay fucked. And if you are afraid of being fucked publicly I will fuck you privately. I will tear off a few hairs from your cunt and paste them on Boris' chin. I will bite into your clitoris and spit out two franc pieces. . . .

Describing another sexual episode, at page 18 of the book the central character says:

In the lavatory I stand before the bowl with a tremendous erection; it seems light and heavy at the same time, like a piece of lead with wings on it. And while I'm standing there like that two cunts sail in—Americans. I greet them cordially, prick in hand. They give me a wink and pass on. In the vestibule, as I'm buttoning my fly, I notice one of them waiting for her friend to come out of the can. The music is still playing and maybe Mona'll be coming to fetch me, or Borowski with his gold-knobbed cane, but I'm in her arms now and she has hold of me and I don't care who comes or what happens. We wriggle into the cabinet and there I stand her up, slap up against the wall, and I try to get it into her but it won't work and so we sit down on the seat and try it that way but it won't work either. No matter how we try it it won't work. And all the while she's got hold of my prick, she's clutching it like a lifesaver, but it's no use, we're too hot, too eager. The music is still playing and so we waltz out of the cabinet into the vestibule again and as we're dancing there in the shit-house I come all over her beautiful gown and she's sore as hell about it.

Discussing his experience with a prostitute on a street corner in Paris, he states (p. 42):

. . . there was always a cluster of vultures who croaked and flapped their dirty wings, who reached out with sharp talons and plucked you into a doorway. Jolly, rapacious devils who didn't even give you time to button your pants when it was over. Led you into a little room off the street, a room without a window usually, and, sitting on the edge of the bed with skirts tucked up gave you a quick inspection, spat on your c—k, and placed it for you.

As can be plainly seen, the book is a compilation of a series of *sordid narrations* dealing with sex in a manner designed to appeal to the prurient interest. *It is devoid of theme or ideas.* Throughout its pages can be found a *constant repetition of patently offensive words* used solely to convey debasing por-trayals of natural and unnatural sexual experiences. It is a blow to sense, not merely sensibility. It is, in short, "hard core pornography," dirt for dirt's sake (*United States* v. *'Ulysses,'* 5 F. Supp. 182), and dirt for money's sake (*Kingsley Inter-national Pictures Corp.* v. *Regents,* 360 U. S. 684, 692). We see no reason for adopting an unrealistic appraisal of the nature of this book when there is such overwhelming proof of its incompatibility with the current moral standards of our community. If, as the County Court held, this book is not obscene as a matter of law, it is difficult to conceive when, if ever, a book can be held to be obscene under any established legal standard.

The section given above is from the majority opinion by Judge John F. Scileppi. Only one judge, Adrian P. Burke, com-pletely agreed with the opinion of the majority. Chief Justice

49

Charles S. Desmond wrote a separate opinion, agreeing that the book should be banned and stating in part:

> I concur in the result only because I protest the quoting of offensive material in an opinion issued from this court.
>
> If this book had not been written by a recognized author, if it did not contain some "good writing" and if it were not approved by well-known reviewers, no one, I venture, would deny that it is obscene by any conceivable definition, narrow or tolerant. Its own cover blurb boasts of its "unbridled obscenity." From first to last page it is a filthy, cynical, disgusting narrative of sordid amours. Not only is there in it no word or suggestion of the romantic, sentimental, poetic or spiritual aspects of the sex relation, but it is not even bawdy sex or comic sex or sex described with vulgar good humor. No glory, no beauty, no stars—just mud. The whole book is "sick sexuality," a deliberate, studied exercise in the depiction of sex relations as debasing, filthy and revolting. On page 483 of 370 U.S., Justice Harlan's opinion in *Manual Enterprises* v. *Day* quotes the New International Dictionary's long series of definitions of "obscenity." It is a remarkable fact that "Tropic of Cancer" fits every single one of those numerous meanings.

Judge Marvin R. Dye dissented, saying, among other things, the following:

> It cannot be gainsaid that the profusion of four-letter words used by the author to portray the mental and moral slough into which some of his characters had sunk is unsuited for the drawing room. In "Tropic," as in Joyce's "Ulysses" however, the erotic passages are "submerged in the book as a whole and have little resultant effect" *(United States* v. *One Book Entitled Ulysses,* 72 Fed. 2d. 705, 707). Like "Ulysses," it is a "tragic and very powerful commentary" on the inner lives of human beings caught in the throes of a hopeless social morass. Written in Paris in 1934 at a time when Europe was reeling from the aftermath of the devastating moral and material destruction of World War I, the book reflects the debasing experiences and problems known to many in a city such as Paris in the 1930s. In an effort to escape the clutching insistence of an all-engulfing miasma, the author describes his own and

his companion's sexual indulgences tediously repeated, to re-discover that surrender to such demeaning conduct was the antidote to the underlying human unhappiness caused by the poverty, filth, disease, loneliness and despair in a world in flux. In dealing with Gautier's "Mademoiselle de Maupin" in *Halsey* v. *New York Society for the Suppression of Vice*, (234 N.Y. 1, 4) we said "No work may be judged from a selection [a few] of paragraphs alone. Printed by themselves they might, as a matter of law, come within the prohibition of the statute. So might a similar selection from Aristophanes or Chaucer or Boccaccio, or even from the Bible." The book should neither be appraised nor condemned by the tone of a few passages wrested from context and viewed in a vacuum. "It must be considered broadly as a whole." (*Halsey* v. *N. Y. Society*, 234 N. Y. 4).

When so read, its content does not meet the test of "hard core pornography" which we announced in *People* v. *Richmond County News* (9 N. Y. 2d 578, 586), nor does the book contain, in the words of Mr. Justice Harlan, "patently offensive" material and have its predominant appeal to the "prurient interest"—the criteria enunciated by the Supreme Court in *Manual Enterprises* v. *Day* (370 U.S. 478, 486) .

This so-called "obscenity case" and those that preceded it all call to mind the book-burning of eighteenth-century Europe and New England which fortunately did not stop the forces of the inquisitive and curious minds for long but, as might well have been expected and as we are now witnessing, released forces which today are demanding attention through-out the democracies of the world. To hold this book obscene necessarily places one in the role of the censor, a role which is incompatible with the explicit powers and obvious purposes of this court. Obscenity is variously defined, but it does not follow that the printed word which is in bad taste, disgusting, and offensive is obscene as a matter of law requiring sup-pression by the censor, and that is what we must say beyond any reason of doubt in order to find ground for reversal here. Such a view in no way minimizes the right of the state to suppress what is obscene and pornographic. However, when material is so characterized to charge commission of a crime, the courts should be ever-mindful before rendering a judgment of conviction that the evidence of guilt is free from reasonable doubt, else what is done in the name of the law will so fritter away the free speech and free press guarantees of the First Amendment and due process under the Fourteenth Amendment as to make the remedy more dangerous than the ill, for the effect will be to substitute the fleeting ad hoc opinion of men, whether we realize it or not, for the rule of law envisioned by the framers of the Constitution.

Judge Stanley H. Fuld also dissented in a separate opinion, stating:

Since "Tropic of Cancer" is a serious expression of views and reactions toward life, however alien they may be to the reader's philosophy or experience, and since the book is not without literary importance as attested by recognized critics and scholars, it is our judgment that the First Amendment does not permit its suppression. And this, we note, is the conclusion recently reached by the high courts of California, Massachusetts and Wisconsin. . . . In short, the book before us, to cull from what we said in the *Richmond County News* case "appraised" . . . in the light of First Amendment concepts may not be adjudged obscene without impairing the vital social interest in freedom of expression.

Justice John Van Voorhis concurred in both dissenting opinions of Judges Dye and Fuld.

On June 22, 1964, the United States Supreme Court finally decided for the entire United States the problem of *Tropic of Cancer*. The District Court of Appeal of Florida had ruled that *Tropic of Cancer* was obscene and the case went to the Supreme Court, which ruled on it in a peremptory opinion without discussion.[26] Justices Black, Douglas, Brennan, Goldberg, and Stewart created a five-justice majority to reverse the Florida court. Justices Clark, Harlan, White, and Chief Justice Warren voted to support the Florida court and hold the book obscene. Thus, by the narrow margin of one United States Supreme Court Justice the people are now permitted to buy and read *Tropic of Cancer*.

II

History

IN THE BEGINNING

The history of the doctrine of obscenity is generally believed to have started with the case of Sir Charles Sedley of Kent.[1] Sedley was an intimate of King Charles II and a typical profligate, gay blade of the madcap court. One day Sedley, Charles Sackville (Lord Buckhurst, later the Earl of Dorset), and Sir Thomas Ogle engaged in an extended drinking bout at "The Cock," a tavern near Covent Garden. Seeking additional amusement, the inebriated trio climbed to the balcony of the public house and staged an uninhibited performance which would today be termed as "obscene show." The three undressed themselves and pantomimed a series of indecent proposals to the passing public. Then, growing bored with pantomime, they shouted indecencies to the passersby, and Sir Charles boasted loudly of magical sexual powers that caused women to pursue him. Finally, they climaxed the orgy by urinating in bottles and throwing them at the rapidly increasing audience. This indignity turned the crowd into a mob which stoned the performers until they fled from the scene.

Arrested and tried, Sedley "was fined 2000 mark, committed without bail for a week, and bound to his good behaviour for a year, on his confession of information against him, for shewing himself naked in a balcony, and throwing down bottles (pist in) *vi et armis* among the people in Covent Garden, *contra pacem* and to the scandal of the government." [2]

Although the conduct of the roistering lords was unquestionably illegal on a number of counts, the case is generally accepted as the first involving criminal obscenity under the common law.[3]

Not until almost half a century had passed did a court really consider a case of obscenity without accompanying illegal conduct. In 1708, in *Queen vs. Read*,[4] the publisher Read was brought into the dock for the publication of the pamphlet *The Fifteen Plagues of a Maiden-Head*. The Queen's Bench Court found that the publication created "no offense at common law" and observed on the side that whatever punishment could be meted out had to be exercised by the ecclesiastical courts. With remarkable restraint Judge Powell observed that he wished the publication of obscene literature could be punished but concluded that the courts "cannot make law."

This is the full pamphlet that came before the Court (this is, apparently, its first publication in the United States) :

THE FIFTEEN PLAGUES OF A MAIDEN-HEAD

The First Plague

The Woman Marr'y'd is Divinely Blest,
But I a Virgin cannot take my Rest;
I'm discontented up, as bad a Bed,
Because I'm plagued with my Maiden-head;
A thing that do's my blooming Years no good
But only serves to freeze my youthful Blood,
Which slowly Circulates, do what I can,
For want of Bleeding by some skilful Man;
Whose tender hand his *Launcet* so will guide,
That I the Name of *Maid* may lay aside.

The Second Plague

When I've beheld an am'rous Youth make Love
And swearing Truth by all the Gods above,
How has it strait inflam'd my sprightly Blood
Creating Flames, I scarcely should withstood,
But bid him boldly march, not grant me leisure
Of Parley, for 'tis Speed augments the Pleasure

But ah! tis my Misfortune not to meet
With any Man that would my Passion greet,
Till he with balmy Kisses stop'd my Breath,
Than which one cannot die a better Death.
O! stroke my Breasts, those Mountains of Delight,
Your very Touch would fire an Anchorite;
Next let your wanton Palm a little stray,
And dip thy Fingers in the milky way:
Then having raiz'd me, let me gently fall,
Love's Trumpets found, so Mortal have at all.
But why wish I this Bliss? I wish in vain,
And of my plaguy Burden do complain;
For sooner may I see whole Nations dead,
'er I find one to get my Maiden-head.

The Third Plague

She that her Maiden-head does keep, runs through
More Plagues than all the Land of *Egypt* knew;
A teasing Whore, or a more tedious Wife,
Plagues not a Marry'd Man's unhappy Life,
As much as it do's me to be a Maid,
Of which same Name I am so much afraid,
Because I've often heard some People tell,
They that die Maids, must all lead Apes in Hell;
If so, 'twere better I had never been,
Than thus to be perplex'd: *God Save the Queen.*

The Fourth Plague

When trembling Pris'ners all stand round the Bar,
In strange suspence about the fatal Verdict,
And when the Jury crys they Guilty are,
How they astonish'd are when they have heard it.
When in mighty Storm a Ship is toss'd,
And all do ask, What do's the Captain say?
How they (poor Souls) bemoan themselves a loss
When his Advice at last is only, Pray!
So as it was one Day my pleasing Chance,

THE
Fifteen PLAGUES
OF A
Maiden-Head.

Written by Madam *B-----le*.

LONDON:
Printed by *F. P.* near *Fleet-street*, 1707.

THE

Fifteen Plagues of Maiden-Head, &c.

The First Plague.

THE Woman Marry'd is Divinely Bleſt,
But I a Virgin cannot take my Reſt;
I'm diſcontented up, as bad a Bed,
Becauſe I'm plagued with my Maiden-head;
A thing that do's my blooming Years no good
But only ſerves to freeze my youthful Blood,
Which ſlowly Circulates, do what I can,
For want of Bleeding by ſome ſkilful Man;
Whoſe tender hand his *Launcet* ſo will guide,
That I the Name of *Maid* may lay aſide.

The Second Plague.

When I've beheld an am'rous Youth make Lo
And ſwearing Truth by all the Gods above,
How has it ſtrait inflam'd my ſprightly Blood
Creating Flames, I ſcarcely ſhould withſtood,
But bid him boldly march, not grant me leiſur
Of Parley, for 'tis Speed augments the Pleaſu

To meet a handsome young Man in a Grove,
Both time and place conspir'd to advance
The innocent Designs of Charming Love.
I thought my Happiness was then compleat,
Because 'twas in his Pow'r to make it so;
I ask'd the Spark if he would do the Feat,
But the unperforming Blockhead answer'd *No*.
Poor Pris'ners may, I see, have Mercy shewn,
And Shipwreck'd Men may sometimes have the Luck
To see their dismal Tempests overblown,
But I poor Virgin never shall be *Focked*.

The Fifth Plague

All Day poor I do sit Disconsolate,
Cursing the grievous Rigor of my Fate,
To think how I have seven Years betray'd,
To that dull empty Title of a Maid.
If that I could my self but Woman write,
With what transcendent Pleasure and Delight,
Should I for ever, thrice for ever Blest,
The Man that led me to such Happiness.

The Sixth Plague

Pox take the thing Folks call a Maiden-head,
. For soon as e'er I'm sleeping in my Bed,
I dream I'm mingling with some Man my Thighs
Till something more than ord'nary does rise;
But when I wake and find my Dream's in vain,
I turn to Sleep only to Dream again,
For Dreams as yet are only kind to me,
And at the present quench my Lechery.

The Seventh Plague

Of late I wonder what's with me the Matter,
For I look like Death, and am as weak as Water,
For several Days I loath the sight of Meat,
And every Night I chew the upper Sheet;

I've such Obstructions, that I'm almost moap'd,
And breath as if my Vitals all were stop'd,
I told a Friend how strange with me it was,
She, an experienc'd Bawd, soon grop'd the Cause,
Saying, *for this Disease, take what you can,*
You'll ne'er be well, till you have taken Man.
Therefore, before with Maiden heads I'll be
Thus plagu'd, and live in daily Misery,
Some Spark shall rummage all my Wem about,
To find this wonderful Distemper out.

The Eighth Plague

Now I am young, blind *Cupid* me bewitches,
I scratch my Belly, for it always itches,
And what it itches for, I've told before,
Tis either to be Wife, or be a Whore;
Nay any thing indeed, would be poor I,
E'er Maiden-heads upon my Hands should lie,
Which till I lose, I'm sure my watry Eyes
Will pay to Love so great a Sacrifice,
That my Carcass soon will weep out all its Juice,
Till grown so dry, as fit for no Man's use.

The Ninth Plague

By all the pleasant Postures of Delight,
By all the Twincs and Circles of the Night,
By the first Minute of those Nuptial Joys,
When Men put fairly for a Brace of Boys,
Dying a Virgin once I more do dread,
Than ten times losing of a *Maiden head*;
For tho' it can't be seen, nor understood,
Yet is it troublesome to Flesh and Blood.

The Tenth Plague

You heedless Maids, whose young and tender Hearts,
Unwounded yet, have scap'd the fatal Darts;
Let the sad Fate of a poor Virgin move,
And learn by me to pay Respect to Love.

If one can find a Man fit for Love's Game,
To lose one's Maiden-head it is no Shame:
'Tis no Offence, if from his tender Lip
I snatch a tonguing Kiss; if my fond Clip
With Loose Embraces oft his Neck surround,
For Love in Debts of Nature's ever bound.

The Eleventh Plague

A Maiden head! Pish, in it's no Delight,
Nor have I Ease, but when returning Night,
With Sleep's soft gentle Spell my Senses charms,
Then Fancy some Gallant brings to my Arms:
In them I oft the lov'd Shadow seem
To grasp, and Joys, yet blush I too in Dream.
I wake, and long my Heart in Wonder lies,
To think on my late pleasing Extasies:
But when I'm waking, and don't yet possess,
In Sleep again I wish to enjoy the Bliss:
For Sleep do's no malicious Spies admit,
Yet yields a lively Semblance of Delight.
Gods! what a Scene of Joy was that! how fast
I clasp'd the Vision to my panting Breast?
With what fierce Bounds I sprung to meet the Bliss,
While my wrapt Soul flew out in ev're Kiss!
Till breathless, faint, and softly sunk away,
I all dissolv'd in reaking Pleasures lay.

The Twelfth Plague

Happen what will, I'll make some Lovers know
What Pains, what raging Pains I undergo,
Till I am really Heart-sick, almost Dead,
By keeping that damn'd thing a Maiden-head.
Which makes me with Green Sickness almost lost,
So pale, so wan, and looking like a Ghost,
Eating Chalk, Cindars, or Tobacco-Pipes,
Which with a Looseness scowers all my Tripes;
But e'er I'll longer this great Pain endure,
The Stews I'll search, but that I'll find a Cure.

The Thirteenth Plague

Let doating Age debate of *Law* and *Right*,
And gravely state the Bounds of Just and Fit;
Whose Wisdom's but their Envy, to destroy
And bar those Pleasures which they can't enjoy.
My blooming Years, more sprightly and more gay,
By Nature were design'd for Love and Play:
Youth knows no Check, but leaps weak Virtue's **Fence**,
And briskly hunts the noble Chase of Sense!
Without dull thinking I'll Enjoyment trace,
And call that lawful whatsoe'er do's please.
Nor will my Crime want Instances alone,
Tis what the Glorious Gods above have done;
For *Saturn*, and his greater Off-spring, *Jove*,
Both stock'd their Heaven with Incestuous Love.

The Fourteenth Plague

If any Man do's with my Bubbies play,
Squeeze my small Hand, as soft as Wax or Clay,
Or lays his Hands upon my tender Knees,
What strange tumultuous Joys upon me seize!
My Breasts do heave, and languish do my Eyes,
Panting's my Heart, and trembling are my Thighs;
I sigh, I wish, I pray, and seem to die,
In one continu'd Fit of Ecstacy;
Thus by my Looks may Man know what I mean,
And how he easily may get between
Those Quarters, where he may surprize a Fort,
In which an Emperor may find such Sport,
That with a mighty Gust of Love's Alarms,
He'd lie dissolving in my circling arms;
But 'tis my Fate to have to do with Fools,
Who're very loth and shy to use their Tools,
To ease a poor, and fond distressed Maid,
Of that same Load, of which I'm not afraid
To lose with any Man, tho' I should die,
For any Tooth (good Barber) is my Cry.

The Fifteenth Plague

Alas! I care not, Sir, what Force you'd use,
So I my Maiden-head could quickly lose:
Oft do I wish one skill'd in *Cupid's* Arts,
Would quickly dive into my secret Parts;
For as I am, at Home all sorts of weather,
I skit,—as Heaven and Earth would come together,
Twirling a Wheel, I sit at home, hum drum,
And spit away my Nature on my Thumb;
Whilst those that Marry'd are, invited be
To Labours, Christnings, where the Jollitry
Of Women lies in telling, as some say,
When 'twas they did at Hoity-Toity play;
Whose Husband's Yard is longest, whilst another
Can't in the least her great Misfortune smother,
So tells, her Husband's Bauble is so short,
Then when he Hunts, he never shews her Sport.
Now I, because I have my Maiden-head,
Mayn't know the Pastimes of the Nuptial Bed;
But mayn't I quickly do as Marry'd People may,
I'll either kill my self, or shortly run away.

FINIS

The unresolved situation, fortunate from the viewpoint of writers and publishers, was not to continue. Edmund Curll, a printer and bookseller, was indicted and tried for the sale of obscene literature. Although counsel argued that the *Read* case had already established that the publication *or sale* of obscenity did not constitute an offense punishable in the common-law courts, the court overruled itself on the ground that it was obviously an offense against religion, and religion was a part of the common law.[5]

The item involved in this case was *Venus in the Cloister or The Nun in Her Smock*. The book was an anti-Catholic tract written around 1682 by one "Abbé DuPrat," probably a pseudonym for one of the better known anti-Catholic French writers of the period—possibly Chavigny or Barrin. The book was first published in Paris, and Curll pirated a translation.

The story is a dialogue between nuns (two sets) in a convent and primarily concerns lesbian love. The following excerpt constitutes a fair sample:

> *Angelique:* Oh! let me look at you uncovered, at this beautiful face [*real reference is buttocks*] that always goes veiled! Kneel down on the couch, and kiss the top a little so that I may watch the violence of your blows. Ah! divine kindness, what a medley of colors! It seems to me that I am seeing Chinese taffetas or rather some striped fabric of times long past! Is it necessary to have a great devotion to the Mystery of Flagellation in order to color up the buttocks like this?
>
> *Agnes:* Well, have you gazed enough at the outrage of this innocent? Oh God! how you handle it! Give it a rest, let it recover its first tint, let that foreign hue subside. What, you kiss it?
>
> *Angelique:* Don't oppose me, my child. I have the most compassionate soul in the whole world, and since it is a work of mercy to console the afflicted, I believe that I could not make too many caresses for the worthy performance of this duty. Ah! but you have this part well shaped! It has such a pallor and plumpness that it appears to be really brilliant! I notice too another spot which is no less well divided by nature. No, it is *nature itself.*
>
> *Agnes:* Draw your hand, I beg you, away from that place, if you don't wish to cause an arousing that could not be easily put out. I have to admit my weakness to you: I am the most sensitive girl you will find anywhere, and something that would not cause in others the least emotion often throws me into wild disorder.
>
> *Angelique:* So! then you are not so cold as you would have persuaded me you were when we began our conversation. And I think you would conduct yourself as coolly as any person I know if you should be placed by me in the hands of five or six good monks.

*   *   *   *   *

Agnes: I am struck by this fantasy; I myself would be ravished just to see in you what you have observed so attentively in my body.

Angelique: Alas, my child, the request you make of me does not surprise me at all; we are all shaped from the same clay. There, I set myself in your posture. Good, now lift my skirt and my chemise as high as you can.

Agnes: I have a strong desire to show my control and do it in a way that will not give these two sister-cheeks any excuse to blame me.

Angelique: Ouch! ouch! ouch! how you go at it! This sort of game doesn't please me much when it is not rough. Truce, truce! If your devotion is going to renew your strength, I am lost. Oh God! but you have a flexible arm! It is my intention to make you a partner in my job, but you have to have a little more moderation.

Agnes: You certainly have a lot to complain about! This isn't one tenth of the blows that I have received. I will ply you with the rest another time; we must make some allowance for your scarcity of courage. Do you know that this portion of you is growing ever more lovely? A certain fire animates it, conveying through the flesh a vermillion more pure and more radiant than all the scarlet of Spain. Come a little closer to the window, so I may see what light discovers of all your beauty. Just so, that's good. I will never tire of looking at it. I see everything I desire right up to your naturehood. Why do you hide that part with your hand?

Angelique: Oh, dear, you can examine it as well as the rest. If this occupation of ours has any badness about it, it still is not prejudicial to anybody, and does not disturb in the least the public peace.

* * * * *

Virginie: That's good! I see it, I feel it, I am overjoyed with it. But now it is my turn to frolic, to take my little friskers and exercise them on your organs, sweet as those that Helen of Troy had or Cleopatra. I want them to perform on you like gallant pirates whom nothing can escape, who go ferreting everywhere with a gentleness equal to their curiosity. Let's go, let me kiss the pavilion of the Graces, and let me see if I am as skilful a buccaneer as you are in carrying out amorous banditries! From buccaneer to a scourer of the sea is only a hand-span. So touch me there, my own one, and set yourself lively in the position for a good ransacking and thorough groping until I tell you, There, that will do! Enough! Oh, for the blow, I have in front of me a little labyrinth of jet, of coral and alabaster and in its windings my fingers go to do their duty and delight. By Venus! but it's narrow, erect, well placed, brisk, ticklish and passionate! It moves by itself and without propulsion in a kind of systole and diastole. Already I feel there a soft wetness, the advance messenger of the pleasures of love. Ah, ah! How you wriggle! Courage, my child: act on your side just as I do on mine. There's no task here like shelling an oyster. You have to assist, to stir yourself, spring and prance; you have to know how to maneuver for the finest profit the talent of an agile hand, fit for high office and a contest which begins and concludes on the throne of ecstasy.

Like so many other items in the field of obscenity, if this book had not had religious overtones it probably would have passed unnoticed. But because of the setting it became an item forever banned. Apparently it has not been printed in English since Curll was punished. (The above material was translated from the French edition. It has been reprinted by Paris publishers at regular intervals. They were never indicted.)

It is amazing that this book, unquestionably a classic to have survived since 1682, is still on the prohibited list of literary imports of the Bureau of Customs. The book was released to me solely on my assurance that I wanted it only for this study and not to sell, distribute, or republish! The letter forwarding the book is reprinted to give the flavor of the problems encountered in this field.

TREASURY DEPARTMENT
BUREAU OF CUSTOMS
NEW YORK, N.Y.

January 15, 1965
REFER TO
9.DIC/ES:vhc

Mr. Albert B. Gerber
c/o Gerber & Galfand
Third Floor, 1512 Walnut Street
Philadelphia, Pa. 19102

Dear Mr. Gerber:

There is enclosed, herewith, the mail package addressed to you from France containing the book entitled, "Venus dans le Cloiture", detained by this office under the provisions of Section 305 of the Tariff Act; and the subject of our recent correspondence. The book is being released to you in connection with your present study.

Sincerely yours,

JOSEPH P. KELLY
Collector of Customs

BY *Eleanor M. Suske*
ELEANOR M. SUSKE
Supervisory Administrative Aid
Division of Imports Control

"THAT DEVIL WILKES"

The matter rested for another half century. Then, as might have been anticipated, the next use of the doctrine of obscenity was for purely political purposes. The case involved the famous John Wilkes, "one of the most astonishing men thrown up during a bewildering century." [6] Despite his general ugliness, enhanced by crossed eyes, the female sex adored him to such an extent that he boasted: "If any man grant me ten minutes with his wife or mistress I can and will win the woman." Politically he was an agitator and active opponent of George III, who gave him the name, "That devil Wilkes." Although consistently refused a seat in Parliament, his constituents in Middlesex regularly reelected him. He may be the only man refused admission to Parliament on three separate occasions.

Wilkes supported the American colonies against George III and this fact as much as anything else probably got him into his real trouble. Wilkes could be termed a "pornographic man" —this is indisputable. He became a member of the infamous Medmenhan monks, an order which purported to base itself upon anti-Catholicism but which in fact was a secret organization dedicated to mass sexual satisfaction. Wilkes' leading biographer describes the activity of the order.

> What were the enjoyments to which they were invited? They seemed to have been simple and, in contrast with the lurid imaginations of the Victorian age, almost innocent. Sexual vice is after all very limited: it has in England only taken four main forms—normal fornication, homosexuality, flagellation and fetishism. To the first the Medmenhan monks were devoted. All their architecture, sculpture and poetry celebrated it—even their art, for there was a huge oil painting which for years afterward hung in the King's Arms in Old Palace Yard showing the 'Father Superior,' Dashwood, kneeling in full costume before a young woman with nothing on but a

halo which blazed out from her loins. To anyone who has read John Cleland's *Memoirs of Fanny Hill,* the most famous (and the best written) of eighteenth-century pornographic works, it is easy to deduce what was the usual 'ritual.' It was an example of what the next century was to call 'voyeurism.' The chosen 'friar' advanced with his collaboratress to the bed which took the place of an altar, to the accompaniment of prayers or incantations; they were stripped or stripped each other; the woman was laid out as a 'sacrifice' to the Bona Dea; they then completed the sexual act in public under such exhortations or comments as the congregation chose to offer. Either before or after there was a fine dinner with plenty of 'libations', and the rest of the brotherhood, in cubicles or otherwise, went on to show what they could do as well. It is as certain as anything can be in so veiled a subject, that this rather adolescent orgy was all that occurred.[7]

This, then, is the background of the man who furnishes the clue to the reason for the modern doctrine of obscene literature. Wilkes became aroused over the corruption of the Tory government under George III and in 1762 published a satirical introduction to the play *The Fall of Mortimer,* in which he exposed debasement in the government and hinted at the imbecility of George III. Finally, as the coup de grace, he made veiled references to a meretricious relationship between the king's mother and the prime minister, Lord Bute. The publication and dissemination of this bit of prose created an explosion on the continent. In Paris Madame Pompadour asked, "How far does the liberty of the press extend in England?" Wilkes promptly replied, "I do not know. I am trying to find out." Lord Bute resigned, but Wilkes, in the newspaper *North Briton,* of which he was the publisher, suggested that the resignation was a mockery.

The government, unable longer to ignore his barbs, arrested Wilkes and held him for trial. While in jail Wilkes reached the crest of his popularity both at home and abroad—especially in the colonies. He became known as "The Liberty Boy" and appeared to enjoy enough popularity to lead a revolution against the government. The government was afraid to arrest and try Wilkes on any of the standard charges such as "seditious libel," "treason," or the rest of the bag of tricks kept in reserve for the punishment of nonconformists. In desperation it tried to buy Wilkes' silence, but he was not for sale.

At this point the authorities received information that Wilkes had written a parody of Alexander Pope's *Essay on Man* entitled *Essay on Women*. Wilkes had in truth written the essay and had had twelve copies printed privately, for the Society of the Medmenhan Monks. However, a former employe in Wilkes' printing shop had secretly run off a thirteenth copy, which fell into the hands of the government.

With the Essay for support, a careful but strenuous campaign was inaugurated against Wilkes. He was denounced in both the House of Commons and the House of Lords. Parliament adopted a resolution that Wilkes' *Essay on Women* was a "most scandalous, obscene and impious libel."

Lord Mansfield, well known for his loyalty to George III, presided at the trial. Mansfield made short shrift of Wilkes' arguments that, although he wrote and printed the essay, he did not publish or circulate it. The case, obviously political, made bad law under any theory. No less than a Supreme Court Justice of the United States has observed that men may amuse themselves as they please in private. The *sine qua non*, the essence of obscenity, has always been publication. The denial of Wilkes' argument that he never published or circulated any obscenity creates a theory which is radically unsound in law.

Wilkes' *Essay on Women* today hardly seems to merit the furor it caused.[8] Yet the poem has apparently never been printed in the United States, and the few copies available are all in privately printed editions. In all its dubious glory here is the complete poem that acted as the stimulus for the entire modern theory of legal obscenity:

Awake, my Fanny, leave all meaner things;
This morn shall prove what rapture swiving brings!
Let us (since life can little more supply
Than just a few good fucks, and then we die)
Expatiate free o'er that loved scene of man,
A mighty maze, for mighty pricks to scan;
A wild, where *Paphian Thorns* promiscuous shoot,
Where flowers of Monthly Rose, but yield no Fruit.
Together let us beat this evil field,
Try what the open, what the covert yield;
The latent tracts, the pleasing depths explore,
And my prick clapp'd where thousands were before.
Observe how Nature works, and if it rise
Too quick and rapid, check it ere it flies;
Spend when we must, but keep it all we can:
Thus Godlike will be deem'd the ways of man.

I.   Say, first a woman's latent charms below,
What can we reason but from what we know?
A face, a neck, a breast, are all appear
From which to reason, or to which refer.
In every part we heavenly beauty own.
But we can trace it only in what's shewn.
He who the hoop's immensity can pierce,
Dart thro' the whalebone fold's vast universe,
Observe how circle into circle runs,
What courts the eye, and what all vision shuns,
All the wild mode of dress her females wear,
May guess what makes them transform'd appear.
But of their cunts the bearings and the ties,
The nice connexions, strong dependencies,
The latitude and longitude of each
Hast thou gone thro, or can thy Pago reach?
Was that great Ocean, that unbounded Sea,
Where pricks like whales may sport,
Fathom'd by Thee?

II. Presumptuous Prick! The reason would'st thou find
Why form'd so weak, so little, and so blind?
First if thou can'st, the heart or reason guess

72

Why form'd no weaker, meaner and no less.
Ask of thy mother's cunt why she was made
Of lesser bore than cow or hackney'd jade?
Or ask thy raw-boned Scottish Father's Tarse
Why larger he than Stallion, or Jackass?
Of Pago's possible, if 'tis confess'd
That wisdom infinite must form some
Where all must rise, or not coherent be,
And all that rise in due degree;
Then, in the scale of various Pricks,
"Tis plain, God-like erect, BUTE stands the formost
    man,
And all the question (wrangle e'er so long)
Is only this, If Heaven placed him wrong.
Respecting him, whatever wrong we call,
May, must be right, as relative to all.
When frogs would couple, labour'd on with pain,
A thousand wriggles scarce their purpose gain:
In Man a dozen can his end produce,
And drench the female with spermatic juice.
Yet not our pleasure seems God's end alone,
Oft left he when we spend we propagate unknown;
Unwilling we may reach some other goal,
And sylphs and gnomes may fuck in woman's hole.
When the proud Stallion knows whence every vein
Now throbs with lust, and now is shrunk again;
The lusty Bull why now he breaks the clod,
Now he wears a garland, fair Europa's God:
Then shall man's pride Pago comprehend
His actions and erections, use and end.
Why at Celaenae Martyrdom and why
Atlanticus Lampsacus adored Chief Deity.
Then say not man's imperfect, Heaven in fault,
Say rather, Man's as perfect as he ought;
His Pago measured to the female Case,
Betwixt a woman's thighs his proper place;
And if to fuck in a proportion'd sphere,
What matter how it is, or when, or where?
Fly fuck'd by fly may be completely so,
As Hussey's Duchess, or yon well-bull'd cow,

73

III. Heaven from all creatures hide the Book of Fate
All but the page prescribed, the present state,
From boys what girls, from girls what women know
What couldst suffer being here below?
Thy lust the Virgin dooms to bleed today,
Had she thy reason would she skip and play?
Believed to the last, she likes the luscious food,
And grabs the prick just raised to shed her blood.
Oh! Blindness to the Future, kindly given,
That each may enjoy what fucks or mark'd by Heaven.
And seized with equal Eieye, as God,
The Man just mounting, and the Virgin's fall;
Prick, cunt, and bollocks in convulsions hurl'd,
And now a Haymen burst, and now a world.
Hope humbly, then, clean girls; nor vainly soar;
But fuck the cunt, and God adore.
What future fucks he gives not thee to know,
But gives that Cunt to be thy blessing now.

THE TESTS BEGIN

After the case of *That Devil Wilkes,* English history was marked by the indiscriminate use of the new law prohibiting so-called obscenity to attack and ban political and anti-religious books. For example, when Lord Byron's legal representative endeavored to protect his client's poem *Cain* against piracy, Lord Eldon refused to grant the protection on the ground that the work was a "profane libel." [9] The poem *Cain* contains no references to sex and it could have been objectionable only because of its attack on organized religion. Byron again suffered when the Vice-Chancellor of England, Sir John Leach, declined to protect his poem *Don Juan* on the ground that it was obscene. [10] Sir John based his decision on the sixth, seventh, and eighth cantos, the last two of which concerned the siege and assault of Ishmael and constituted a Byronic satire on warfare. Sex played only a minor part in these two cantos. In the sixth canto Don Juan, dressed as a woman, goes into a harem for the night; nothing important happens and it seems a small point upon which to base a theory of obscenity. The true basis for attack could only be that Lord Byron was *persona non grata* in England. It is amusing to note that when a court refuses to grant coypright protection (as it did with respect to Byron's poetry) on the ground that the item is obscene or immoral, the net result is that any publisher may reproduce it and thus very quickly "a multitude of pirated editions from mushroom publishers instantly swamped the country." [11]

The livelier stanzas from *Don Juan* are presented here to furnish some idea of how puritanical the English courts became.

26

Don Juan in his feminine disguise,
    With all the damsels in their long array,
Had bowed themselves before the imperial eyes,
    And at the usual signal ta'en their way
Back to their chambers, those long galleries
    In the Seraglio, where the ladies lay
Their delicate limbs; a thousand bosoms there
Beating for love as the caged birds for air.

35

Their talk of course ran most on the new comer,
    Her shape, her hair, her air, her every thing:
Some thought her dress did not so much become her,
    Or wondered at her ears without a ring;
Some said her years were getting nigh their summer,
    Others contended they were but in spring;
Some thought her rather masculine in height,
While others wished that she had been so quite.

44

Lolah demanded the new damsel's name—
    "Juanna."—Well, a pretty name enough.

Katinka asked her also whence she came—
    "From Spain."—"But where *is* Spain?"—"Don't
        ask such stuff,
Nor show your Georgian ignorance—for shame!"
    Said Lolah, with an accent rather rough,
To poor Katinka: "Spain's an island near
Morocco, betwixt Egypt and Tangier."

46

But here the Mother of the Maids drew near,
    With, "Ladies, it is time to go to rest.
I'm puzzled what to do with you, my dear,"
    She added to Juanna, their new guest:
"Your coming has been unexpected here,
    And every couch is occupied; you had best
Partake of mine; but by to-morrow early
We will have all things settled for you fairly."

47

Here Lolah interposed—"Mamma, you know
    You don't sleep soundly, and I cannot bear
I'll take Juanna; we're a slenderer pair
Than you would make the half of;—don't say no;
    And I of your young charge will take due care."
But here Katinka interfered and said,
"She also had compassion and a bed."
That any body should disturb you so;

48

"Besides, I hate to sleep alone," quoth she.
    The Matron frowned: "Why so?"—"For fear of ghosts,"
Replied Katinka; "I am sure I see
    A phantom upon each of the four posts;
And then I have the worst dreams that can be,
    Of Guebres, Giaours, and Ginns, and Gouls in hosts."
The Dame replied, "Between your dreams and you,
I fear Juanna's dreams would be but few.

49

"You, Lolah, must continue still to lie
    Alone, for reasons which don't matter; you
The same, Katinka, until by and bye;
    And I shall place Juanna with Dudu,
Who's quiet, inoffensive, silent, shy,
    And will not toss and chatter the night through.
What say you, child?"—Dudu said nothing, as
Her talents were of the more silent class;

51

It was a spacious chamber (Oda is
    To bode him no great good, he deprecated
Were couches, toilets—and much more than this
    I might describe, as I have seen it all,
But it suffices—little was amiss;
    Twas on the whole a nobly furnished hall,
With all things ladies want, save one or two,
And even those were nearer than they knew.

59

And then she gave Juanna a chaste kiss;
    Duda was fond of kissing—which I'm sure
That nobody can ever take amiss,
    Because 'tis pleasant, so that it be pure
And between females means no more than this—
    That they have nothing better near, or newer.
"Kiss" rhymes to "bliss" in fact as well as verse—
I wish it never led to something worse.

61

And one by one her articles of dress
    Were laid aside; but not before she offered
Her aid to fair Juanna, whose excess
    Of Modesty declined the assistance proffered:
Which past well off—as she could do no less;
    Though by this politesse she rather suffered,

77

Pricking her fingers with those cursed pins,
Which surely were invented for our sins,—

70

But all this time how slept, or dreamed, Dudu?
    With strict enquiry I could ne'er discover,
And scorn to add a syllable untrue;
    But ere the middle watch hardly over,
And phantoms hovered, or might seem to hover
    Just when the fading lamps waned dim and blue,
To those who like their company, about
    The apartment, on a sudden she screamed out:

73

But what is strange—and a strong proof how great
    A blessing is sound sleep—Juanna lay
As fast as ever husband by his mate
    In holy matrimony snores away.
Not all the clamour broke her happy state
    Of slumber, ere they shook her,—so they say
At least,—and then she too unclosed her eyes,
And yawned a good deal with discreet surprize.

85

As thus Juanna spoke, Dudu turned round
    And hid her face within Juanna's breast;
Her neck alone was seen, but that was found
    The colour of a budding rose's crest.
I can't tell why she blushed, nor can expound
    The mystery of this rupture of their rest;
All that I know is, that the facts I state
Are true as truth has ever been of late.

99

And here she summoned Baba, and required
    Don Juan at his hands, and information
Of what had past since all the slaves retired,
    And whether he had occupied their station;

If matters had been managed as desired,
　　And his disguise with due consideration
Kept up; and above all, the where and how
He had passed the night, was what she wished to know.

102

When Baba saw these symptoms, which he knew
　　to bode him no great good, he deprecated
Her anger, and beseech'd she'd hear him through—
　　He could not help the thing which he related:
Then out it came at length, that to Dudu
　　Juan was given in charge, as hath been stated;
But not by Baba's fault, he said, and swore on
The holy camel's hump, besides the Koran.

Not only were the courts guilty of using the new doctrine of
obscenity for ulterior purposes, but even juries punished on an
extremely questionable basis. In 1841 the publisher of Shelley's
Queen Mab was convicted by a jury of the offense of publishing
obscenity.[12]

We have searched carefully the nearly 20,000 words of the
full thirty pages of *Queen Mab* (one of the most beautiful poems
of all time) for some suggestive verses—a leer—a mild allusion
to sex. Alas, there is nothing! The poem is radical in thought in
its rejection of the perfection of the monarchy and its protest
against then current theology. But of pornography, or sex, there
is nothing. Typical samples follow:

Nature rejects the monarch, not the man;
The subject, not the citizen; for kings
And subjects, mutual foes, forever play
A losing game into each other's hands,
Whose stakes are vice and misery. The man
Of virtuous soul commands not, nor obeys.
Power, like a desolating pestilence,
Pollutes whate'er it touches; and obedience,
Bane of all genius, virtue, freedom, truth,

Makes slaves of men, and of the human frame
A mechanized automaton.

* * * * *

I was an infant when my mother went
To see an atheist burned. She took me there.
The dark-robed priests were met around the pile;
The multitude was gazing silently;
And as the culprit passed with dauntless mien,
Tempered disdain in his unaltering eye,
Mixed with a quiet smile, shone calmly forth;
The thirsty fire crept round his manly limbs;
His resolute eyes were scorched to blindness soon;
His death-pang rent my heart! the insensate mob
Uttered a cry of triumph, and I wept.
"Weep not, child!" cried my mother, "for that man
Has said, There is no God."

A great many people were beginning to experience twinges of
uneasiness because of the broad and blunt aspect of the general
doctrine of obscenity. Then, in 1868, an important, significant,
and dangerous ingredient was added.

ENGLISH COMSTOCKERY

In 1692 the first English society to correct moral standards had
come into being. Although calling itself An Organization for the
Reformation of Manners, it concerned itself primarily with com-
batting the almost universal vices of drunkenness, whoring, and
disregarding the Sabbath. Although the society had more significant problems to contend with than obscenity, certain members
found this particular fight of intense interest and concern. In
1802 a fringe group of the reformation society founded the
Society for the Suppression of Vice. The new organization had as
its avowed purpose the halting of a rapidly increasing flood of

obscene publications, and only secondarily the punishment of blasphemy and the closing of the mushrooming brothels.

The society apparently had cogent leadership, for one of its prime goals was the enactment of appropriate legislation. The first act passed was the Vagrancy Act of 1824 which, among other provisions, punished any public exhibition of an indecent picture with a minimum sentence of three months' hard labor.

In the first fifty years of its existence the Society for the Suppression of Vice started 159 criminal prosecutions and obtained convictions in 154. It succeeded in closing countless stands and shops which sold what the society regarded as questionable literature.

In 1857 the society reached the zenith of its power when it obtained the passage of the famous (infamous?) Lord Campbell's Act which gave magistrates authority to order the destruction of books, pamphlets, prints, and pictures if—in the opinion of the magistrate—the material was obscene. In addition, the act empowered magistrates to issue police warrants to search any premises suspected of containing obscene material. Armed with this legislative weapon the Society for the Suppression of Vice drove the bulk of sex-oriented material underground—as a starter it gave English literature the test of *Regina* vs. *Hicklin*[13] to overcome.

"TO DEPRAVE AND CORRUPT"

The *Regina vs. Hicklin* case probably had more to do with the flowering of censorship in the English-speaking world than any other single factor. This case, which produced a suitable atmosphere for subsequent book-banning and book-burning, involved participants and an item totally unrelated to any concept of obscenity. Henry Scott, highly repected metal broker in the town of Wolverhampton, was a devout member of a militant Protestant group which took umbrage at many of the practices of the

Roman Catholic Church. Activities of this group included the sale of pamphlets exposing what it regarded as dangerous and depraved customs. Mr. Scott personally purchased a number of these pamphlets for a shilling each and subsequently sold them for a shilling each in an attempt to disseminate information about what he regarded as the depravity of the confessional. An examination of the pamphlet titled *The Confessional Unmasked: Showing the Depravity of the Romish Priesthood, the Iniquity of the Confessional, and the Questions Put to Females in Confession,* leads to the inescapable conclusion that it was intended to accomplish only its avowed purpose. There was no evidence of ulterior motive or "dirty" intent. The booklet is divided into two columns, printed in Latin on the left and in English on the right. It runs the gamut of the sex life—primarily of married people—and endeavors to give moral or religious answers to sex questions. For example, one question posed is whether a woman is ever exempt from granting her husband's request for sexual intercourse. (With interesting delicacy, the pamphlet refers to the act as "rendering the marriage debt.") The answer states that the husband should not demand it too carelessly, be drunk, make his request too often or immoderately, and concludes "the debt can neither be paid nor demanded in a public place, nor before children or domestics, nor in the manner which is contrary to nature."

The objection of the pamphleteer to questions of this nature is that theoretically women, including wives, were questioned during confessionals as to whether they engaged in this type of conduct.

A careful search of *The Confessional Unmasked* to see what might have offended the Puritan judges of the mid-nineteenth century reveals the following discussion of fellatio:

> But is it always a mortal sin, if the husband introduces his —— into the mouth of his wife? It is denied by Sanchez and others, provided there be no danger of pollution. But it is

more truly affirmed by Spor. de Matrim,[14] and others, both because in this case, owing to the heat of the mouth, there is proximate danger of pollution, and because this appears of itself a new species of luxury, repugnant to nature (called by some, *Irrumation*), for as often as another vessel than the natural vessel ordained for copulation, is sought by the man, it seems a new species of luxury. However, Spor. and others make an exception, if that be done casually; and, in truth, Sanchez seems to be of this opinion, whilst he excuses that act from mortal sin, should all danger of pollution cease. Pal., also, makes an exception, 'if the husband does this to excite himself for natural copulation.' But, from what has been said before, I think neither ought to be admitted. In the same manner, Sanchez condemns a man of mortal sin, who, in the act of copulation, introduces his finger into the hinder vessel of the wife, because (he says) in this act there is a disposition to sodomy. But I am of opinion that such effect may be found in the act; but, speaking of itself, I do not acknowledge this effect natural in the act. But I say that husbands practising a foul act of this nature, ought always to be severely rebuked.

The pamphlet also takes up the following problem:

We now give a few extracts on the above subjects, which the ingenuity of very fiends could not surpass. Yet it is for teaching this filth that Maynoooth College[15] receives a Parliamentary Grant of 30,000 a year. We hope the days of that iniquitous grant are numbered. If Oxford, Cambridge, and Dublin are to be interfered with, surely so also may Maynooth.

You will ask, whether, and at what times, touches, looks, and filthy words are permitted among married persons?

Ans. Such acts are of themselves lawful to them because, to whom the end is lawful, the means are also lawful; and to whom the consummation is lawful, so also is the beginning; consequently, they lawfully excite nature to copulation by such acts. But, if these acts are performed separately and without order to copulation, as, for example, for the purpose of pleasure alone, they are venial sins, because, in respect of the state which renders those acts honourable, they have a right to them; unless, however, as often happens, they are joined with danger of pollution, or the married parties have a vow of chastity, for in that case they are mortal sins, as has been said above.

Despite the obvious religious aspect of the pamphlet and the lack of true pornographic content, the local obscenity group, then called the "Watch Committee," arranged for the arrest of Scott and the seizure of 252 copies of the pamphlet which he had for sale. The case came to trial before the Court of Quarter Sessions and the lower court judge (then called the Recorder) ordered Scott freed and the seized material released on the ground that the pamphlet was not obscene, would not have the effect of corrupting public morals, and was intended solely to discredit the Roman Catholic Church. The Queen appealed to the Court of Queen's Bench presided over by Sir Alexander Cockburn. Chief Justice Cockburn reversed the Recorder, ordered the pamphlets destroyed, and laid down the first and probably the most famous of all tests for obscenity: "I think the best test of obscenity is this, whether the tendency of the matter charged as obscenity is to deprave and corrupt those whose minds are open to such immoral influences, and into whose hands a publication of this sort may fall."

A thoughtful reading of this definition reveals a series of fallacies. The first is that it requires merely a *"tendency"* of the matter, not a certainty, not a sureness, not even a likelihood. Now what is the "tendency" of the matter likely to do? It simply will have this tendency to deprave and corrupt. Deprave and corrupt whom? The answer is: those whose minds are open to the immoral influences. This means that, if any judge can interpret the material as possibly having a tendency to deprave and corrupt anyone, the answer is given. The judge need only say that *he believes* that this material *might* have a tendency to deprave or corrupt a child or weak-minded person. Thus the contest is over. There exists no burden to *prove* that there are people who might be open to the immoral influences. It is sufficient if the judge simply *believes* they exist.

It is true that at the end of the definition a few additional words state that there should be some demonstration that the publication might fall into the hands of the people who might be corrupted or depraved by it. However, this proviso was studiously ignored. Even in the *Hicklin* case, which established the opinion, obviously no attention could have been given this point, for surely whoever saw this pamphlet would recognize that it would never conceivably or possibly deprave or corrupt any child, adolescent, teenager, or weak-minded person. Unless the youth of 1868 were much better educated than the youth of today none of them would ever have taken a second glance at the pamphlet. The inescapable conclusion must be that the Hicklin case used a rule of obscenity as an excuse to burn anti-religious pamphlets.

Modern doctrine holds that although an item may "deprave and corrupt" youngsters or teenagers, this does not constitute sufficient grounds for ruling the matter obscene. Therefore, when police officials impound items on alleged obscenity charges it becomes important to know what class of person is being protected. Consequently, the following information is frequently forthcoming after cross examination of the law enforcement officer involved in the particular case:

QUESTION: Why did you pick up this magazine *Scream* and the book *Sex at the Fireside?*
ANSWER: I believe that this magazine and that book are both bad and should not be offered for sale.
Q. I assume you did it because you believe that tendency of *Scream* and *Sex at the Fireside* will be to deprave and corrupt?
A. Yes.
Q. Having looked at this book and magazine, do you believe they will have a tendency to deprave and corrupt *you?*
A. Of course not. I have had too much experience and I don't think there's anything I haven't seen and there is no book or magazine that could affect me in any way.

Q. Well, whom do you think a book and magazine of this nature will affect?

A. Young people, teenagers, adults with weak and juvenile minds, and all kinds of people.

The preceding dialogue, although fictitious as reported here, is typical of the type of response that we get when proper legal procedures are employed in order to elicit the information. These officials always believe they are protecting someone other than themselves. In the same way the judges in the century following Lord Cockburn's ruling never believed that any of the material could "deprave and corrupt" them, but they were always protecting some segment of the community "whose minds are open to such immoral influences."

The next element of the Cockburn test is the audience which might be influenced. As stated in the test, this is any person or group whose mind or minds are open to "immoral influences" and into whose hands such a publication might fall. This, of course, creates a theoretical composite omnipresent audience exposed to a vague potential possibility of becoming the recipient of an obscene publication. The language clearly states "may fall," not with certainty *will fall* or with some degree of reasonable foresight probably *shall reach,* but actually only *may* fall. Consequently, so long as an item (in the opinion of the judges) could possibly deprave and corrupt some group into whose hands it *might* fall, then the item is obscene. Under such a test it is not surprising that as late as 1930 the Supreme Judicial Court of Massachusetts found one of America's greatest novels—Theodore Dreiser's *An American Tragedy*—obscene and unfit for sale.[16]

Despite the tons of criticism that have been heaped on the obscenity test laid down by Chief Justice Cockburn it remains basically the law in England. In 1959 the English Parliament enacted the Obscene Publication Act, which law provides:

For the purposes of this Act an article shall be deemed to

be obscene if its effect or (where the article comprises two or more distinct items) the effect of any one of its items is, if taken as a whole, such as to tend to deprave and corrupt persons who are likely, having regard to all relevant circumstances, to read, see or hear the matter contained or embodied in it.

However, although the words did not change, attitudes did. For most of the century following the Hicklin test, almost anything that could be called sexy could also be banned in England. A comparatively recent case, although resulting in a conviction, shows the present split in English law and thinking. *Shaw's* case, which was tried before a judge and jury in Old Bailey, September, 1960, is not as clear as might be desired because the defendant was held on three different charges: (1) conspiracy to corrupt public morals, (2) publishing an obscene book, *The Lady's Directory,* and finally (3) living off the earnings of a prostitute.

Mr. Shaw endeavored to assist prostitutes in the pursuit of their trade when a 1959 English law, the Street Offenses Act, prohibited them from streetwalking and from accosting men in order to solicit trade. He published a business directory of women engaged in sexual commerce, which gave names and addresses, displayed photographs, and even carried advertisements in which the enterprising businesswomen indicated their proficiency in certain sexual practices. The directory was, in fact, merely a successor to a number of such books published in other years. One historian found a book published in 1780 entitled the *List of Covent Garden Ladies.*

Essentially the case turned on whether publication of a directory of this nature constituted publication of an obscene item. In earlier years all judges and juries would have made short shrift of the case, rendered a conviction, and there would have been no appeals. In this case the judge charged the jury as follows:

> The test, therefore, that you have got to apply is laid down by the act of Parliament—is the effect of this publication,

taken as a whole, such as to tend to deprave and corrupt persons who are likely to read it. . . . if the effect of this document is thought by you to encourage or induce readers of it to resort to prostitutes for fornication and/or for the other deviations which we have heard about, and if that is a thing which corrupts and depraves such people, and if you think they are then acting in a depraved and corrupt way, then in my view the effect of this article would be to tend to deprave and corrupt and it would be obscene within the definition of this Act. Whether to induce or encourage a person likely to read this article to resort to prostitution for this purpose, does, in fact, tend to deprave and corrupt is of course a matter for you in the light of my previous observations to you on this subject.

On appeal, the next court (the Court of Criminal Appeal) held the defendant guilty but indicated its uncertainty by authorizing further appeal to the House of Lords.

This august body actually split. Lord Reid, dissenting, wrote a full opinion and included an argument that there was no such thing as a conspiracy to corrupt public morals.

EARLY AMERICAN DEVELOPMENTS

In the colonies no one bothered to prosecute for obscenity. The first case involving obscenity in the United States, *Commonwealth vs. Sharpless*,[17] was heard in 1815. The charge was displaying an obscene picture depicting a man in an obscene posture with a woman. The Mayor's Court of Philadelphia convicted, and the appeal to the Supreme Court was heard by Chief Justice William Tilghman, who made short shrift of the argument that sexual pictures do not create crimes. The Chief Justice ruled:

That actions against public decency were always crimes, as tending to corrupt the public morals, I can have no doubt;

because, even in the profligate reign of Charles II, Sir Charles
Sedley was punished by imprisonment and a heavy fine, for
standing naked on a balcony, in a public part of the City of
London. It is true, that besides this shameful exhibition, it is
mentioned in some of the reports of that case, that he threw
down bottles, containing offensive liquid, among the people;
but we have the highest authority for saying, that most criminal part of his conduct and that which principally drew upon
him the vengeance of the law, was the exposure of his person.

In the mid-eighteenth century there came in rapid succession
three significant English novels. In 1748 Samuel Richardson
wrote and published *Clarissa: or the History of a Young Lady,*
Tobias Smollett published *The Adventures of Roderick Random,* and in 1749 Henry Fielding presented to the world *Tom
Jones.* In the midst of these publications came *The Memoirs of a
Woman of Pleasure* by John Cleland, reputedly published in
1749, although advertisements as early as 1748 can be located.

The first three books became classics of the novel, and *Memoirs,* commonly known as *Fanny Hill,* achieved fame as the great
sex novel. An excerpt from it is included later in this book.

The origins of *Fanny Hill* are obscure, but many literary histo-
rians subscribe to the view that John Cleland made a bet with
some friends that he could write the "dirtiest" book in the
English language without using a single "dirty" word.[18] Probably many a college lad would agree with Cleland, who did
create what was (up to recently) the most vivid word picture of
sexual activity ever written in the English language.

At first the book circulated freely in England, was advertised
in the newspapers, and had a reasonably good and legitimate
sale. At the end of the eighteenth century, with the rise of Puritanism, Victorianism, and the Societies for the Suppression of
Sex, the book was outlawed. This made it possible for any
printer, with impunity, to publish an edition of the book. Its
publication rapidly became a bookprinter's method of picking
up extra money from an under-the-counter edition.

Fanny Hill is of particular interest today because in 1963 G. P. Putnam's Sons published the first open edition and thereby set off a new series of court decisions of what constitutes "obscenity."

Memoirs holds the dubious distinction of being the first book to be banned in the United States. A printer named Holmes produced an under-the-counter edition and was arrested and convicted. The highest court in Massachusetts sustained the conviction. [19]

It is significant that Jesse Sharpless, for exhibition of a picture, and Peter Holmes, for publishing a book, were convicted and punished under the so-called "common law." At this time there had been no legislation on obscenity.

In 1821, Vermont became the first state in the United States to enact a law against the distribution of obscene books or pictures. Connecticut followed in 1824 and Massachusetts the following year.

In 1842 the first Federal act was passed. In its first pronouncement Congress limited its activity to the control of "imports." The law provided that there should not be admitted into the United States and, if admitted, there should be destroyed upon arrival at customs, "all indecent and obscene prints, paintings, lithographs, engravings and transparencies."

Significantly, the first law did not cover books, pamphlets, or any other printed material. The first objective was to stop French postcards and offensive (to Puritan America) European nudist art. However, as nineteenth-century sexual morality became more and more jealous of its prerogatives in governing the lives of Americans, the Customs Law was gradually amended. In 1857 a clause on indecent and obscene "articles" was added, and later all forms of photographs and printed materials were included.

The middle of the nineteenth century witnessed the emergence of a young man who probably had more effect on English

literature than any writer, publisher, or critic. The man—
Anthony Comstock[20]—born in Connecticut and raised under the
harsh Puritan discipline of a Connecticut Congregational household, volunteered for service in the Union army in 1863. Upon
his return from an eventful eighteen months of duty he began a
campaign destined to last forty years. The basis of his campaign
was the slogan: "Morals, not Art or Literature." He formed the
Committee for the Suppression of Vice, which later became the
famous Society for the Suppression of Vice. The society captured
the imagination of many wealthy people who, in some cases for
ulterior reasons, wanted to continue a Victorian morality. Even
J. P. Morgan made substantial contributions to the society.

Comstock became a crusader. From early morning to late at
night he was a sleuth on the trail of what he regarded as obscenity. Some insight into his mentality can be gained from the
following points:

One of his earliest slogans was: "Books are feeders for
brothels." He insisted that in art, regardless of artist or purpose,
the human figure should be clothed. He objected to statues of
nudes unless there were fig leaves over the genitals and coverings
for the breasts. He objected to pictures or stories about Lady
Godiva, and on one occasion he seized and endeavored to destroy
117 prime examples of French classical art.

An inkling of Comstock's power may be gleaned from the fact
that in 1873 Comstock and his supporters lobbied through both
houses of Congress the law that governed the depositing of
"obscenity" in the mails. Not only did he obtain the enactment
of this law, which is still known as the "Comstock Act," [21] but he
accomplished the result with less than an hour of Congressional
debate. The law was hurried through in the closing hours of an
active Congressional session, the final vote taken at two o'clock of
a Sunday morning with the clock being stopped to preserve the
legislative fiction that it was still Saturday. The Comstock Act

provided that no obscene, lewd, or lascivious book, pamphlet, picture, or publication could be carried in the mails. For the first time, it became a felony to use the mails to carry such material. The law provided for a fine of $5,000 and imprisonment up to five years for the first offense, with $10,000 and ten years as a limit for subsequent offenses.

Not only did Comstock obtain the passage of the law but he got himself appointed as a special agent of the Post Office to enforce the law. And to gild the lily, he contrived to obtain for himself or the Society a portion of the fines collected on successful prosecutions. In the first year under the law, Comstosk boasted he seized 200,000 pictures and photographs, 100,000 books, and more than 60,000 rubber articles (probably rubber contraceptives). On the amusing side he also seized more than 5,000 packs of playing cards and 30,000 boxes of pills and powders having aphrodisiac qualities.

In the same year the Comstock Act was passed, the validity of the Postal Inspection Service received its first test in *United States vs. Bott.*[22] In that case the Federal District Court for the Southern District of New York quickly affirmed the conviction of two men charged with sending through the mails powder intended to cause abortions. The District Court stated without reservation that Congress had the power to eliminate material from the mails.

In 1878 the *Orlando Jackson*[23] case constituted the first test of the Comstock Act. The Supreme Court affirmed the authority of Congress to prohibit the use of mails for the distribution of materials which it regarded as contrary to public morals. However, the court created an interesting reservation when it denied the authority of the postal officials to invade the privacy of first-class mail. To this day first-class mail is accorded complete exemption from examination, and any interference with this right is illegal.

THE HICKLIN RULE ARRIVES IN
THE UNITED STATES

Shortly after the pronouncement by Chief Justice Cockburn of the infamous *Hicklin* rule, the lower courts of the United States adopted and used it. However, more than a decade passed before an appellate court had an opportunity to write a thorough opinion on the subject. In 1879 Circuit Judge Samuel Blatchford wrote a fully considered opinion in *United States vs. Bennett,*[24] in which the defendant Deboigne M. Bennett had been convicted for mailing a booklet entitled *The Binding Forces of Conjugal Life.* The prosecution was initiated by Anthony Comstock, and for the first time the defendants vigorously defended. Notwithstanding the defense that the booklet had no relationship to obscenity but was intended as an educational pamphlet, the court ruled that under the Hicklin decision conviction could be sustained.

The Hicklin rule reached at least one high point when in 1859 a physician was found guilty of using the mails to circulate a treatise on venereal disease.[25]

The United States Supreme Court sustained the first conviction under the Comstock Act when Lew Rosen, publisher of the periodical *Broadway,* was sentenced to thirteen months in prison for publishing a newspaper which contained photographs of almost nude females.[26]

Anthony Comstock died in 1915. Already a few dissident voices could be heard. For example, in *United States vs. Kennerly,*[27] (1913) a young progressive judge named Learned Hand went along with the existing law, but set forth in his opinion the following protest, which has become a landmark in the fight against censorship:

I hope it is not improper for me to say that the rule as laid down, however consonant it may be with mid-Victorian morals, does not seem to me to answer to the understanding and morality of the present time, as conveyed by the words, "obscene, lewd or lascivious." I question whether in the end men will regard that as obscene which is honestly relevant to the adequate expression of innocent ideas, and whether they will not believe that truth and beauty are too precious to society at large to be mutilated in the interests of those most likely to pervert them to base uses. Indeed, it seems hardly likely that we are even today so lukewarm in our interests in letters or serious discussion as to be content to reduce our treatment of sex to the standard of a child's library in the supposed interest of a salacious few, or that shame will for long prevent us from adequate portrayal of some of the most serious and beautiful sides of human nature.

However, despite the straws in the wind, it took another decade and a half for the protest to become real rather than verbal.

In 1930 Judge Hand's words first became meaningful (as the next section will show) and Massachusetts upheld the conviction of David Friede, for offering one of America's best novels, Theodore Dreiser's *An American Tragedy*, for public sale.[28]

Dreiser's great novel was defended by none other than Arthur Garfield Hayes, who brought forth a whole battery of arguments why the book should not be held obscene or banned. The high court, in what is probably the high-water mark of bias against literature, ruled against Hayes on every point. The court accepted the *Hicklin* rule without modification and decided that passages could be quoted out of context from the book to show that it was obscene and might—in the hands of youth—corrupt morals.

This decision created so much controversy that it forced the Massachusetts legislature to amend its obscenity law. The then-existing Massachusetts law provided that any book containing obscene or impure language could be held to be obscene. The law was amended to apply only to a book which in itself was "obscene, indecent or impure." [29]

Ironically the leading fighter of the Massachusetts decision was the redoubtable H. L. Mencken, who, although he thought very little of *An American Tragedy* and regarded it as a sloppy, chaotic piece of junk, battled hard and vigorously for Dreiser's right to publish such material.

THE FIRST BREAK

In the 1920's a distinguished American woman, Mary Ware Dennett, wrote a paper for the sexual education of her two sons. It included the unpopular statement that the major evil of masturbation was the feeling of guilt it created and the excess it might encourage. This was written at a time when church and state uniformly condemned all forms of masturbation as activity designed by the devil. Secondly, Mrs. Dennett pointed out methods of avoiding venereal disease and indicated that it was curable. This, too, offended the bluenoses, who frequently argued that venereal disease ought not be curable, but rather should be fatal punishment for sexual transgressors.

The essay to the Dennett boys became so widely read that the *Medical Review of Reviews* published it and subsequently the Voluntary Parenthood League reprinted it in pamphlet form and offered it for sale. The Post Office Department obtained a copy through one of its hired entrappers and requested the Federal District Attorney to obtain an indictment of Mrs. Dennett. The Brooklyn Grand Jury obliged. Mrs. Dennett stood trial before a judge and jury and was convicted and sentenced to pay a $300 fine. This time the bluenoses had picked an adversary with the courage to speak out. Mrs. Dennett stood before the court proudly and declaimed in ringing tones, "If I have in fact corrupted youth a fine of $300 is too light a penalty. I will appeal and should go to jail if my conviction is sustained."

The following excerpts are taken from the pamphlet's *Introduction for Elders*:

On the moral side I have tried to avoid confusion and dogmatism in the following ways by eliminating fear of venereal disease as an appeal for strictly limited sex relations, stating candidly that venereal disease is becoming curable; by barring out all mention of "brute" or "animal" passion, terms frequently used in pleas for chastity and self-control, as such talk is an aspersion on the brute and has done children much harm in giving them the impression that there is an essential baseness in the sex relation; by inviting the inference that marriage is "sacred" by virtue of its being a reflection of human ideality rather than because it is a legalized institution.

Unquestionably the stress which most have laid upon the beauty of nature's plans for perpetuating the plant and animal species, and the effort to have the child carry over into human life some sense of that beauty has come from a most commendable instinct to protect the child from the natural shock of the revelation of so much that is unesthetic and revolting in human sex life. The nearness of the sex organs to the excretory organs, the pain and messiness of childbirth are elements which certainly need some compensating antidote to prevent their making too disagreeable and disproportionate an impression on the child's mind.

The results are doubtless good as far as they go, but they do not go nearly far enough. What else is there to call upon to help out? Why, the one thing which has been persistently neglected by practically all the sex writers—the emotional side of sex experience. Parents and teachers have been afraid of it and distrustful of it. In not a single one of all the books for young people that I have thus far read has there been the frank, unashamed declaration that the climax of sex emotion is an unsurpassed joy, something which rightly belongs to every normal human being, a joy to be proudly and serenely experienced. Instead there has been all too evident an inference that sex emotion is a thing to be ashamed of, that yielding to it is indulgence which must be curbed as much as possible, that all thought and understanding of it must be rigorously postponed, at any rate till after marriage.

In discussing the emotions created by the sex act, the pamphlet states:

It means that a man and a woman feel that they belong to no one else; it makes them wonderfully happy to be together; they find they want to live together, work together, play together, and to have children together, that is, to marry each other; and their dream is to be happy together all their lives. The idea of sex relations between people who do not love each other, who do not feel any sense of belonging to each other, will always be revolting to highly developed sensitive people.

People's lives grow finer and their characters better, if they have sex relations only with those they love. And those who make the wretched mistake of yielding to the sex impulse alone when there is no love to go with it, usually live to despise themselves for their weakness and their bad taste. They are always ashamed of doing it, and they try to keep it secret from their families and those they respect. You can be sure that whatever people are ashamed to do is something that can never bring them real happiness. It is true that one's sex relations are the most personal and private matters in the world, and they belong just to us and to no one else, but while we may be shy and reserved about them, *we are not ashamed.*

When two people really love each other, they don't care who knows it. They are proud of their happiness. But no man is ever proud of his connection with a prostitute and no prostitute is ever proud of her business.

Sex relations belong to love, and love is never a *business.* Love is the nicest thing in the world, but it can't be bought. And the sex side of it is the biggest and most important side of it, so it is the one side of us that we must be absolutely sure to keep in good order and perfect health, if we are going to be happy ourselves or make any one else happy.

97

Three distinguished circuit judges: Augustus N. Hand, Thomas W. Swan, and Harrie B. Chase, heard the appeal, reversed the district court, and acquitted Mrs. Dennett.[30] In pure reasoning the case is not too helpful. It does not purport to change any rules and simply offers an *ad hoc* argument that a sex pamphlet cannot be, if properly written, obscene. The major point of the court is made in the following language:

> Mrs. Dennett's discussion of the phenomena of sex is written with sincerity of feeling and with an idealization of the marriage relation and sex emotions. We think it tends to rationalize and dignify such emotions rather than to arouse lust. While it may be thought by some that portions of the tract go into unnecessary details that would better have been omitted, it may be fairly answered that the curiosity of many adolescents would not be satisfied without full explanation, and that no more than that is really given. It also may reasonably be thought that accurate information, rather than mystery and curiosity, is better in the long run and is less likely to occasion lascivious thoughts than ignorance and anxiety. Perhaps instruction other than that which Mrs. Dennett suggests would be better. That is a matter as to which there is bound to be a wide difference of opinion, but, irrespective of this, we hold that any accurate exposition of the relevant facts of the sex side of life in decent language and in manifestly serious and disinterested spirit cannot ordinarily be regarded as obscene. Any incidental tendency to arouse sex impulses which such a pamphlet may perhaps have is apart from and subordinate to its main effect. The tendency can only exist in so far as it is inherent in any sex instruction, and it would seem to be outweighed by the elimination of ignorance, curiosity, and morbid fear. The direct aim and the net result is to promote understanding and self-control.

The importance of the case lies more in what it did rather than in what it said. In reversing a lower court and a jury which had found that the pamphlet was obscene, the court implied that a decision on such a case was a question of law. Up to this point, it was generally regarded that what was or was not "obscenity" was a question of fact for a jury or a judge (acting as a trier of facts.)

FUCKING BECOMES LEGAL

In 1922, after years of unsuccessful endeavor, James Joyce obtained the publication of his lengthy novel *Ulysses* in Paris. It was banned in this country by the customs authorities and more than a decade of American tourists could show at least one tangible result of their trips abroad by returning to the United States with a coveted copy of *Ulysses*. In 1926 Samuel Roth, who later became famous for Supreme Court litigation, serialized a bowdlerized version of the book strictly as an act of literary piracy. More than a hundred distinguished authors signed a complaint in an effort to protect Joyce's literary rights. These included T. S. Eliot, Ernest Hemingway, D. H. Lawrence, Virginia Woolf— all widely known figures in the literary world. However, nobody made a legal test of whether *Ulysses* could be brought into the United States until the courageous Bennett Cerf of Random House arranged for the book to be sent into the Port of New York in such fashion as to be seized by the port authorities.

District Judge John M. Woolsey tried the case. The government attacked the book on two grounds: the use of Anglo-Saxon four-letter words, and the frankness of thought employed by Joyce in his stream of consciousness.

Morris L. Ernst, counsel for Random House, believes the following colloquy between counsel and the court may have contributed much to the forthright decision of the judge.[31]

> COUNSEL: Judge, as to the word "fuck," one etymological dictionary gives its derivation as from *facere*—to make—the farmer fucked the seed into the soil. This, your honor, has more integrity than a euphemism used every day in every modern novel to describe precisely the same event.

JUDGE WOOLSEY: For example . . .
COUNSEL: Oh—"They slept together." It means the same thing.
JUDGE WOOLSEY (smiling): But, Counselor, that isn't even usually the truth!

After considerable study, Judge Woolsey rendered his opinion that the book was not obscene.[32] The key point in the decision is the following statement:

> Whether a particular book would tend to excite [sexual] . . . impulses and thoughts must be tested by the Court's opinion as to its effect on a person with average sex instincts—what the French would call *l'homme moyen sensuel*—who plays in this branch of legal inquiry, the same role of hypothetical reagent as does the "reasonable man" in the law of torts and "the man learned in the art" on questions of invention in patent law.

If sustained, this opinion would change the entire law on the subject. It was no longer a question of whether the material would arouse the sex instincts of *any* person, even a weak-minded adult or a child, but would it arouse the sex instincts of a knowledgeable man?

The government appealed to the Second Circuit Court. Judges Learned Hand and Augustus N. Hand (cousins) affirmed the decision and Judge Martin T. Manton dissented. The circuit court lays down some interesting rules. It clearly adopts the rule that even though a book may "to some extent and among some people . . . tend to promote lustful thoughts" it will not be regarded as obscene unless obscenity is "the dominant note of the publication."

A second major point the court makes is that passages of an isolated nature cannot be taken out of context and tested in the law. Any book must be treated as a unit and the "dominant effect" of the book is the key to whether it would be regarded as obscene. Finally, the court decides that even though portions of the book "justly may offend many" people since it is a "book of originality and sincerity of treatment" it cannot be banned. (This is very close to the law as it exists in the 1960's.)

Circuit Court Judge Manton dissented vigorously, basing his opinion almost entirely on the case of *Regina v. Hicklin,* 1868.

The government did not appeal the circuit court decision and after 1933 *Ulysses* became a commonplace item in public libraries in the United States.

The following material, illustrative of James Joyce's *Ulysses,* is taken from the Modern Library Giant edition. The book is extremely difficult to describe and impossible to summarize. These excerpts can only give the flavor.

> Bello: Well, I'm not. Wait. (*He holds in his breath.*) Curse it. Here. This bung's about burst. (*He uncorks himself behind; then, contorting his features, farts loudly.*) Take that! (*He recorks himself.*) Yes, by Jingo, sixteen three quarters.

* * * * *

Yes I think he made them a bit firmer sucking them like that so long he made me thirsty titties he calls them I had to laugh yes this one anyhow stiff the nipple gets for the least thing Ill get him to keep that up and Ill take those eggs beaten up with marsala fatten them out for him what are all those veins and things curious the way its made 2 the same in case of twins theyre supposed to represent beauty place up there like those statues in the museum one of them pretending to hide it with her hand are they so beautiful of course compared with what a man looks like with his two bags full and his other thing hanging down out of him or sticking up at you like a hatrack no wonder they hide it with cabbageleaf the woman is beauty of course thats admitted when he said I could pose for a picture naked to some rich fellow in Holles street when he lost the job in Helys and I was selling the clothes and strumming in the coffee palace would I be like that bath of the nymph with my hair down yes only shes younger

* * * * *

they want everything in their mouth all the pleasure those men get out of a woman I can feel his mouth O Lord I must stretch myself I wished he was here or somebody to let myself go with and come again like that I feel all fire inside me or if I could dream it when he made me spend the 2nd time tickling me behind with his finger I was coming for about 5 minutes with my legs around him I had to hug him after O Lord I wanted to shout out all sorts of things fuck or shit or anything at all only not to look ugly or those lines from the strain who knows the way hed take it you want to feel your way with a man theyre not all like him thank God some of them want you to be so nice about it I noticed the contrast he does it and doesnt talk I gave my eyes that look with my hair a bit loose from the tumbling and my tongue between my lips up to him the savage brute Thursday Friday one Saturday two Sunday three O Lord I cant wait till Monday

* * * * *

he must have come 3 or 4 times with that tremendous big red brute of a thing he has I thought the vein or whatever the dickens they call it was going to burst though his nose is not so big after I took off all my things with the blinds down after my hours dressing and perfuming and combing it like iron or some kind of a thick crowbar standing all the time he must have eaten oysters I think a few dozen he was in great singing voice no I never in all my life felt anyone had one the size of that to make you feel full up he must have eaten a whole sheep after whats the idea making us like that with a big hole in the middle of us like a Stallion driving it up into you because thats all they want out of you with that determined vicious look in his eye I had to half shut my eyes still he hasn't such a tremendous amount of spunk in him when I made him pull it out and do it on me considering how big it is so much the better in case any of it wasnt washed out properly the last time I let him finish in me nice invention they made for women for him to get all the pleasure but if someone gave them a touch of it themselves theyd know what I went through with Milly nobody would believe cutting her teeth too and Mina Purefoys husband give us a swing out of your whiskers filling her up with a child or twins once a year

as regular as the clock always with a smell of children off her
the one they called budgers or something like a nigger with a
shock of hair on it Jesusjack the child is a black the last time
I was there a squad of them falling over one another and
bawling you couldn't hear your ears supposed to be healthy
not satisfied till they have us swollen out like elephants or I
dont know what supposing I risked having another not off him
though still if he was married Im sure hed have a fine strong
child but I don't know Poldy has more spunk in him yes thatd
be awfully jolly I suppose it was meeting Josie Powell and the
funeral and thinking about me and Boylan set him off well
he can think what he likes now if thatll do him any good I
know they were spooning a bit when I came on the scene he
was dancing and sitting out with her the night Georgina
Simpsons housewarming and then he wanted to ram it down
my neck on account of not liking to see her a wallflower that
was why we had the standup row over politics he began it not
me when he said about Our Lord being a carpenter . . . .

* * * * *

Private Carr: (*Tugging at his belt*) I'll wring the neck of any
bugger says a word against my fucking king.

* * * * *

Ill put on my best shift and drawers let him have a good eyeful
out of that to make his micky stand for him Ill let him know
if thats what he wanted that his wife is fucked yes and damn
well fucked too up to my neck nearly not by him 5 or 6 times
handrunning theres the mark of his spunk on the clean sheet
I wouldnt bother to even iron it out that ought to satisfy him
if you dont believe me feel my belly unless I made him stand
there and put him into me Ive a mind to tell him every scrap
and make him do it in front of me serve him right its all his
own fault if Im an adulteress as the thing in the gallery said
O much about it if thats all the harm ever we did in this
vale of tears God knows its not much doesnt everybody only
they hide it I suppose thats what a woman is supposed to be
there for or He wouldnt have made us the way He did so attrac-
tive to men then if he wants to kiss my bottom Ill drag open
my drawers and bulge it right out in his face as large as life

he can stick his tongue 7 miles up my hole as hes there my brown-part. . . .

LEGAL CONTRADICTIONS BEGIN—
GOD'S LITTLE ACRE

One would expect after the enlightened viewpoint and erudite opinion rendered in the *Ulysses* case that the law would take a liberal turn in the direction of freedom and permissiveness. The opinion was clear, the rules were intelligent, and the results should have been excellent. However, because this field of law tends to be more emotional than logical, the results were completely contrary to those which normally would have been anticipated. The opinions of the courts began to express not law but the personal prejudices of the opinion-writers.

This period produced the interesting phenomenon of the same book or play being held a fine work of art in one court and a piece of the devil's obscenity in another.

An excellent example of this confusion is furnished by Erskine Caldwell's *God's Little Acre* which was published by Viking Press in the early 1930's. Caldwell, one of the new school of realistic writers, faithfully recorded the language of his characters and described their sexual activities. The book derives its name from the fact that one of the major characters has set aside one of his acres of land for God, but, fearing that the acre could be the lucky acre on which he might find gold, he continually changes it. The New York Society for the Prevention of Vice took violent exception to the book and obtained a criminal indictment of Viking Press for publishing it. The case was tried before an enlightened New York magistrate, Judge Greenspan, and was one of the first of the obscenity trials in which modern-day methods were used on behalf of the defense. Some of the greatest literary figures of the day testified on behalf of the book.

These included Franklin P. Adams, John Mason Brown, Marc Connelly, James T. Farrell, Lewis Gannett, Sinclair Lewis, Elmer Rice, and Carl Van Doren.

The magistrate ruled that the book was not obscene because it "has no tendency to incite its readers to behave like its characters."[33] Furthermore, the judge said: "The Court may not require the author to put refined language in the mouths of primitive people."

Such a decision plus the approval of the great literary figures of the day, and with the years adding to the reputation of Caldwell as a man of letters, should have disposed of obscenity charges against *God's Little Acre* for all time. However, in the Alice in Wonderland field of obscenity, the logical rarely happens. Over the next two decades the book was banned in some cities and cleared in others. It was banned in St. Paul as late as 1946 and in Denver in 1947, but cleared in Philadelphia in 1946 and in Los Angeles in 1948.

Controversy over this book reached a peak when, after being banned in Boston, the case of *Attorney General vs. Book Named "God's Little Acre"* [34] came before the highest court of Massachusetts.

The attorney general used the provisions of a 1945 Massachusetts law to file a petition before the court to have *God's Little Acre* adjudicated "obscene, indecent, or impure." The lower court judge, ruling in favor of the book, found that "the book as a whole would not stimulate sexual passions or desires in a person with average sex instincts." He concluded that the book would not have "a substantial tendency to deprave and corrupt its readers by inciting lascivious thoughts or arousing lustful desires."

The Supreme Judicial Court of Massachusetts (highest court) reversed the Superior Court on the following grounds:

The book abounds in sexual episodes and some are portrayed

105

with an abundance of realistic detail. In some instances, the author's treatment of sexual relations descends to outright pornography. Nothing would be gained by spreading these portions of the book on the pages of this opinion.

In discussing the literary nature of the book and the evidence produced at the hearing, the court stated:

> Evidence was introduced at the hearing below by literary critics, professors of English literature, and a professor of sociology touching the "literary, cultural and educational character" of the book. In general, the literary experts regarded the book as a sincere and serious work possessing literary merit. The sociologist was of the opinion that the book was of value as a sociological document in its portayal of life of the so-called "poor whites" in the south.

Notwithstanding the foregoing the court concluded that regardless of how literary or how much of a work of art a book is it does not "necessarily dispel obscenity."

The high court recognized that both New York and Pennsylvania had found this specific book by specific judicial opinion not obscene. However, it quickly, if not cogently, disposed of these decisions simply by saying: "A discussion of these decisions would not be profitable."

Finally, the court had to dispose of the argument of the attorneys representing Erskine Caldwell that a decree declaring the book to be obscene was a violation of the Constitution of the United States. The court's brilliant and scintillating answer to that argument was: "The contention that a decree adjudicating the book as obscene, indecent or impure would be an abridgement of the rights of freedom of the press guaranteed by the . . . Constitution of the United States requires no discussion."

In *God's Little Acre* Ty Ty Walden's son Buck is married to Griselda. Ty Ty is very fond of Griselda and makes no attempt to conceal his feelings. He says concerning his daughter-in-law:

"I ain't ashamed of nothing," Ty Ty said heatedly. "I reckon Griselda is just about the prettiest girl I ever did see. There ain't a man alive who's ever seen a finer-looking pair of rising beauties as she's got. Why, man alive! They're that pretty it makes me feel sometime like getting right down on my hands and knees like these old hound dogs you see chasing after a flowing bitch. You just ache to get down and lick something. That's the way, and it's God's own truth as He would tell it Himself if He could talk like the rest of us."

Will, Ty Ty's son-in-law, frustrated by the painful loss of a labor strike, said to Griselda, in the presence of his wife Rosamund and despite the threat of his brother-in-law Buck to kill him:

"I'm going to look at you like God intended for you to be seen. I'm going to rip every piece of those things off of you in a minute. I'm going to rip them off and tear them into pieces so small you'll never be able to put them together again. I'm going to rip the last damn thread. I'm a loomweaver. I've woven cloth all my life, making every kind of fabric in God's world. Now I'm going to tear all that to pieces so small nobody will ever know what they were. They'll look like lint when I get through. Down there in the mill I've woven ginghams and shirting, denim and sheeting, and all the rest; up here in this yellow company house I'm going to tear hell out of the cloth on you. We're going to start spinning and weaving again tomorrow, but tonight I'm going to tear that cloth on you till it looks like lint out of a gin."

He went toward her. The veins on the backs of his hands and around his arms swelled and throbbed, looking as if they would burst. He came closer, stopping at arm's length to look at her.

Griselda stepped backward out of his reach. She was not afraid of Will, because she knew he would not hurt her. But she stepped backward out of his reach, afraid of the look in his eyes. Will's eyes were not cruel, and they were not murderous—he would not hurt her for anything in the world—they were too tender for that now—and his eyes were coming closer and closer.

107

Will caught the collar of her dress, a hand on each side, flung his arms wide apart. The thin printed voile disintegrated in his hands like steam. He had ripped it from her, tearing it insanely in his hands, quickly, eagerly, minutely. She watched him with throbbing excitement, following the arcs of his flying fingers and the motions of his arms. Piece by piece he tore like a madman, hurling the fluffy lint in all directions around the room while he bent forward over the cloth. She watched him unresistingly when he flung the last of the dress aside and ripped open the white slip as though it were a paper bag. He was working faster all the time, tearing, ripping, jerking, throwing the shredded cloth around him and blowing the flying lint from his face. The final garment was silk. He tore at it frantically, even more savagely than he had at the beginning. When that was done, she was standing before him, waiting, trembling, just as he had said she would stand. Perspiration covered his face and chest. His breathing was difficult. He had worked as he had never done before, and the shredded cloth lay on the floor at his feet, covering them.

"Now!" he shouted at her. "Now! God damn it, now! I told you to stand there like God intended for you to be seen! Ty Ty was right! He said you were the most beautiful woman God ever made, didn't he? And he said you were so pretty, he said you were so God damn pretty, a man would have to get down on his hands and knees and lick something when he saw you like you are now. Didn't he? Yes, so help me God, he did! And after all this time I've got you at last, too. And I'm going to do what I've been wanting to do ever since the first time I saw you. You know what it is, don't you, Griselda? You know what I want. And you're going to give it to me. But I'm not like the rest of them that wear pants. I'm as strong as God Almighty Himself is now. And I'm going to lick you, Griselda. Ty Ty knew what he was talking about. He said that was what a man would do to you. He's got more sense than all the rest of us put together, even if he does dig in the ground like a God damn fool."

He paused for breath, going toward her. Griselda backed toward the door. She was not trying to escape from him now, but she had to go away from him until he caught her and dragged her to another part of the house. He ran, throwing his hands on her.

Later, we get a hint that cunnilingus was involved when Griselda, after Will is killed, had this conversation with her father-in-law:

> Griselda stopped crying until she could tell Ty Ty. She pushed her hands tighter into his, laying her head on his shoulder.
>
> "You remember what you said about me sometimes—you used to say that and I'd try to make you stop—and you never would stop—that's what I mean."
>
> "Now, I don't know. Maybe I do."
>
> "Of course you know—those things about what a man would want to do when he saw me."
>
> "I reckon I know what you mean."
>
> "You and Will were the only two men who ever said that to me, Pa. All the other men I've known were too—I don't know what to say—they didn't seem to be men enough to have that feeling—they were just like all the rest. But you and Will weren't like that."
>
> "You and Will— were the only two men who ever said that."
>
> "A woman can never really love a man unless he's like that. There's something about it that makes everything so different— it's not just liking to be kissed and things like that—most men think that's all. And Will—he said he wanted to do that—just like you did. And he wasn't afraid, either. Other men seem to be afraid to say things like that, or else they aren't men enough to want to do them. Will—Will took my clothes off and tore them to pieces and said he was going to do that. And he did, Pa. I didn't know I wanted him to do it before, but after that I was certain. After a woman has that done to her once, Pa, she's never the same again. It opens her up, or something. I could never really love another man unless he did that to me. I suppose if Will had not been killed, I would have stayed over there. I couldn't have left him after that. I would have been like a dog that loves you and follows you around no matter how mean you are to him. I would have stayed with Will

the rest of my life. Because when a man does that to a woman, Pa, it makes love so strong nothing in the world can stop it. It must be God in people to do that. It's something, anyway. I have it now."

Ty Ty patted her hand. He could think of nothing to say, because there beside him sat a woman who knew as he did a secret of living. After a while he breathed deeply and lifted her head from his shoulder.

Not only did Erskine Caldwell give rise to a *cause célèbre* among books but it was his dramatized version of *Tobacco Road* which created one of the first cases of a court ban of a play. *Tobacco Road* enjoyed one of the longest runs on Broadway of any play of modern times. An unexpurgated version ran without incident or difficulty on a road tour throughout the eastern United States. However, when it reached Chicago in 1935 Mayor Edward J. Kelly, acting under existing Chicago ordinances, banned the play on the ground of obscenity. In following what was then regarded as the proper latitude allowed to administrative officials, the Federal District Court and later the 7th Circuit Court of Appeals upheld the mayor's rule.[35]

God's Little Acre, among other books, was instrumental in bringing into existence a superlative legal opinion. Although never accepted as a rule of law itself, it had a profound effect on the existing law. In this case—*Commonwealth vs. Gordon*[36]—the vice squad of the Philadelphia Police Department, in March, 1948, seized a large quantity of books, including *God's Little Acre,* James T. Farrell's *The Studs Lonigan Trilogy,* William Faulkner's *Sanctuary,* and certain others.

Judge Curtis Bok, who tried the case, reviewed all the significant case law in the United States—and particularly in Pennsylvania—on the subject of obscenity and literature. He concluded that the Constitution prohibited interference with literature unless it could be shown there was a clear and present danger that the particular work of literature would under normal circumstances cause a crime to be committed. Judge Bok said in effect that if it could be demonstrated that the reading of a particular book would cause the commission of a crime such as rape then that book would be held obscene and sellers of the book would be punished for the sale of obscene literature. However, in the absence of such proof the Pennsylvania judge decided that no conviction could be sustained.

III

U. S. Supreme Court at Bat

TIE SCORE

In 1946 Doubleday & Co., Inc., one of America's largest and most reputable publishing houses, published Edmund Wilson's *Memoirs of Hecate County*.

Publication of the book was regarded as a major literary event because the author was at that time the most distinguished literary critic in the United States, if not in the English-speaking world. It was a major work of fiction by a man who had spent a quarter of a century criticizing other literary offerings. A book review in the *Saturday Review of Literature* recorded the occasion as follows:

> When the man who was the sharpest and most readable literary critic of our time produces a long work of fiction he is laying himself wide open to attack. He who has assaulted so many fly-blown reputations and flattened so many writers who were hailed as budding geniuses may expect to find himself in a direful position of the armed knight of old who was pushed off his horse and lay helpless on his back where the common soldier might have a go at him.

Although Wilson had published many works of literary and social criticism and books on travel, plays, and poems, he had up to that time written only one novel—*I Was a Daisy*—published in 1929.

A book produced by an author with such a background inevitably would be thoroughly reviewed. The reviews cannot really be called mixed because they ranged through extremes of opinion. Some reviewers praised it to the skies and others damned it to hell. Ralph Bates in the *New York Times* called it "a good, a distinguished book." *Time* called it the first literary event of the year and "pretty certainly the best contemporary chronicle, so far, of its place and period." *Commonweal* characterized *Memoirs* as a "pathological joke—a string of satiric stories, which, in their aimless offensive vulgarity . . . defied description." *Harper's Magazine* stated that: "There is a blindness in the book that robs it of any ultimate effectiveness."

Regardless of how critical any individual reviewer was, the book was regarded as an important and significant contribution to the world of American letters. Most reviewers made the point, perhaps best expressed by Malcolm Cowley in the *New Republic,* that: "Morally it (Hecate County) is a scene of a conflict between good and evil, in which evil is stronger and more personalized—one of the characters is, or appears to be Satan himself—and wins minor victories one after another, but never achieves a complete triumph."

Shortly after publication the Comstocks attacked the book, obtaining a hung jury in San Francisco and a conviction in Los Angeles. However, the real battle was fought in New York.

The New York Society for the Suppression of Vice, in one of its last gasps for life, obtained an obscenity indictment of Doubleday & Co. for publication of the book. In line with modern theory, the defendant produced experts such as Professor Lionel Trilling, noted literary critic on the staff of Columbia University, who offered testimony concerning the literary and moral quality of the book. However, a three-judge court in a New York Court of Special Sessions found the book obscene. *Time* reported, "The decision made thousands of citizens more impatient than ever to get their morals ruined."

After the state courts sustained the lower court decision, the publishing house appealed to the United States Supreme Court.

The particular story in *Memoirs* which gave rise to obscenity charges was "The Princess with the Golden Hair," which describes the author's affairs with two women. One is a neighbor whom the writer, after considerable effort, persuades to visit him one hot summer afternoon in his room. Obviously she arrives expecting to have sexual intercourse and the author describes his experience as follows:

> She did not, however, lend herself readily to my ardent and expert induction. She had thought the thing out for herself. When I tried to have her lie on the couch, she insisted on finishing her cigarette; and when I tried it the second time, she said decisively: "Let me go into the other room." But she remained on the couch a moment, brooding with her great round brown eyes, as Anna had done on the evening when she had first been unfaithful to Dan. "Don't frighten me, will you?" she begged, at once pleading and giving me orders.
> She picked up a small overnight suitcase. "You let me go in here," she said, and disappeared into the bedroom. When I heard her close the bathroom door, I slipped in and snatched my bathrobe and got into it and hovered in the other room. I waited a long time till I feared I had waited too long; then I softly called out "Hello!" and she answered from the bedroom, "Hello." I went in and found her under the covers in a dressing gown of dull rose red. I put my arms around her and kissed her, and then told her how pretty the dressing gown was. "I just got it—it's new," she said. I found to my surprise that she was nude underneath, and I did not at that moment remember that there had ever been a question of a brace. I wondered at her breast. It was perfect; round and white, with a small pink nipple; and it inspired me almost with awe, like an object of luxury and ornament, after Anna's meager little breasts that seemed scarcely more than cute spots for kisses. "I'm afraid they're not pretty," she said. "Oh, yes, they are: they're marvelous—incredibly so!" "That one was spoiled when it was held in too tight at the time I was having a baby. The other one is better." "But you didn't have a baby?" "No: the doctor thought I oughtn't to have one." They're both perfectly lovely!"—I kissed them. It seemed to be true that she doubted her beauty; but this somehow made it harder to praise it. I was actually embarrased and baffled by a body

which surpassed in its symmetry anything I had ever expected. I suppose that, though I had not imagined it, I had been fearing some deformity or at least defect; but, even if I had not, I should hardly have been prepared for a woman who—alone in my experience—did really resemble a Venus. She seemed perfectly developed and proportioned, with no blight from her spinal disease; she was quite straight and had the right kind of roundness. I found that I was expressing admiration points as if she were some kind of museum piece, and that she seemed to enjoy being posed in the setting of the fresh rose sheath, as if some frank and unashamed self-complacency coexisted with her morbid self-doubt. "I have too much flesh on my stomach," she said; and "I know you don't approve of stained toenails— but I like them": she had colored them red. But what struck and astonished me most was that not only were her thighs perfect columns but that all that lay between them was impressively beautiful, too, with an ideal aesthetic value that I had never found there before. The mount was of a classical femininity: round and smooth and plump; the fleece, if not quite golden, was blond and curly and soft; and the portals were a deep tender rose, like the petals of some fleshly flower. And they were doing their feminine work of making things easy for the entrant with a honeysweet sleek profusion that showed I had quite misjudged her in suspecting as I had sometimes done that she was really unresponsive to caresses. She became, in fact, so smooth and open that after a moment I could hardly feel her. Her little bud was so deeply embedded that it was hardly involved in the play, and she made me arrest my movement while she did something special and gentle that did not, however, press on this point, rubbing herself somehow against me—and then consummated, with a self-excited tremor that appeared to me curiously mild for a woman of her positive energy. I went on and had a certain disappointment, for, with the brimming of female fluid, I felt even less sensation; but— gently enough—I came, too.

Dramatically, attorneys for the defense argued the case before the United States Supreme Court. Justice Felix Frankfurter abstained because of his long friendship with the author, Edmund Wilson. After argument and study the balance of the court divided equally,[1] thus allowing the decision by the New York Supreme Court to remain in effect. *Memoirs of Hecate County* stood condemned as obscene in the state of New York.

A DECADE OF STUPIDITY

After the United States Supreme Court refused to reverse the New York courts on *Memoirs,* many quarters interpreted the action as approval of censorship of almost anything. This ushered in a period in which it was dangerous to sell anything left of center in the obscenity field. Not many actual cases are reported because attorneys saw little reason to appeal. Since it was unlikely that a higher court would reverse a decision, the defendant had to concentrate on obtaining the lightest possible sentence or, at best, a suspended one. Although the subject matter does not make the case a good illustration of the point, the language used by the court in *United States vs. Two Obscene Books*[2] is significant. Ernest J. Bessig, then Director of the American Civil Liberties Union in San Francisco, attempted in 1951 to bring into the United States Henry Miller's *Tropic of Cancer* and *Tropic of Capricorn.* The customs authorities brought action to prevent the import and Judge Louis E. Goodman, in upholding them, ruled with considerable emphasis that the books were "filthy, revolting and obscene." This itself would be not especially significant except that the court specifically went far out of its way to state that it was not approving *United States vs. Ulysses.*

Similarly, in a Missouri case involving nudist magazines, the Supreme Court of that state refused to permit an expert opinion on the ground that it was obvious that nudist magazines aroused lustful desires.[3] The court stated that it would not under any circumstances refuse to recognize a clear law "which has as its obvious purpose the protection of the morals of the *susceptible* into whose hands these publications may come." This was unques-

tionably a return to the original *Hicklin* test. The court knew
that it was returning to this test and was not doing it accidentally
because, in referring to the *Ulysses* idea and the subsequent decisions, the court stated: "The apparent rationale of these . . .
cases . . . seem to be confounded of confusions and artificialities
and seem not to have considered certain basic concepts and teach-
ings which we deem important." Arkansas,[4] Kentucky,[5] and many
other jurisdictions[6] adopted similar views during this period
following the Supreme Court refusal to reverse in the *Memoirs*
case and before the next great landmark of *Butler vs. Michigan.*[7]

In order to appreciate the case of *Butler vs. Michigan,* the
background must be understood. During the early 1950's the
Comstocks of the United States were riding high. Prosecutors
willingly indicted and juries gladly convicted. New organizations formed to replace the old societies for the suppression of
vice. The first of these organizations was the National Organization for Decent Literature, which changed its name to the National Office for Decent Literature. Later it was replaced by a
new type of organization called the Citizens for Decent Literature (which organization still exists). These citizens' groups
stimulated district attorneys to prosecute vigorously any alleged
obscene material.

Detroit became a hotbed of censorship activity.[8] In fact, the
situation became so tense at this time that the distributor of
paperback books submitted copies of all questionable books to
the police for pre-censorship. Police officers would examine the
books for what they regarded as illegal or obscene words or sections and, if they found anything, the book would be sent to an
assistant county prosecutor for an opinion as to whether any violation of the Michigan law existed.

Assistant Prosecutor John J. Rusinack devised a simple test
to reach his opinion. He stated to the *Detroit News:*[9] "If I feel
that I wouldn't want my thirteen-year old daughter reading it, I
decide it's illegal. Mind you, I don't say it is illegal in fact. I

120

merely say that in my opinion it would be a violation of the law to distribute it. Distributors usually cooperate by withholding the book."

There is no question that the Michigan statute of that time, enacted in 1938, would bar the sale of such books: The statute provided that any person who sold a book containing obscene language or obscene pictures, tending to incite minors to violent or depraved acts, manifestly tending to the corruption of the morals of youth, was guilty of a misdemeanor.

Finally, desperate and disgusted with their cavalier treatment, the local sellers and the American Civil Liberties Union arranged for a test case: the sale of the book *The Devil Rides Outside,* a novel by John H. Griffin.

This book was one of the least obscene or pornographic books that ever became part of a test case. It is the story of a musicologist who spends a period of time in a French monastery in order to take advantage of the music records of the monks. The book was written by a blind Texas veteran and primarily involves the conflict between a man's search for inner peace and the devil of temptation who prowls outside the monastery walls.

During the trial the best that the prosecution could produce as examples of the obscenity in the book were these:

The young musician is walking to town on a cold November morning and thinks of warm things like a fire, a small black stove that warmed his room in Paris. "I think of sleeping warm sleep, with an arm thrown across the soft belly of my Lucette."

At another point in the story, the musician is having a conversation with a monk who has fallen in love with a girl and is leaving the monastery in order to marry her. After the musician suggests that he wait, the monk says, "And tell me, do you think maybe I should try to keep her satisfied? I've never had any sexual experience, I'm just asking you."

Also the prosecution objected to the use of certain words: "bastard" and "whore." In fact, the prosecution set forth 101

121

brief excerpts—all of which follow precisely the above pattern. It would appear that, in the absence of real obscenity, it became necessary to manufacture the illusion of obscenity.

To illustrate the innocuous nature of *The Devil Rides Outside* here is a small but typical section. For reasons of health, the young musicologist moves out of the monastery (continuing to study there during the day) and into a nearby house. He falls ill, and after the fever crisis . . .

Finally, the drunken sleep of sweat and broken fevers. The vague, muffled impression of pouring rivers of perspiration and urine into my bed, of being lifted protestingly out of my nest, of my terror in realizing that they intend bathing me. Voices return, the ones croaking at my embarrassment as they undress and prepare me for the tub, the others lost in a confusion of clean sheets replacing the soiled sheets on my bed.

I can't stand alone. Agony of soap and water and strong hands holding me in place, while women scrub and click their teeth and laugh, cajole, scold. Humiliation of being held vice-like in a half-crouching position by two of them, while another washes soapy water from my behind into the tub. A hazed blushing as they dry me, rubbing and hurting, still holding me as they find nothing but a clean shirt for me to wear.

Old Mother Nourrie, flustered, busy, taking command, is resentful that the others have seen. She supports me as another woman buttons my shirt. "There, there, sweet pup," she murmurs soothingly. "Feeling better now, eh? Feels good to be rid of four days' pipi and sweat. Feels good to be clean. Hold still, hold still. Bless him, he's too watery to stand of himself. Here, back to bed. Back to the nice clean sheets. He's my washed young trump, washed and powdered and clean. Hurry and button him, woman. Ah, don't button the bottom one, the child needs his freedom. Now turn over, and zoom! up with the covers. Go to sleep, child. You need to sleep it out, now the poison's left you."

The cracked sweetness of aged voices as they throw out the bath-water and straighten the room. I settle down between the clean, the wondrously clean sheets. Immediate sleep, ever conscious of the newness of fresh bedclothes, of the lightness of my body washed free of filth. Dreamless sleep, lasting forever. Last thought that Madame René wasn't there for the bath, that she'll never forgive herself when she learns what has happened. Warmth of gratefulness that it was old Mother Nourrie. Glimpse of her sitting near me, knitting, humming softly to herself, looking well content.

Despite a cogent argument by eminent counsel concerning the constitutionality of the Michigan statute, the Detroit Recorder's Court, Judge John A. Ricca presiding, peremptorily ruled the book obscene and in violation of the statute. The seller, Mr. Butler, was found guilty and fined $100.

Like similar cases involving petty crimes, no absolute right of appeal existed and the Supreme Court of Michigan had to be petitioned for leave to appeal. That court denied the petition, setting the stage for a ruling by the United States Supreme Court. Distinguished counsel participated in the case. Horace S. Manges appeared for the American Book Publishers, Inc.; Osmond K. Frankel filed a brief for The Authors League of America, Inc., and Irwin B. Ellman appeared for the metropolitan Detroit branch of the American Civil Liberties Union.

The appeal to the United States Supreme Court contained three basic arguments contending that the Michigan statute was unconstitutional as being in violation of the First and the Fourteenth Amendments to the United States Constitution.

Basically, the First Amendment (not as written, but as interpreted by the courts) prohibits any abridgement of freedom of speech or press. The Fourteenth Amendment prohibits a state from acting without proper or due process of law.

The defendant appealed on three grounds: that it was unconstitutional to prohibit the sale to an adult of books unfit or unsuitable for minors; that the prohibitions of the Michigan statute were too vague to be enforced; and that prohibiting the sale of a book containing "obscene language" was invalid since a book had to be considered as a whole, not with respect to individual passages or individual words.

123

The Supreme Court rendered its historic decision in the *Butler vs. Michigan* case on February 25, 1957. Justice Frankfurter wrote the brief opinion joined in by the other eight justices in a display of unanimity rare in the field of obscenity. All nine judges agreed that the conviction had to be reversed and that the Michigan statute was unconstitutional. Unfortunately, the court accepted only the first ground, disregarding the other two grounds of the arguments. The court's ruling follows:

> It is clear on the record that Butler was convicted because Michigan made it an offense for him to make available for the general reading public (and he in fact sold to a police officer) a book that the trial judge found to have a potentially deleterious influence upon youth. The State insists that, by thus quarantining the general reading public against books not too rugged for grown men and women in order to shield juvenile innocence, it is exercising its power to promote the general welfare. Surely, this is to burn the house to roast the pig. Indeed, the Solicitor General of Michigan has, with characteristic candor, advised the Court that Michigan has a statute specifically designed to protect its children against obscene matter "tending to the corruption of the morals of youth." But Butler was not convicted for violating this statute.
>
> We have before us legislation not reasonably restricted to the evil with which it is said to deal. The incidence of this enactment is fit for children. It thereby arbitrarily curtails one of those liberties of the individual, now enshrined in the Fourteenth Amendment, that history has attested as the indispensable conditions for the maintenance and progress of a free society. We are constrained to reverse this conviction.

The case was momentous for many reasons: First, it sets the pattern for holding state obscenity statutes unconstitutional. Secondly, the unanimous Supreme Court declared that state statutes must be limited to reasonableness in the obscenity field —the first time that any responsible authority had suggested that this might be so. Thirdly, the court made a constitutional rule out of the simple thought that state statutes and state courts (and police officers, too) cannot limit the reading matter of adults in order to protect children. This is what Justice Frankfurter called "burning the house to roast the pig."

In the *Louisiana News Co.*[10] case (1960) Circuit Judge John Minor Wisdom expressed the same idea, when he said:

> While we have no occasion here to pass on the constitutionality of such a law, it would seem that a state might enact a valid statute "specifically designed to protect its children" from suggestive books and magazines that are not too rugged for grown men and women, without at the same time burning the house down to roast the pig by restricting everyone else to reading such fiction as *Boy's Life* at the magazine stand and *The Five Little Peppers* at the bookstand.

THE SUPREME COURT ESSAYS A TEST

In the *Butler* case the Supreme Court of the United States for the first time squarely undertook to decide the constitutionality of obscenity legislation. It was not a difficult decision, and all the court had to do was to say that the statute went too far by (to all intents and purposes) ruling out all but children's books. It was not necessary for the Supreme Court to set up any test of what constituted obscenity. Four months later, in the same term of court, the Supreme Court had the problem again. The case involved Samuel Roth, who has been aptly described by one authority in this field as "an experienced dealer in not-very-erotic erotica."[11] Roth had an interesting history. About a decade before, the Post Office had issued a series of fraud orders against him because he advertised books as salacious when in fact they were not. In general, Roth did not present a good case for the foes of censorship. He unquestionably catered to the desire of a broad segment of the American public to be titillated by erotica. He sold such magaines as *A Review of the World of Pleasure,* and *An American Aphrodite,* at prices as high as $10.00 per volume! He sold nude photographs under such headings as: *Wallet Nudes, French Nudes at Play, Stereoptic Nude Show,* and *Two Undraped Stars.* He offered publications entitled *Good Times, Photo and Body,* and *Chicago Sex-Dimensional Issue.* He was under close surveillance at all times by the Federal Postal Inspectors, had had numerous brushes with the law and some convictions, and was finally indicted by the Federal Grand Jury in New York for violation of the Federal mail statute[12] in the mailing of obscene matter.

The case was tried before a jury which, following a weird charge by the trial judge, brought in a most unusual verdict. The indictment had specified twenty-six different counts, and the jury acquitted Roth on most of them. He was found guilty on one count, which involved the quarterly *An American Aphrodite* and certain other material, but he was acquitted for the nude photographs, including titles like *French Nudes at Play.* After the conviction Roth received a sentence of five years' imprisonment and a $5,000 fine. On appeal, the circuit court affirmed the conviction,[13] although that brilliant jurist, Judge Jerome Frank, concurred reluctantly and invited a review by the Supreme Court, stating that "since ours is an inferior court, we should not hold invalid a statute which our superior has thus often said is constitutional (albeit without any full discussion) ."

The Supreme Court of the United States granted certiorari, limiting the issues to whether the Federal obscenity statute violated the Constitution.

Simultaneously, that court accepted another case, coming out of California. By so doing the court brought before itself a case that had gone through the federal courts on the Federal Obscenity Statute and one that had gone through the state courts on a state obscenity statute. This gave the court an opportunity to render a significant opinion that would possibly set up rules in the obscenity field applicable to both state and federal law, and to settle the myriad cases that were cropping up throughout the country.

The *Alberts* case involved David S. Alberts and his wife Violet, who operated a mail-order business in Los Angeles. The Alberts, who had numerous brushes with the law, specialized in the sale of photographs of nude women. One night Los Angeles deputy sheriffs raided the Alberts' warehouse and seized hundreds of items. A judge without a jury tried them in the Beverly Hills Municipal Court and found David Alberts guilty. He was sentenced to sixty days in jail and $500 fine with probation for two years. (Violet Alberts, because she acted under the direction of her husband, was acquitted.) The higher California courts affirmed the conviction, and the defendant then appealed to the United States Supreme Court.

Both the *Roth* case and the *Alberts* case were unfortunate selections for review by the United States Supreme Court because they involved typical cases of commercial pandering as opposed to a struggle for freedom of speech. Moreover, as the cases developed, they became abstractions not involving the material facts but rather pure ideas or principles: whether the federal and California obscenity statutes, in the abstract, violated the freedom of speech guarantee and the definiteness requirements of the federal Constitution.

The federal government fought hard to insure the upholding of laws against obscenity. The Solicitor General set up three categories of material which should be regarded as obscene: (1) Novels of quite serious literary interest like *Tropic of Cancer* but obscene because "they concentrate on an explicit discussion of sex conduct in a vocabulary based on four letter words"; (2) borderline material, mostly photographic, of nudes and the like; (3) the bulk of obscenity—hard-core pornography, including pictures depicting sex activity and perversion.

The Solicitor General really stacked the deck by sending to the clerk of the United States Supreme Court a box of what he regarded as samples of "hard core pornography."

The Supreme Court ruled[14] through Justice William J. Brennan, Jr. that obscenity was not protected by the Constitution because it was utterly without redeeming social importance. Justice Brennan was joined by Justices Felix Frankfurter, Harold H. Burton, Tom C. Clark, and Charles E. Whitaker. The decision that the prohibition of obscenity was constitutional was already a foregone conclusion. But the court went on to attempt to rule on *what constituted* obscenity, by setting up a test: "Whether to the average person, applying contemporary community standards, the dominant theme of the material taken as a whole appeals to prurient interest."

Justices William O. Douglas and Hugo L. Black dissented on the ground that obscenity legislation or censorship was unconstitutional unless it could be demonstrated that "the particular publication has an impact on action that the government can control." Basically, these two judges adopt the attitude of Judge Curtis Bok that the government must prove a clear and present danger in order to prohibit the publication of a book.

Justice John M. Harlan concurred in the conviction of Alberts but dissented in the conviction of Roth because he believed that the *federal* law should be limited to hard-core pornography but he would permit the states to have broader powers.

Chief Justice Warren concurred in the result but wrote a separate short opinion expressing his belief that material relating to sex should get constitutional protection. He set up as a criterion that the important item in an obscenity case should be *not* "the obscenity of a book or picture" but the "conduct of the defendant." The Chief Justice significantly states: "The history of the application of laws designed to suppress the obscene demonstrates convincingly that the power of government can be invoked under them against great art or literature, scientific treatises, or works exciting social controversy. Mistakes of the past prove that there is a strong countervailing interest to be considered in the freedoms guaranteed by the First and Fourteenth Amendments."

The United States Supreme Court in the *Alberts* and *Roth* cases established the following test for prohibitable or suppressible obscenity: "Whether to the average person, applying contemporary community standards, the dominant theme of the material taken as a whole appeals to prurient interest." If this test is analyzed slowly and carefully on a word-for-word basis it becomes evident that, far from being a test, it is a meaningless conglomeration of words purporting to set forth a profound equation but really saying practically nothing.

First the objective of the test is the effect upon "the average person." The law does have a theoretical person known as "a reasonable man." This never refers to an actual person but rather to a theoretical one who behaves properly at all times. The Supreme Court could not have meant a "reasonable man" because the court is too familiar with that concept to use the term "average person" when meaning "reasonable man." Consequently, the Supreme Court must have meant someone other than a "reasonable man"—an idea foreign to the law and alien to any concept to date.

At best the Supreme Court might have been referring to a person with a statistically average education, the completion of one and one-half years of high school. Next the person should have an intelligence quotient of 100. Now, having established these two great levelers, what comes next? What religion does this "average person" follow? This makes a great difference, because to the average Catholic a matter may become obscene at a much earlier stage than it might to a Jew, simply because in the Catholic pattern nudity and sex are recurring anti-religious themes, whereas in the typical American Hebrew religion they are concepts rarely treated or discussed, except as matters of per-

129

sonal preference. Furthermore, many of the Protestant religions such as the Unitarians possess a liberality not tolerated in the Baptist bible belt. In other words, once an analysis of statistical averages such as I.Q. and education—and perhaps physical characteristics—is completed, nothing remains but whether or not a person experiences an emotional reaction from a given item. Since the cultural and religious background, rather than those items which comprise an average, determines this effect, the court basically appears to have set forth a new and impossible concept of an "average person."

The next point of the definition is the application of "contemporary community standards." It means what it says: That, in making a decision, the court should apply the concepts in current vogue as opposed to yesterday's outmoded theories. However, the following words, "community standards," lack clarity. Do they mean the neighborhood standards? Do they refer to an entire city? Perhaps the state creates a standard? What about regional standards such as the "community standards" of New England or the Deep South? Actually, as the test emerged later, it appeared that those who promulgated it meant the use of a national standard—in other words, the contemporary community standards prevalent in the United States. Of course, this is a completely fictitious creation, because the United States does not have a *single* community standard. Many sections in suburban New York City, Hollywood, Miami Beach, and other points throughout the country permit and accept the bikini and perhaps even the topless bathing suit. However, in the Ozarks, the small towns of New England, the Midwest or bible belt, the small towns of Utah, and in many other places in the United States, even the brief two-piece suit has barely gained acceptance as suitable garb for public sun or water-bathing. It is necessary to recognize that this is a heterogeneous country in its definition of morality, and obscenity legislation exists only as an element in the field of morality.

The Supreme Court test that the "dominant theme" of the material must be taken as a whole is an improvement on the general idea that a word or sentence could be taken out of context and, if found questionable, could cause an entire work to be prohibited. Undoubtedly this is a helpful step in the right direction.

The final portion of the test draws a blank. Analysis has shown that obscenity may (albeit with difficulty) be tested by application to someone called an "average person" and by "contemporary standards," probably on a national basis. It has further shown the need to test the "dominant theme" of the entire material rather than isolated words, sentences, or portions. Having resolved these problems, what is supposed to happen next? The Supreme Court contends that in these circumstances the last question is: Does the material "appeal to prurient interest?"

What does the word *prurient* mean? It is an adjective derived from the Latin verb *prurire,* which means to itch. *Webster's New International Dictionary* defines *prurient* as follows: "itching; longing; uneasy with desire, or longing; of persons having itching, morbid or lascivious longings; of desire, curiosity or propensity, lewd." *Webster's* further obliges with two examples of the use of the word *prurient.* Taylor states: "The eye of the vain and prurient is darting from object to object of illicit attraction." And Kingsley says: "The reading public . . . in its usual prurient longing after anything like personal gossip." By these definitions the word *prurient* does not have an especially sexual connotation. The Supreme Court clarified this to some extent by saying in another part of the opinion: "Obscene material is material which deals with sex in a manner appealing to prurient interest. . . ." Thus the Supreme Court has made clear only that obscenity must have something to do with sex, which completes the circle back to the original question.

On that same final Monday in June, 1957, the Supreme Court decided two other cases. Both cited *Roth and Alberts,* both related to the identical subject matter, but actually neither contributed much to the history of the obscenity field. However, for the sake of completeness a report on the two cases follows.

In *Kingsley Books, Inc., vs. Brown,*[15] the corporation counsel of the City of New York brought an action under a special statute to enjoin book dealers from selling a series of books which he regarded as obscene. These volumes were essentially torture books and included details of such acts as cauterizing a woman's breasts with a hot iron, or ringing the nipples of the breasts in blood with a needle. A considerable amount of space was devoted to accounts of blood sucking, and one book related the classic torture of putting honey on a female's breasts, into the vagina, and in the anus, and then letting loose hundreds of great red ants on the honey.

The lower court granted the injunction against the sale of the books, the court of appeals affirmed, and the case went to the United States Supreme Court. Under the existing state of the law many attorneys would have predicted a unanimous decision sustaining the New York court. However, curiously enough, the New York court was sustained by a close vote of 5 to 4, with the Chief Justice and Justices Brennan, Black, and Douglas dissenting. Actually, the major issue before the court was the constitutionality of the statute, which by that time had become reasonably common.

The other case involved the constitutionality of a city ordinance that would license burlesque performances. Here, the city of Newark, New Jersey, prohibited "lewd, obscene, or indecent" shows or performances and specifically prohibited a particular series of acts. These included removal of clothing by a female performer in such a way as to give the appearance of nudeness of the genital organs, buttocks, or breasts. The ordinance added a new twist of its own by prohibiting "the performance of any dance, episode, or musical entertainment, the purpose of which is to direct the attention of the spectator to the breasts, buttocks, or genital organs of the performer." Before the city had an opportunity to enforce the new law, a test case reached the United States Supreme Court. Taking a theoretical view of an academic situation, the court sustained the constitutionality of the statute. [16]

After careful study of the decisions of the United States Supreme Court in the *Roth* case, the *Kingsley* case and the *Burlesque* case, the Comstocks of America took heart. The Postmaster General, the various Committees for Decent Literature, the blue-noses throughout the country—all issued statements exuding exultation. The Executive Secretary of the National Office for Decent Literature, in referring to the decisions, stated with satisfaction, "The cause of decency has been strengthened." Postmaster General Arthur Summerfield declared self-righteously, "The Post Office Department welcomes the decisions of the Supreme Court as a forward step in the drive to keep obscene materials out of the mails."

THE SUPREME COURT DIDN'T MEAN IT

In June, 1957, the United States Supreme Court closed its term with these decisions which so heartened the censors. The modern Comstocks, aware of the number of cases pending, waited with eager anticipation for that long-desired moment when the "pornographers" would get their come-uppance in the High Court. But, when the court convened again in October, 1957, a series of brief and peremptory opinions disposed of four cases in such fashion as to begin to set the record straight: Clearly, the judicial guardians of American freedom wished no censorship except in the most extreme cases. The High Court was truly solicitous of the freedom to communicate ideas and would not permit censorship to interfere. It was one thing to convict a New York or Los Angeles vendor of selling French postcards to juvenile Peeping Toms and another thing entirely to ban a motion picture or magazine. The Supreme Court quickly acted to make this distinction apparent.

The City of Chicago banned the French motion picture—*The Game of Love*—which the Seventh Circuit Court of Appeals described as follows:

> The thread of the story is supercharged with a series of illicit sexual intimacies and acts. . . . A flying start is made when a sixteen year old boy is shown completely nude on a bathing beach in the presence of a group of younger girls (as a result of a boating accident). On that plane the narrative proceeds to reveal a seduction of this boy by a physically attractive woman old enough to be his mother. Under the influence of this experience and an arrangement to repeat it, the boy thereupon engages in sexual relations with a girl of his own age. The erotic thread of the story is carried, without deviation toward any wholesome idea, through scene after scene. The narrative is graphically pictured with nothing omitted except those sexual consummations which are plainly suggested but meaningfully omitted and thus, by the very fact of omission, emphasized.[17]

Basing its opinion on the theory that the Constitution did not protect obscenity, the intermediate federal court sustained the censorship of the movie in question. On appeal, the Supreme Court peremptorily reversed,[18] simply citing the *Roth* case. Here for the first time it became evident that the Supreme Court did not intend to open the gates of censorship but rather to close them. In the second case,[19] instead of reversing the Court of Appeals as it did in three of the four cases at that term, the High Court simply recognized that governments can make a "confession of error," and remanded the case to the district court for reconsideration in the light of the *Roth* case. In spite of the seeming unimportance of this case, the facts and handling shocked the censors. Involved was a forfeiture proceeding against a series of imported publications of both the nudist variety and the artists and models type. The lower court found the artists and models issues obscene because they "contained many large closeup, full front-views of nude men and women, plainly showing the genital and pubic areas." Similarly, the lower court found the nudist publications obscene, stating: "Although an avowed purpose of the books is to explain the nudist movement, its principles, and its practices, there are relatively very few photographs of the mixed groups of all ages which ordinarily would be found in a nudist park. The great preponderance of the illustrations depicts shapely, well-developed young women appearing in the nude, mostly in front exposures." Yet, the Supreme Court encouraged reversal.

The censors suffered a major traumatic shock in the case of *One, Inc. vs. Olesen.* [20] The Post Office Department ruled that a magazine entitled *One—The Homosexual Magazine* could not be sent through the mails because it was obscene. Both the district and appellate courts sustained this ruling, and in due time the case reached the United States Supreme Court.

The magazine was published deliberately to cater to the tastes of the non-heterosexual. Lower court arguments maintained that the magazine dealt with homosexuality from its scientific and historical point of view. The court of appeals denied this contention, stating that the magazine did not meet its purported "purpose of dealing primarily with homosexuality from the scientific, historical, and critical point of view—to . . . promote among the general public an interest, knowledge and understanding of the problems of variation." The lower court pointed to a story in the magazine in which a young girl eschewed her opportunity for normal married life in order to live with a lesbian. It also contained a poem about the alleged homosexual activities of Lord Montague and other British peers, containing a warning to all men to avoid the public toilets while "Lord Samuel is sniffing around the drains of Piccadilly."

The following is the material out of the 1954 (Oct.) issue of *One* to which the lower court objected:

SAPPHO REMEMBERED

Jane Dahr

On the way from the airport to their hotel they had no chance to talk for Joe Rich, the manager of the Antoinette Room where Pavia was opening that night, was giving her all the information he'd given Jill, her secretary, at least four times already. Joe Rich was obviously the itchy type.

"And Miss Orr," he said ridding himself of yet another hangnail with his small bright teeth, "your secretary and I decided to let your accompanist do a whole number by himself tonight before you sing. Then, when he's half way through the second number, you start singing softly out beyond the spot and just sort of wander into it. Ignore the audience, sort of, you know."

Beneath her mink coat, folded over her knees, Pavia pressed her knee conspiratorily against Jill's. The routine was as old as the ballad singer, but an effective opening for any *diseuse* with her poise, and Jill knew Pavia was delighted to have it accepted without a row. She said in that silky, famous voice of hers, "That's a very shrewd idea. Yours, Mr. Rich?"

"Well, I suppose," he admitted modestly. "If it's done right, it sort of catches 'em napping, you know. And wear that slinky silver and white job your secretary showed me yesterday — Gad! you've got a figure!" His eyes appraised the firm lines beneath her beige jersey dress with a buyer's gleam. "She says it's a Fath original — I'll see the word gets around where it'll do the most good — and it fits you like the hide on an earthworm." He leaped ahead of himself and rushed on, "And keep that pianist of yours out of trouble. This town's hot as a rivet since they picked up the mayor's kid queening a drag ball. We're sold out for the next three weeks and we can't afford any bad publicity. Didja notice I had three photographers at the airport? Not bad for a town this size!" But before they could reply, "Oh, here's the hotel. Want me to come up awhile. I can."

"No, thank you, Mr. Rich, I really need to relax." Pavia cleared her throat and Rich jumped with fright.

"Something wrong with your throat? I know a specialist—"

"Everything's fine, Mr. Rich. I'll see you this evening."

"Nine o'clock! Don't forget! Don't be late! Remember, nine o'clock!"

As they entered the lobby, where Pavia instinctively took Jill's elbow to assist her at the few marble steps, she said, "Poor darling, have you had to put up with that for three days?"

"That and more! Pavia, don't be surprised if he drops dead before your first number. He's a dynamo, but too big for what he's supplying."

"Everything all right, if you'll excuse a foolish question?"

"Perfect. And how did Dr. Kaegel impress you?"

"Jill, that man's a marvel. He has facts that will make Kinsey's look like copy book exercises. But everyone's afraid of him, so I promised —"

"Oh, darling! How much this time?"

"I said five thousand, but if you —" Pavia trailed off sheepishly.

"Pavia, *five* thousand! You're so generous, and even though you're —"

Pavia closed the door of their suite behind them, tossed her coat on a chair and gently drew the girl to her.

"Forgiven?" she asked at last. She touched the delicate pulse beat beneath the light golden hair on the child-like temple. "Will there ever be a day when you won't blush when I do that," she murmured.

"I hope not," Jill sighed. "It's so good to have you back."

"Sweet." Pavia touched her earring. "Coral flowers on little shell ears. Coral suits your coloring, Jill; pearl, ivory, coral, gold. But aren't those the ones we saw in the shop in New York?"

Jill nodded. "I showed them to Jerry and he bought them. I couldn't resist taking them even though they're far too dear. They had a necklace too, each little flower was a perfection of carving and it was all worked into several strands of tiny seed pearls. But it was sold." She sounded heartbroken. She was such a child, Pavia thought with annoyance.

"Never mind, you're pretty enough without it. Any mail?"

"Pavia, you don't mind my taking presents from Jerry occasionally?"

"Of course not. You're free to do as you please — until you decide. You know that." Pavia's rich voice had grown ominously flat as she took off her hat and fluffed her short dark hair in the mirror. "Any mail?"

Jill picked up a stack of letters and two unopened notes that had been delivered by hand. "Do you know a Mrs. Leah Brake," Jill asked.

"Why yes, she's —" Pavia stopped short, feeling herself flush.

"— the girl who had you expelled from college," Jill finished for her. "The one I remind you of so much. The notes are from her. She has called three times, wanting you have cocktails and dinner with her tonight — just the two of you — out at her home. She said she's a widow now."

"I know," Pavia put the mail down unexamined. "I think I'll shower."

"Pavia, Jerry's calling from New York tonight for a definite answer."

"Have you made up your mind?"

"I *think* so."

"When will you *know?*"

"I don't quite know. It's rather up to you, isn't it?"

Pavia took a cigarette from her bag and lighted it. "Nothing is up to me. That decision is yours. I've explained why." She started out. "Call Mrs. Brake and tell her to pick me up here at five."

"I . . . I've found a girl here in town who can take my place," Jill said quietly. "She's a good secretary, a wonderful girl. I knew her sister."

"I'll interview her tomorrow." And Pavia left the room.

She dressed in the new gown that Jill had put out for the show, and as she caught up her long ermine wrap and shimmering bag, she called to Jill, who was staring out of the tall windows at the snow falling over the lake, "Will I see you before the show? I'm not coming back here."

"I suppose so," Jill replied, not turning, "but if you don't—"

"If you want, you may wait here for your call."

"Thank you. Mrs. Brake's chauffeur is waiting in the lobby."

"Good night."

"Good night."

How could she, Pavia reproached herself as she stared at the back of the chauffeur's sleek, well groomed head. She was numb with misery and yet she had done nothing to alleviate the pain. She had practically pushed the girl out of her life, even before she knew what her decision was to be. But Jill was so dependent; she had to learn to think more for herself. And hadn't Jill said she'd found another secretary? Of course, that had been after she'd told her to call Leah. Still, she had been searching for a substitute.

Pavia massaged her throat which suddenly had begun to ache with suppressed emotion. The chauffeur was staring at her in the mirror again. Now that they'd left the downtown traffic, he had divided his attention almost equally between her and the road, yet his eyes held neither admiration nor curiosity for the famous. It was plain hatred. Did he know about her, Pavia wondered. If he did, how did he know? Did Leah send for other women now that she was a widow? She picked up the small microphone at her elbow and said, "Will you keep your eyes on the road, please?" His face and neck turned scarlet, but he did not look at her the rest of the drive.

She wondered again about Leah. Was it possible for the personality of such a woman to change? Vividly she remembered their sorority room at the university, the faces of their House Mother and the Dean of Women as the door had burst open upon them, that nightmare of an inquisition in the office downstairs with Leah hysterically screaming accusations at her, her parents' faces as they had come to take her home. Ten years ago, and yet the agony could still bleed freely. Was it possible she still loved Leah? She had thought she wanted never to see her again, yet here she was on her way to answer the first summons the woman had sent her. But how much had Jill to do with her going — and Jill's young man.

Jill was so helplessly young, only twenty and actually nearer sixteen in many essential ways of maturity. She'd known this Jerry all her life; they'd been in love in a way, until she'd come to work for Pavia. Pavia had met the fellow several times, a nice young man, good job, good prospects, he would give Jill a good life with healthy babies and her share of bliss and mediocrity. Could I do more, Pavia thought with a sharp ache in her heart,

Then she remember what Dr. Kaegel had said to her in New York: "We, as individuals, are not important; but as a part of some scheme of Nature we have yet to understand, we're terribly important. As individuals it doesn't matter if we're big or little, wise or foolish, so long as, together, we generate enough energy, or enlightenment, to reveal the darkened stage upon which Nature has set us. We *have* to find the main switch before we are all lost or dead! *That* is how we are important to mankind!"

He was right. It must not matter what the Jills did. There were always the Leahs to provide the essentials, Pavia told herself fiercely.

But she was wrong. She knew it the moment she walked into the beautiful drawing room, cold and correct like its mistress. Leah had not changed. As one slow minute dragged forth a fresh one, Pavia saw the old faults grown bigger, the few virtues nearly dead. Pavia's mind could not leave her hotel suite, where the girl she loved above all else was waiting for a fatal call.

And Leah, receiving no encouragement, nor even interest, became more aggressive, and after dinner in the middle of a plea for forgiveness and understanding, with tears, and "can't we try just once more, darling," the sleek young chauffeur had strolled in, out of uniform, his collar open, as if he had owned the house! The situation was as ludicrously clear as Leah's face. Pavia could hardly keep from laughing aloud. Of course, the man had apologized, thinking, "Madame was alone," which only made matters worse for Leah. After that, even a fool would have understood that Leah didn't care where her pleasures came from — so long as the supply was tremendous, varied and unending. Pavia went back to town in a cab, leaving Leah's paramour to justify his deliberate intrusion in ways best known to them alone. She hoped they would be very happy, as she laughed in spite of her misery.

But the episode had helped to restore enough perspective to get her through her first performance at the Antoinette Room. She had told Joe Rich, "I'll just do three numbers," and afterward, "I don't think I should do a second show the first night — bad psychology to crowd them on an opening," and miraculously, he had agreed with her. She escaped to her suite where she expected to find her secretary at least ecstatic, and probably packed.

To Pavia's surprise, there was a candlelit table laid for two overlooking the city, the lake and the night. Jill, who had been weeping, was dressed in the gown Pavia liked best. But she barely spoke as Pavia took off her wrap.

"Well," Pavia tried to sound cheerful, "is this for *Auld Lang Syne.*"

"It *is* an occasion," Jill said, biting her lip and not looking at her. Then she burst forth, "I can't leave you, Pavia. Jerry called just a few minutes ago. My answer was *no*. He . . . he was even drunk!"

"But why *no?* He has a right to get drunk once in a while, surely?"

"It wasn't that! Drunk or sober, I don't love him . . . like I do you!" She started to cry. "Mrs. Brake may be more important to you than I am — but she won't go with you everywhere as I will, and you *do* need me . . . in spite of what you may think . . . as I need you!"

Pavia felt the fatigue within her melt from her mind down through her muscles. She felt like a girl again herself, living in the imagery of Millay and Dickinson. But she knew Jill too well. She must not give in too quickly to her for the girl had to be taught to be stronger and more self reliant somehow, and Pavia knew how she must teach her. It would be difficult, but it would be heaven.

"Jill, dear," she said quietly, "I've a surprise for you — two of them, in fact, before we have a long, long talk. First, Mrs. Brake is sleeping with her chauffeur, and I'm glad she is. Second, if you found a jeweler's box when you unpacked for me, it's for you. You see, I remembered what day it is too," she nodded to the roses and candlelight. "Why don't you get the box?"

"Pavia! It can't be the —" Jill ran from the room.

"But it is, dear," Pavia said softly as the girl brought the box back and opened it. "*Every flower a perfection of the carver's art, all worked into several strands of tiny pearls.*' Something out of the same gentle sea from which Aphrodite arose, and over which Sappho gazed as she wrote her lyrics. It might have been my going away gift, but thank God, it isn't. Come, my mouse, let me help you put it on."

Lord Samuel
and
Lord Montagu

(A New and Very BAB BALLAD by Brother Grundy, Hollywood 1954)

". . . now . . . we find to our dismay that the vices of Sodom and Gomorrah appear to be rife among us . . . we may indeed be on the eve of a new Elizabethan age."

Viscount Samuel, News of the World

"And Samuel said, What meaneth then this bleating of the sheep in mine ears, and the lowing of the oxen which I hear?"

I Samuel, 15-14

Lord Samuel says that Sodom's sins
Disgrace our young Queen's reign,
An age that in this plight begins
May well end up in flame.

As if to show his words are true
Of commoner and peer —
It's goal for Baron Montagu
For upwards of a year!

His ins and outs with various Scouts
Had caused a mild sensation.
Accomplice airmen take the stand —
Secure the Lord's damnation.

A Labour Member, Mr. Field
For "importuning" fined is,
The spivs, the M.P's. richly heeled,
Discover Justice blind is.

The GENT'S at Piccadilly says
The press, both tame and raucous,
Of places the most silly is
To hold a party caucus!

Lord Samuel is a legal peer
(While real are Monty's curls!)
Some peers are seers but some are queers —
And some boys WILL be girls.

18

In good Victoria's glorious days
When Sammy was a child
Were things perverse a great deal worse?
Is Wildeblood worse than Wilde?

This new Elizabethan age
The ancient pattern fits —
When Roister Doister held the stage
And boys were Honest Kit's.

Gomorrah, Pompeii, Corinth, Tyre,
Rome, London — all a piece —
It seems the fat's been in the fire
Ere Athens was in Greece.

While Priestley tell the B.B.C.
About the "invert clique"
Why should this Second Samuel flee
The bleating of the sheep?

Had he beheld — this Statesman Eld' —
The vice of other reigns,
Would he thus the "Lily" geld
Or throw him to the flames?

Would he idly waste his breath
In sniffing round the drains
Had he known "King Elizabeth"
Or roistering "Queen James"?

MORAL

They say the sins of Sodom
In these Isles have come to roost —
So if your flying east from GANDER
Watch you don't get fairly "goosed".

And if you wish to Pick a Dilly
When you're strolling out at night,
Just make sure it's not a "Lily"
Or a male transvestite.

For there's blackmail in the woodpile
And there's blackmail by the fence,
But to black male and to white male
It's: AVOID THE PUBLIC "GENTS"!

The reversal in the case of *One Inc.* could be interpreted as a refusal by the court to permit censorship of ideas. Basically, the advocacy of the right to be—or the necessity to be—a homosexual is still the expression of an idea or thought and it could reasonably be argued that the Supreme Court was simply protecting the communication of ideas. In *Sunshine Book Co. vs. Summerfield*,[21] however, came the first *definite* indication that the Supreme Court was departing from the limited area of protection of ideas. Until that case the general dogma was that while nudity as such did not constitute obscenity the nudity had to be tempered with what is called in the vernacular "blocked pictures." This means that the male genitals and both male and female pubic hair had to be removed from the photographs. The magazine photographs on which the Supreme Court ruled in 1958 were of the "unblocked" variety and showed clearly male and female genitals and pubic hair.

THE COURT PROTECTS NUDITY

In December, 1954, the publisher of the magazines *Sunshine & Health* and *Sun Magazine*, located at Mays Landing, New Jersey, was notified by the postmaster of this little town that future issues of these magazines would not be accepted for mailing until reviewed by administrative hearing of the Post Office Department. The Solicitor of the Post Office Department held a hearing in January and found after a review of the entire official record that the magazines in question contained photographs of "naked men, women and children, principally women clearly revealing genitals, breasts, and other portions of the body normally covered in public." Based upon this finding the Post Office Department concluded that:

> The photographs appear obscene and indecent when judged by the ordinary community standards of a vast majority of the citizens of this country.

Thereafter the publisher filed an action in the United States District Court in the District of Columbia to obtain relief and a declaratory judgment that the two magazines were not obscene. Judge James R. Kirkland heard the case and quickly concluded that the magazines were obscene.

The judge decided that in order for the magazines to be obscene they must "be calculated to lower that standard which we regard as essential to civilization or calculated with the ordinary person to deprave his morals or lead to impure purposes."

Based upon this test the district judge found that simple nudity either in the form of a photograph or a pen sketch was not obscene and would not be barred. The court also stated that practically any picture of a "posterior view of a nude" male or female, young or old, was not obscene. However, the court concluded: "Where photographs are taken of the pubic area at very close range they are as a matter of fact obscene, and, it will follow as a consequence, as a matter of law obscene."

Four of the most extreme photographs which appeared in the two magazines involved in this action are reprinted here together with the comments of the court. About Plate A the court states:

> This is a picture of two persons: a woman seated beside a pool and a man standing to her side. The woman, by crossing of one leg partly over the other, has obscured the pubic area and genitalia, and hers is not an obscene picture. The man, on the other hand, is standing with a side view. By artful use of shadow his face is completely obliterated, his entire pubic area is obliterated by the shadow, but prominently shown in front of the pubic area and against this dark background is his male organ; the corona of the penis is clearly discernible; in fact even a casual observation of it indicates that the man is circumcised. This obviously has no place even in illustrating the principles of nudism. It is filthy, it is foul, it is obscene, and the Court will hold such as a matter of fact.

A

B

C

D

With respect to Plate B the court states:

> In a mixed group there is one man revealed at the corner where his genitals are clearly shown and the Court will rule as a matter of fact that this is obscene.

With respect to Plate C, the court categorizes it as a "most unusual picture," and continues:

> Here are two women who appear to be in their late twenties or early thirties. The woman to the left appears to be approximately five feet seven. She must weigh in the neighborhood of 250 pounds. She is exceedingly obese.
>
> I assume the illustration not retouched by the photographer, is to represent the normal, natural person and reveals her as she was in fact when the picture was taken. This picture was taken within approximately twelve feet of the camera. First of all, so far as the demonstration of nudism goes, the picture shows a very clear sunburned "V" at her neck—V-shaped sunburn—whereas the rest of her skin is white as the snow on which she stands. The Court might gather she is a new member or a non-conformist. She has large, elephantine breasts that hang from her shoulder to her waist. They are exceedingly large. The thighs are very obese. She is standing in snow, wearing galoshes. But the part which is offensive, obscene, filthy and indecent is the pubic area shown.
>
> Being most liberal, one might say that the area shown of the pubic hair is caused by shadow, that the same is not to be noticed on both sides. The hair extend outwardly virtually to the hipbone. It looks to the Court like a retouched picture because the hairline instead of being straight is actually scalloped in a half-moon shape, which makes the woman grotesque, vile, filthy, the representation is dirty, and the Court will hold that this picture is obscene as a matter of fact; because of the closeness of the view the woman to her left and the viewer's right is likewise held to be obscene.

Plates A, B, and C appeared originally in the magazine *Sun-*

shine and Health, and Plate D was in *Sun Magazine.* With respect to this latter picture the court holds "that the picture of the young girl photographed on page 6, standing within approximately six feet of the camera, showing the pubic area, is obscene; that it is lewd, lascivious, and tending to excite lust and sensual ideas."

Based on an examination of these pictures the district court found for the Postmaster General and sustained him completely.

The publisher appealed to the next highest court: the United States Court of Appeals for the District of Columbia. Chief Judge Henry W. Edgerton and Circuit Judges George Thomas Washington and John A. Danaher heard the appeal. Circuit Judge Washington rendered the opinion on March 31, 1956 (more than a year later). This court adopted a different view. It set up a test to consider how much the item involved would arouse "the salacity of the reader to whom it is sent" as against what "literary, scientific or other merits it may have in the reader's hands."

With this test as a guide, the court found that both the examiner, acting on behalf of the Post Office Department, and the district judge "showed no effort to weigh the material considered objectionable against the rest of the contents, or to weigh the risk of permitting the former to circulate against the limitations on freedom of the press implicit in halting circulation of the latter."

Finally, this three-judge court also found that the Post Office Department had not proceeded properly. Therefore the court reversed the district judge with instructions that he should issue an injunction permanently restraining the Post Office Department from interfering with the magazines.

Circuit Judge Danaher dissented. Judge Danaher believed that the pictures "were obscene by any standards" and that the district judge should be affirmed.

Subsequently the Post Office Department applied for a rehearing before the complete District Court of Appeals. After the full court heard the case, they rendered a new decision on October 3, 1957 (fifteen months later—these magazines were getting stale!).

The court consisted of Chief Judge Edgerton, and Associate Judges E. Barrett Prettyman, C. Wilbur, Wilbur K. Miller, David L. Bazelon, Charles Fahy, Washington, and Daneher.

The full court, on rehearing, reversed the smaller District of Columbia court. This time the majority of the court decided that the District judge was right in banning the magazines. They found that the magazines in question were properly held to be obscene and should be barred from the mails. Chief Judge Edgerton and Circuit Judges Washington and Bazelon dissented. The minority continued to urge their test that the material considered objectionable should be weighed against the balance of the contents and also against the injury to freedom of the press in prohibiting circulation.

The case was promptly appealed to the United States Supreme Court and, in a remarkable burst of speed (within three months), on January 13, 1958, a unanimous court entered a "per curiam order"[22] reversing the judgment of the United States Court of Appeals for the District of Columbia. At long last the litigation came to rest when on April 18, 1958, a new judge, United States District Judge James W. Morris, signed a declaratory judgment that the February, 1956, issues of *Sunshine and Health* and *Sun Magazine* were not obscene and enjoined the Post Office from restraining the magazines from the mail.

The case itself constantly shifted between two basic problems: what constituted obscenity, and whether the Post Office Department had followed the proper procedure. The United States Supreme Court in its opinion unquestionably ruled *only on the obscenity* because it cited only the case of *Roth vs. United States.* This case involved a criminal conviction and consequently would not have any relationship to proper procedure by the Post Office Department.

150

Although the 1957 decisions of the United States Supreme Court indicated that the Court would not permit the banning of an idea on the ground of obscenity, this indication was not clearly spelled out until 1959 in the *Lady Chatterley's Lover* movie decision.[23] The movie was made in France and the importer filed an application in New York with the Motion Picture Division of the Education Department for a permit to exhibit the film. That division, after examination, found three scenes "immoral" and ordered them cut prior to public showing. This was standard operating procedure in the movie fields in most states of the United States as well as in most civilized countries of the world. The constitutionality of this kind of censorship had been tested before the United States Supreme Court prior to this occasion and had been upheld. Few lawyers, if any, doubted that this was an appropriate procedure, sanctioned by society, and hoary with age.

The exclusion orders are worth noting:

The exhibitor was directed to eliminate all views of the gardener, Mellors, and Lady Chatterley in a cabin from a point in time when they are seen lying on a cot together, undressed, until the end of the sequence. In another reel all views of the gardener caressing Lady Chatterley's buttock and unzipping her dress had to be eliminated.

The Board directed that the following dialogue be deleted:

Mellors: But you're nude . . . you're nude under your dress and you didn't say so. . . .

The exhibitor appealed from the decision of the Motion Picture Division to the highest administrative authority—the Regents of the University of the State of New York. The Regents affirmed the decision of the Division on the ground that the scenes to be cut were definitely immoral and that furthermore "the whole theme of this motion picture is immoral . . . for that theme is the presentation of adultery as a desirable, acceptable

151

and proper pattern of behavior." The inference was clear: The Regents believed that the picture should not be shown at all.

The First Appellate Court, after hearing the appeal, reversed,[24] held the movie not obscene and stated that the administrative authorities had interpreted obscenity too broadly. The New York Court of Appeals considered the problem and solemnly reinstated the original decision, refusing to grant a license to the picture and holding that the administrative authorities were correct in denying licenses to exhibitors of "motion pictures which are immoral, in that they portray acts of sexual immorality . . . as desirable, acceptable or proper patterns of behavior." At this high level of "is it or isn't it" the highest court in New York found that even though a picture was not *technically* obscene it should not be granted a license if it showed adultery in a favorable light. And then, to compound the confusion, the New York court went on to find that the picture *was* obscene.

The court stated: "The dominant theme of the film may be summed up in a few words—exaltation of illicit sexual love and derogation of the restraints of marriage . . . and this entire theme was woven about scenes which unmistakably suggested and showed acts of sexual immorality."

In another point the court said: "We reiterate that this case involved the espousal of sexually immoral acts (here adultery) plus actual scenes of a suggestive and obscene nature."

Because the seven-man court rendered a four-to-three decision, the case was heard by the United States Supreme Court, which accepted jurisdiction and reversed. Although the agreement to reverse the New York court was unanimous, the basis for the reversal was expressed by the nine justices in six different legal opinions.

Mr. Justice Stewart, in the majority opinion, found the New York statute itself unconstitutional on the ground that it violated the First Amendment to the Federal Constitution which guarantees the right to advocate ideas. His opinion stated: "What New

York has done is to prevent the exhibition of a motion picture because that picture advocates an idea—that adultery under certain circumstances may be proper behavior. Yet the First Amendment's basic guarantee is freedom to advocate ideas." Supporting Justice Stewart were the Chief Justice and Justices Black, Brennan, and Douglas.

Mr. Justice Harlan, joined by Justices Frankfurter and Whittaker, wrote a separate concurring opinion in which, although they did not hold the statute of New York unconstitutional, they found that the New York Court of Appeals had misinterpreted the law. The decision of these judges would leave both the statute and the film intact.

Mr. Justice Clark in a separate opinion made the curious suggestion that the New York statute should be employed to fight only the improper pictorialization of immoral acts. Justices Black and Douglas added a warning that they concurred in the result primarily on the basis that the First Amendment prohibited any forms of censorship.

THE SUPREME COURT
ADDS ANOTHER INGREDIENT

From the time obscenity was first outlawed, the subject was treated with such scorn, contempt, and revulsion that most lawyers and judges put it in the same classification with such reprehensible items as narcotics, adulterated foods, poisons, and firearms. In these lethal fields the interest of society in suppression is so great that the law permits punishment and other acts (for example, seizure) without proving the legal fact of "knowledge."

In other words, if a person is walking down the street and someone running away from a policeman surreptitiously slips a packet of heroin or morphine into his pocket or purse, and the innocent bystander is arrested for "possession of illegal narcotics" he will have no legal defense. The laws on this subject generally are clear: Anyone found in possession of an illegal narcotic is guilty of a crime. The law does not say *"knowingly* in possession,"* because the law believes that it would be very unusual for an innocent person to be—as described in the hypothetical illustration above—unknowingly in possession of a narcotic. It is theoretically possible but highly improbable, says the law. Furthermore, constitutional law holds that the suppression of traffic in illegal narcotics is of such paramount importance to all citizens that the slight occasional danger of punishing an innocent person is not too great a price to pay to achieve efficiency in the elimination of all narcotics peddling. Many legal authorities believe that so-called obscene pictures and literature fall into the same class. Rarely has an attorney defended an obscenity charge on the grounds that the possessor did not have knowledge of the nature of the book or picture.

Such a defense did indeed come before the United States Supreme Court in the significant case of *Smith vs. California,*[25] decided in 1959. A Los Angeles ordinance provided that it "shall be unlawful for any person to have in his possession any obscene or indecent book . . . in any place of business where ice cream, soft drinks, candy . . . magazines, books . . . are sold or kept for sale." Eleazer Smith, a book dealer, maintained a stock of thousands of new and used books (most of which he obtained from dealers in New York City) selected from advertising leaflets and catalogues which he received. A Los Angeles police officer bought a copy of a book entitled *Sweeter Than Life* and then arrested the clerk and Smith.

At the trial the defense waged a vigorous argument, presenting a literary critic and a clinical psychologist who were both prepared to testify that the book was not obscene. Unfortunately for Smith, the trial judge refused to permit the expert testimony.

Smith testified that he had not read the book and had no reason to believe that it was objectionable. The trial judge made short shrift of the case, finding that knowledge of the obscenity was not an ingredient of the offense, and he sentenced Smith to thirty days' incarceration.

On appeal to the appellate department, that court approved of the decision of the trial judge. Under California law no further appeals could be made at a state level, so Smith carried the problem to the United States Supreme Court, which unanimously reversed the California court. The majority, speaking through Mr. Justice Brennan (joined by the Chief Justice and Justices Clark, Stewart, and Whittaker) found that the ordinance on its face violated the First Amendment to the Federal Constitution because it eliminated knowledge as an element of a crime and therefore was too restrictive with regard to the dissemination of reading matter. Basically, the court said that it imposes too burdensome a duty on any bookseller to have a complete knowledge of all his books. The famed passage is:

> By dispensing with any requirement of knowledge of the contents of a book on the part of the seller, the ordinance tends to impose a severe limitation on the public's access to constitutionally-protected matter. For if the book seller is criminally liable without knowledge of the contents, and the ordinance fulfills its purpose, it will tend to restrict the books he sells to those he has inspected; and thus the State will have imposed a restriction upon the distribution of constitutionally protected as well as obscene literature.

Justices Black and Douglas continued their fight for elimination of *all* censorship. Justice Harlan wanted to reverse only because the literary critic and the psychologist were prohibited from testifying. Justice Frankfurter agreed with Justice Harlan and also went on to say that the knowledge requirement (generally called *scienter*) should be developed more fully by the majority and he protested that they failed to give "some indication of the scope and quality of *scienter* that is required."

The decision of the court making it a constitutional requirement to have *knowledge* that the obscene matter existed and to possess some idea of its nature infuriated the Comstocks. They complained long and bitterly that the new requirement was "unrealistic and absurd." Others declared that this was a "maddening complication" and very frustrating to those who would fight the good fight against obscene literature. The local police assured the public that this would cripple the efforts of the municipalities to curb obscene publications.[26]

FIRST THE MOVIE—THEN THE BOOK

Once the movie based upon *Lady Chatterley's Lover* was found not obscene and permitted to be shown in its original and unexpurgated version, it was not long before Grove Press, Inc., brought forth an unexpurgated edition of D. H. Lawrence's *Lady Chatterley's Lover*. Both the Federal District Court[27] and the Court of Appeals[28] ruled against the Postmaster General, finding the book not obscene, utilizing the test of the *Roth* case. Judge C. Clark in the Circuit Court stated that it was his opinion that "Courts, not Post Offices, are the proper places for determination of what is and what is not protected by the Constitution." On the merits Judge Clark says, "Obviously a writer can employ various means to achieve the effect he has in mind, and so probably Lawrence could have omitted some of the passages found 'smutty' by the Postmaster General and yet have produced an effective work of literature. But clearly it would not have been the work he planned, because for what he had in mind his selection was most effective, as the agitation and success of the book over the years has proven."

Thus, we enter the 1960's with general agreement that there

are few if any limitations upon the language which may be employed by an author in writing his material and creating his scenes and moods. The following are some typical scenes from *Lady Chatterley's Lover*:

"Have you left your underthings off?" he asked her.

"Yes!"

"Ay, well, then I'll take my things off too." ·

He spread the blankets, putting one at the side for a coverlet. She took off her hat, and shook her hair. He sat down, taking off his shoes and gaiters, and undoing his cord breeches.

"Lie down then!" he said, when he stood in his shirt. She obeyed in silence, and he lay beside her, and pulled the blanket over them both.

"There!" he said.

And he lifted her dress right back, till he came even to her breasts. He kissed them softly, taking the nipples in his lips in tiny caresses.

"Eh, but tha'rt nice, tha'rt nice!" he said, suddenly rubbing his face with a snuggling movement against her warm belly.

And she put her arms round him under his shirt, but she was afraid, afraid of his thin, smooth, naked body, that seemed so powerful, afraid of the violent muscles. She shrank, afraid.

And when he said, with a sort of little sigh: "Eh, tha'rt nice!" something in her quivered, and something in her spirit stiffened from the terribly physical intimacy, and from the peculiar haste of his possession. And this time the sharp ecstasy of her own passion did not overcome her; she lay with her hands inert on his striving body, and do what she might, her spirit seemed to look on from the top of her head, and the butting of his haunches seemed ridiculous to her, and the sort of anxiety of his penis to come to its little evacuating crisis seemed farcical. Yes, this was love, this ridiculous bouncing of the buttocks, and the wilting of the poor insignificant, moist little penis. This was the divine love! After all, the moderns were right when they felt contempt for the performance; for it was quite true, as some poets said, that the God who created man must have had a sinister sense of humor, creating him a reasonable being, yet forcing him to take this ridiculous posture,

and driving him with blind craving for this ridiculous performance. Even a Maupassant found it a humiliating anti-climax.
Men despised the intercourse act, and yet did it.

Cold and derisive her queer female mind stood apart, and
though she lay perfectly still, her impulse was to heave her
loins, and throw the man out, escape his ugly grip, and the
butting overriding of his absurd haunches. His body was a
foolish, impudent, imperfect thing, a little disgusting in its
unfinished clumsiness. For surely a complete evolution would
eliminate this performance, this "function."

And yet when he had finished, soon over, and lay very still,
receding into silence, and a strange, motionless distance, far,
farther than the horizon of her awareness, her heart began to
weep. She could feel him ebbing away, leaving her there like a
stone on the shore. He was withdrawing, his spirit was leaving
her. He knew.

And in real grief, tormented by her own double consciousness and reaction, she began to weep. He took no notice, or did
not even know. The storm of weeping swelled and shook her,
and shook him.

"Ay!" he said. "It was no good that time. You wasn't
there."—So he knew! Her sobs became violent.

"But what's amiss?" he said. "It's once in a while that way."

"I . . . I can't love you," she sobbed, suddenly feeling her
heart breaking.

"Canna ter? well, dunna fret! There's no law says as tha's
got to. Ta'e it for what it is."

He still lay with his hand on her breast. But she had drawn
both her hands from him.

His words were small comfort. She sobbed aloud.

"Nay, Nay!" he said. "Ta'e the thick wi' th' thin. This wor'
a bit o' thin for once."

She wept bitterly, sobbing: "But I want to love you, and I
can't. It only seems horrid."

He laughed a little, half bitter, half amused.

*   *   *   *   *

He took her in his arms again and drew her to him, and
suddenly she became small in his arms, small and nestling. It
was gone, and she began to melt in marvellous peace. And as

158

she melted small and wonderful in his arms, she became infinitely desirable to him, all his blood vessels seemed to scald with intense yet tender desire, for her, for her softness, for the penetrating beauty of her in his arms, passing into his blood. And softly, with that marvellous swoon-like caress of his hand in pure soft desire, softly he stroked the silky slope of her loins, down, down between her soft warm buttocks, coming nearer and nearer to the very quick of her. And she felt him like a flame of desire, yet tender, and she felt herself melting in the flame. She let herself go. She felt his penis risen against her with silent amazing force and assertion, and she let herself go to him. She yielded with a quiver that was like death, she went all open to him. And oh, if he were not tender to her now, how cruel, for she was all open to him and helpless!

She quivered again at the potent inexorable entry inside her, so strange and terrible. It might come with the thrust of a sword in her softly-opened body, and that would be death. She clung in a sudden anguish of terror. But it came with a strange slow thrust of peace, the dark thrust of peace and a ponderous, primordial tenderness, such as made the world in the beginning. And her terror subsided in her breast, her breast dared to be gone in peace, she held nothing. She dared to let go everything, all herself, and be gone in the flood.

And it seemed she was like the sea, nothing but dark waves rising and heaving, heaving with a great swell, so that slowly her whole darkness was in motion, and she was ocean rolling its dark, dumb mass. Oh, and far down inside her the deeps parted and rolled asunder, in long, far travelling billows, and ever, at the quick of her, the depths parted and rolled asunder, from the center of soft plunging, as the plunger went deeper and deeper, touching lower, and she was deeper and deeper and deeper disclosed, and heavier the billows of her rolled away to some shore, uncovering her, and closer plunged the palpable unknown, and further and further rolled the waves of herself away from herself, leaving her, till suddenly, in a soft shuddering convulsion, the quick of all her plasm was touched, she knew herself touched, the consummation was upon her, and she was gone. She was gone, she was not, and she was born: a woman.

Ah, too lovely, too lovely! In the ebbing, she realized all the

159

loveliness. Now all her body clung with tender love to the unknown man, and blindly to the wilting penis, as it so tenderly, frailly, unknowingly withdrew, after the fierce thrust of its potency. As it drew out and left her body, the secret, sensitive thing, she gave an unconscious cry of pure loss, and she tried to put it back. It had been so perfect! And she loved it so!

And only now she became aware of the small, bud-like reticence and tenderness of the penis, and a little cry of wonder and poignancy escaped her again, her woman's heart crying out over the tender frailty of that which had been the power.

"It was so lovely!" she moaned. "It was so lovely!" But he said nothing, only softly kissed her, lying still above her. And she moaned with a sort of bliss, as a sacrifice, and a new-born thing.

And now in her heart the queer wonder of him was awakened. A man! the strange potency of manhood upon her! Her hands strayed over him, still a little afraid. Afraid of that strange, hostile, slightly repulsive thing that he had been to her, a man. And now she touched him, and it was the sons of god with the daughters of men. How beautiful he felt, how pure in tissue! How lovely, how lovely, strong, and yet pure and delicate, such stillness of the sensitive body! Such utter stillness of potency and delicate flesh! How beautiful! How beautiful! Her hands came timorously down his back, to the soft, smallish globes of the buttocks. Beauty! What beauty! a sudden little flame of new awareness went through her. How was it possible this beauty here, where she had previously been repelled? The unspeakable beauty to the touch, of the warm, living buttocks! The life within life, the sheer warm, potent loveliness. And the strange weight of the balls between his legs! What a mystery! What a strange heavy weight of mystery, that could lie soft and heavy in one's hand! The roots, root of all that is lovely, the primeval root of all full beauty.

* * * *

He was ashamed to turn to her, because of his aroused nakedness.

He caught his shirt off the floor, and held it to him, coming to her.

160

"No!" she said, still holding out her beautiful slim arms from her drooping breasts. "Let me see you!"

He dropped the shirt and stood still, looking towards her. The sun through the low window sent a beam that lit up his thighs and slim belly, and the erect phallus rising darkish and hot-looking from the little cloud of vivid gold-red hair. She was startled and afraid.

"How strange!" she said slowly. "How strange he stands there! So big! and so dark and cocksure! Is he like that?"

The man looked down the front of his slender white body, and laughed. Between the slim breasts the hair was dark, almost black. But at the root of the belly, where the phallus rose thick and arching, it was gold-red, vivid in a little cloud.

"So proud!" she murmured, uneasy. "And so lordly! Now I know why men are so overbearing. But he's lovely, *really*. Like another being! A bit terrifying! But lovely really! And he comes to *me—*" She caught her lower lip between her teeth, in fear and excitement.

The man looked down in silence at his tense phallus, that did not change.—"Ay!" he said at last, in a little voice. "Ay ma lad! Tha'rt theer right enough. Yi, tha mun —rear thy head! Theer on thy own, eh? an ta'es no count o' nob'dy! Tha ma'es noowt o' me, John Thomas. Art boss? of me? Eh well, tha'rt more cocky than me, an' tha says less. John Thomas! Dost want *her?* Dost want my lady Jane? Tha's dipped me in again, tha hast. Ay, an' tha comes up smilin."—Ax 'er then! Ax lady Jane! Say: Lift up your heads o' ye gates, that the King of glory may come in. Ay, th' cheek on thee! Cunt, that's what tha'rt after. Tell lady Jane tha wants cunt. John Thomas, an' th' cunt o' lady Jane!—"

"Oh, don't tease him," said Connie, crawling on her knees on the bed towards him and putting her arms round his white slender loins, and drawing him to her so that her hanging, swinging breasts touched the tip of the stirring, erect phallus, and caught the drop of moisture. She held the man fast.

"Lie down!" he said. "Lie down! Let me come!"

He was in a hurry now.

And afterwards, when they had been quite still, the woman had to uncover the man again, to look at the mystery of the phallus.

"And now he's tiny, and soft like a little bud of life!" she said, taking the soft small penis in her hand. "Isn't he somehow lovely! so on his own, so strange! And *so* innocent! And he comes so far into me! You must *never* insult him, you know. He's mine too. He's not only yours. He's mine! And so lovely and innocent!" And she held the penis soft in her hand.

He laughed.

"Blest be the tie that binds our hearts in kindered love," he said.

"Of course!" she said, "Even when he's soft and little I feel my heart simply tied to him. And how lovely your hair is here! quite quite different!"

"That's John Thomas' hair, not mine!" he said.

"John Thomas! John Thomas!" and she quickly kissed the soft penis, that was beginning to stir again.

"Ay!" said the man, stretching his body almost painfully. "He's got his root in my soul, has that gentleman! An' sometimes I don't know what ter do wi' him. Ay, he's got a will of his own, an' it's hard to suit him. Yet I wouldn't have him killed."

"No wonder men have always been afraid of him!" she said. "He's rather terrible."

The quiver was going through the man's body, as the stream of consciousness again changed its direction, turning downwards. And he was helpless, as the penis in slow, soft undulations filled and surged and rose up, and grew hard, standing there hard and overweening, in its curious towering fashion. The woman too trembled a little as she watched.

"There! Take him then! He's thine," said the man.

And she quivered, and her own mind melted out. Sharp soft waves of unspeakable pleasure washed over her as he entered her, and started the curious molten thrilling that spread and spread till she was carried away with the last, blind flush of extremity.

ANOTHER BARRIER TO THE CENSORIOUS

After the *Smith* case in 1959 the Supreme Court took a vacation from decisions on obscenity problems, and did not offer another opinion in the field until 1962. Although this case hardly belonged in the Supreme Court, it nevertheless in its own way added yet another significant obstacle to the path of the prosecutor endeavoring to apply the label of obscenity to any material. The case, *MANual vs. Day*,[29] involved three magazines: *MANual, Trim,* and *Grecian Guild Pictorial.* The publisher deposited the magazines in the mails at Alexandria, Virginia, but the Judicial Officer of the Post Office Department ruled that the magazines were obscene and therefore not mailable. The Federal District Court upheld by the Court of Appeals sustained the prohibition.

The lower court opinion describes the contents of the magazines in the following language:

> The magazines contained little textual material, with pictures of male models dominating almost every page . . . . The typical page consisted of a photograph, with the name of the model and the photographer and occasional references to the model's age (usually under 26), color of eyes, physical dimensions and occupation. The magazines contained little, either in text or pictures, that could be considered as relating in any way to weight lifting, muscle building or physical culture. . . .
> Many of the photographs were of nude male models, usually posed with some object in front of their genitals . . .; a number were of nude or partially nude males with emphasis on their bare buttocks. . . . Although none of the pictures directly exposed the model's genitals, some showed his pubic hair and others suggested what appeared to be a semi-erect penis . . .; others showed male models reclining with their legs (and sometimes their arms as well) spread wide apart. . . . Many of the pictures showed models wearing only loin cloths, "V gowns," or posing straps . . .; some showed the model apparently re-

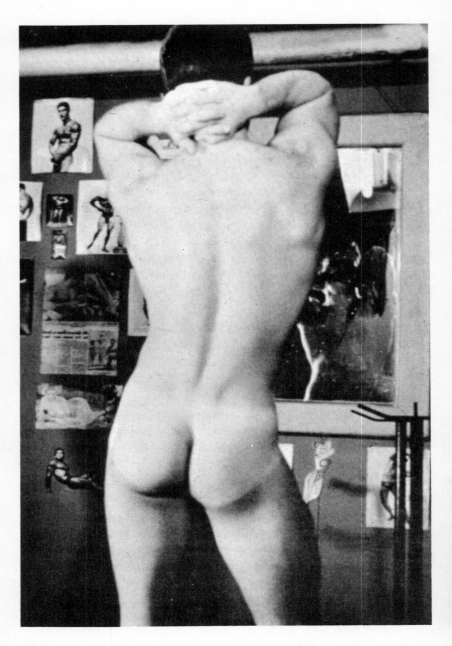

Court: "... nude males with emphasis on their bare buttocks."

Court: "... virtually nude models wearing ... shoes ..."

Court: "Although none of the pictures directly exposed the model's genitals, some showed his pubic hair . . ."

Court: A picture of "one model beating another while a third held his face in his hand as if weeping . . ."

moving his clothing. . . . Two of the magazines had pictures of pairs of models posed together suggestively. . . .

Each of the magazines contained photographs of models with swords or other long pointed objects. . . . The magazines also contained photographs of virtually nude models wearing only shoes, boots, helmets or leather jackets. . . . There were also pictures of models posed with chains or of one model beating another while a third held his face in his hands as if weeping. . . .

The foregoing appears to be the government's description of the magazines. A careful search of all the pictures in the magazines indicates that the four reproduced herein represent to the best extent possible the government's view.

Mr. Justice Harlan wrote the opinion of the court, with only Mr. Justice Stewart joining. Thus, as Judge Alexander Holtzoff, in another case involving the same participants, observed: "The majority opinion was really a minority view because it represented the views of two members of a nine-man court." In any event, whether it was a *majority* or a *minority*, the opinion made one major contribution to the field of obscenity. The court ruled that not only must the material relate to "prurient interest" (whatever that is) but also must have "patent offensiveness." As Justice Harlan stated:

> In most obscenity cases, to be sure, the two elements tend to coalesce, for that which is patently offensive would also usually carry the requisite "prurient interest" appeal. It is only in the unusual instance where, as here, the "prurient interest" appeal of the material is found limited to a particular class of persons that occasion arises for a truly independent inquiry into the question whether or not the material is patently offensive.

The point the court makes is that this material will appeal only to homosexuals and consequently has little general prurient appeal. In addition, Justice Harlan finds that the material lacks offensiveness. In order to best make this determination the judge

168

thinks that the test should be under a national standard of decency.

Mr. Justice Brennan, joined by the Chief Justice and Mr. Justice Douglas, wrote a concurring opinion. The group of three justices did not become much involved in the obscenity issue but instead concentrated on the point that they did not believe that the Post Office had the authority to eliminate material from the mail by simple administrative proceedings. The justices referred to the *Esquire* case and quoted from it, saying that the provisions of the federal law "would have to be far more explicit for us to assume that Congress made such a radical departure from our traditions and undertook to clothe the Postmaster General with the power to supervise the tastes of the reading public of the country."

Justices Frankfurter and White did not render opinions. Justice Black concurred in the result (reversal of the lower court) but without any opinion, probably because he had given this reason throughout the years: that under the Federal Constitution no literature or art material is subject to censorship.

Justice Clark alone dissented, saying:

> The magazines have no social, educational, or entertainment qualities but are designed solely as sex stimulants for homosexuals. They "consist almost entirely of photographs of young men in nude or practically nude poses handled in such a manner as to focus attention on their genitals or buttocks or to emphasize these parts. . . ." Because of this content the magazines do "not appeal to the ordinary male adult . . . [who] would have no interest in them and would not buy them under ordinary circumstances and . . . [therefore] the readers of these publications consist almost entirely of male homosexuals and possibly a few adolescent males. . . ."
>
> The publishers freely admit that the magazines are published to appeal to the male homosexual group. The advertisements and photographer lists in such magazines were quite naturally "designed so as to attract the male homosexual and to furnish him with names and addresses where nude male

pictures in poses and conditions which would appeal to his prurient interest may be obtained." Moreover, the advertisements themselves could leave no more doubt in the publishers' minds than in those of the solicited purchasers. To illustrate: some captioned a picture of a nude or scantily attired young man with the legend "perfectly proportioned, handsome, male models, age 18-26." Others featured a photograph of a nude male with the area around the privates obviously retouched so as to cover the genitals and part of the pubic hair and offered to furnish an "original print of this photo." Finally, each magazine specifically endorsed its listed photographers and requested its readers to support them by purchasing their products. In addition, three of the four magazines involved expressly represented that they were familiar with the work of the photographers listed in their publications.

Turning to Womack, the president and directing force of all three corporate publishers, it is even clearer that we are not dealing here with a "Jack and Jill" operation. Mr. Womack admitted that the magazines were planned for homosexuals, designed to appeal to and stimulate their erotic interests. To improve on this effect, he made suggestions to photographers as to the type of pictures he wanted. For example, he informed one of the studios listed in his publications that "physique fans want their 'truck driver types' already cleaned up, showered, and ready for bed . . . [and] it is absolutely essential that the models have pretty faces and a personality not totally unrelated to sex appeal."

While Justice Clark did not specifically say so, he appeared to be of the opinion that these magazines were obscene and should be banned as obscene.

After *MANual vs. Day* the Supreme Court rendered other decisions but these related more to the field of procedure than to any definition of what constituted obscenity, and these cases are discussed under that section. Then, in June, 1964, the Supreme Court handed down a new series of decisions. Forthrightly, the court supported freedom of speech and restricted the censors.

THE LOVERS

Nico Jacobellis, manager of a motion picture theatre in Cleveland Heights, Ohio, was arrested when he showed a French import motion picture called *Les Amants* [The Lovers]. He was fined $2,500 and sentenced to the workhouse if he did not pay the fine. He carried his appeal through three state courts. The lowest court of three trial judges affirmed the conviction. The intermediate court—the Appellate Court of Ohio—concurred, and the highest court—the Supreme Court of Ohio—concurred and approved. Next step: the United States Supreme Court. Mr. Justice Brennan announced the decision: "We conclude that the film is not obscene and that the judgment must accordingly be reversed." [30]

The movie itself is the story of a bored young French housewife married to a newspaper publisher, who relieves her ennui by taking lovers. The film portrays very little sexual activity or appeal to prurient interest until one scene near the end when the housewife and a young man are seen in a bed where sexual intercourse is obviously taking place. The viewer might also conclude he is witnessing some extra-marital and unusual foreplay but much is left to the imagination and the scenes are neither vivid, revealing, nor frank.

Justice Brennan, in holding the film not obscene (with agreement by Justice Goldberg) makes the following points:

1. There are those who argue that whether "a particular motion picture, book or other work of expression is obscene can be treated as a purely factual judgment on which a jury's verdict is all but conclusive, or that in any event the decision can be left essentially to the State and lower Federal Courts." This idea is appealing because it would remove the Supreme Court from a "difficult, recurring and unpleasant task." However, the abnegation of judicial supervision in this field would be inconsistent

171

with "the duty of the high court to uphold the Constitution. In every case whether anything is obscene is necessarily a final decision of constitutional law and is entitled to review by the United States Supreme Court. There are no substitutes."

2. Because obscenity involves a constitutional judgment, the Supreme Court as well as every other court deciding the matter must examine the material itself to decide whether the Constitution prohibits it.

3. If an item has *any* "redeeming social importance," that is to say, if it has any "literary or scientific or artistic value or any other form of social importance, [it] may not be branded as obscenity and denied constitutional protection." The material cannot be weighed by testing social importance against sex appeal because the mere act of weighing social importance indicates its presence, and thereby negates the possibility of obscenity.

4. In using the test of contemporary community standards, the standard must be national and not local because, if the authorities suppress or permit suppression of a book or film in one locality, it definitely would hinder its freedom of dissemination in other localities since exhibitors, sellers and publishers would be reluctant "to risk criminal conviction in testing the variation between the two places." Although it is recognized that local communities have tremendous variations in their toleration of so-called obscenity and pornography, and reconciling the conflicting rights of the local communities may be difficult, nevertheless the Supreme Court "has not shrunk from discharging that duty in other areas, and we see no reason why it should do so here." The court here affirms the national scope of the Constitution—what governs in the village also governs in the metropolis.

Justice White concurred in the decision. Justice Black (with Douglas joining) concurred in the decision but reiterated that the Supreme Court "is just about the most inappropriate Supreme Board of Censors that could be found." Basically,

Justices Black and Douglas believe that no one can be punished merely for exhibiting a motion picture.

Justice Stewart concurred on the ground that he believed every form of communication was constitutionally protected for everything but hard-core pornography. He then goes on to say, "I shall not today attempt further to define the kinds of material I understand to be embraced within that shorthand description; and perhaps I could never succeed in intelligibly doing so. But I know it when I see it, and the motion picture involved in this case is not that."

The unfortunate part about the *Jacobellis* case was that Chief Justice Earl Warren dissented and apparently has reached the end of his rope in obscenity cases. The Chief Justice pointed out that certainly it was difficult to get a truly satisfactory definition of obscenity. However, he says, this had been true in many other areas of law, as for example, negligence. Although a common concept in the law for centuries, this act is extremely difficult to define. However, courts throughout the land function perfectly well, each defining negligence as it pleases. When it comes to obscenity, the Chief Justice continues, this does not seem to satisfy anyone and the Court has undertaken to rule on alleged obscenity of films or books as they come along. Despite the endeavor of the court to act thus, most of the decisions gave very little guidance. Therefore, maintains the Chief Justice, the Court must end this practice and let the local courts decide, reviewing only by seeing "whether there is sufficient evidence in the record upon which a finding of obscenity could be made."

Warren also doubted the existence of a national standard and argued that the standards of obscenity must be left to each community to decide as it pleases. If, as would undoubtedly happen, books were held obscene in one jurisdiction and cleared in another, the High Court would then have the comparatively simple problems of reconciling conflicting rights.

In general, the opinion of the Chief Justice was extremely

173

vague. It seemed almost querulous in its longing for a simple solution to a complex problem. If (as was so often the case) a book was held obscene in some states and not in others, the Chief Justice concluded that "the Court is confronted with the task of reconciling conflicting rights of diverse communities within our society and of individuals." What precisely the Chief Justice would do to resolve the conflict, he did not indicate.

Justice Warren dealt at length with the fact that the holding of any item obscene should be based upon reasonable findings, but he failed to suggest what these findings were. In the actual case he would have permitted the Supreme Court of Ohio to ban the showing of *The Lovers* in that state, although the only evidence presented was the film itself. The Chief Justice seemed to be saying that the field is too difficult and therefore should be left to the states and lower courts to work out for themselves.

Justice Harlan had a special viewpoint. He would permit any state to have reasonably wide discretion in deciding what constitutes obscenity and he would not interfere except in unusual and special cases. However, in cases involving the federal government, as for example, the Post Office Department, the court should make the final ruling. He said that once a state decided that any item had treated sex in a fundamentally offensive manner with a rationaly established criterion, then the state might prohibit that material. He agreed with the Ohio Supreme Court in condemning the film *The Lovers*.

THE *TROPIC OF CANCER* CASE

On June 22, 1964, the United States Supreme Court handed down what may be its most important decision in the field of obscenity. This brief, peremptory decision in the case of *Grove Press, Inc., vs. Gerstein*[31] ruled at last on the right of Grove

174

Press, Inc., to publish Henry Miller's *Tropic of Cancer*. The details of this case have already been discussed under the section dealing with the present status of the law, but now it becomes important to consider its significance.

The Supreme Court divided along the same lines as it did in ruling on the film *The Lovers*. Justices Black and Douglas would not permit censorship because they believed that nothing should be censored without a demonstration of clear and present danger of the causation of some illegal or criminal act. Justices Brennan and Goldberg wanted to reverse because they could take the national contemporary standards of decency and find sufficient redeeming social importance in this book to keep it from being banned. Justice Stewart reversed because he did not believe *Tropic of Cancer* to be hard-core pornography and he did believe that under the Constitution of the United States only hard-core pornography could be banned.

The Chief Justice and Justices Clark, Harlan, and White did not believe that the decision of the lower court should be reversed, but they gave no reasons. In the past, however, the Chief Justice and Justice Clark had made it apparent that they felt the state has a right "to maintain its moral fibre" and it must take very strong considerations to reverse a lower court finding of obscenity. These two judges obviously saw little reason to reverse here.

It is important to note that Justice White agreed to the reversal in the *Jacobellis* case but supported the Chief Justice and Justice Clark in *Tropic of Cancer*. Apparently he saw a significant distinction between the two cases which could be only the *degree* of so-called obscenity. In considering degree, the major difference between *Tropic of Cancer* and the *Jacobellis* case is that in *Tropic of Cancer* the objectionable four-letter words were spread throughout the book, together with bare and undecorated descriptions of sexual intercourse and sexual deviations, graphically portrayed in frank, unveiled, and untechnical language.

175

The above conclusion is fortified by another case—*Tralins vs. Gerstein* [32]—in which the courts banned the book *Pleasure Was My Business* and the Court lined up the same for this reversal as it did in the *Tropic* case. Yet here there were no four-letter words. The book does contain some passages which would probably offend the squeamish and which could have given Justice White more difficulty than he had with the movie *The Lovers*.

The central character in the story is a woman named Ruth Barnes who, under the name Madam Sherry, opened an elaborate house of prostitution in Miami. The book gives a detailed description of the operation of the house and the whimseys and eccentricities of its customers. The following are some passages from this book:

> Kay, the hillbilly girl from Georgia, always seemed to know the proper way to handle the sadists, the masochists, the flagellants and others who from time to time paid through the nose for their pleasures.
>
> We were tempted to refuse such clients but, because of the very viciousness of some of them we would try to satisfy their whims and idiosyncrasies to avoid having a rumpus. For this service, we provided a soundproof room so other Castle guests wouldn't be disturbed.
>
> I never ceased to be amazed by the social standing of the men involved. Never once did I find a deviate from the lower classes. Almost always they came from the "higher levels" of society: business executives, clergymen and socialites. There were a few lawyers and doctors. They were the most degenerate of the lot.
>
> One couple in particular used to visit us regularly each November. They were in the canning business in Delaware and could well afford the high prices we charged for their "whippings." This couple preferred to disrobe completely and lie down side by side across a bed in the soundproof room while Kay and Felix, completely nude too, except for their shoes and stockings, whipped them on their behinds into a frenzy of excitement. Husband and wife, lying side by side on the bed, would then clasp each other and copulate while they

were being whipped. The cries of agonized passion could hardly be muffled behind those closed doors.

There was another couple who used to wait an entire year to enjoy their pleasure, which was similar to the first couple's, though slightly more ridiculous. The wife would mount one of the male prostitutes and while she was thus impaled, her husband would slap her rump with his palms until she ended her passion in a frenzied orgasm and then collapsed in a dead faint. Then, this couple would go away and we'd see neither one until the following season.

Perhaps the most revolting of all was the sadist who'd come around every third month for his relief. This man was a very prominent banker from Atlanta, who made a special trip to Miami to have his fling. I'll never forget the first time he appeared. A meek, mild-mannered little man about fifty asked to speak to me in private. He handed me five hundred dollars and said that all he wanted was a girl who could "take it" for several hours.

When I asked him what he meant, he hung his head and had difficulty in explaining. I got the implication and sent for Kay. I saw his face light up like a maniac's at the sight of her. Kay, seeming to sense what was afoot, backed off a step and looked at me. I shrugged.

For three hundred dollars—her share—she'd take the beating. I whispered to her that I would give it all to her and she grinned. I did not want her blood money.

And blood money it turned out to be. I told Kay to take the room where the peephole was and then, with several of the girls, followed them upstairs to the secret corridor, ready to rush to her assistance should she need any help.

First, the little guy took his time about undressing and, after he had watched her undress, he stripped and began to slap her. Kay, being experienced in such matters, screamed and pretended to try to elude his slapping hand. Then as his excitement mounted, he began to beat her with his fists and Kay began to whimper and struggle to get free. I knew that she was in all probability enjoying her $500 beating, so we didn't interfere. It is curious how those sadists enjoy causing a woman pain. Perhaps it is something that goes way back into their childhood—perhaps they are inherent woman-haters and are too much men to become fags. I don't know. In any case, we were so sickened that, when he began his descent upon Kay, none of us could bear to watch any longer. The whole idea was that he wanted to rape a woman, and just didn't have the nerve—thank God—to try it with an innocent woman.

In some cases, perhaps, a whorehouse does a community service in providing a harmless outlet—for perverts and deviates. However, I don't mislead myself that legalizing prostitution would eliminate rape. I never did believe that, although I might have said it from time to time. Sex deviates are mentally disturbed and should be helped—not by madams in whorehouses, but by competent medical and mental doctors.

That's what I told Dr. Kinsey when he called at my establishment to question me on matters pertinent to his research. I also told him I thought he was too far ahead of his time and that people would laugh at his findings when and if they were made public. He smiled and said he knew it was so.

I found that some women are just as guilty as some men of odd-ball sex desires. For example, one married woman used to come to us with her husband in tow and ask to have a party with another couple.

Then there was the wealthy real estate woman, recently named Clubwoman of the Year in Miami, who used to come to me and ask that not one, but *two* of our biggest men have a birthday party with her in the same bed at the same time. And believe me, she wore out both of them in due time. Her excuse for her actions? "Every time I make a big sale and earn a large commission, I get passionate. So I come to you for assistance, Madam Sherry. Then I can behave like a normal loving wife when I go home to my husband."

The odd balls that came in from time to time could not be told apart from the average client by their appearance.

The exhibitionists who liked to strip naked while still downstairs in the parlor and then go upstairs in full view of everyone in the house were usually impotent when they were behind closed doors. There were deviates who would beg to watch the customers come and go and then, upon finding someone they particularly fancied, asked to have the same girl *quick*, before she dried her deck.

And then there were others I absolutely wouldn't allow. The

one who'd ask to have a girl who was having her period. The other who'd ask if he could wait while the girl took a purgative for him. And still others who wanted things even more unspeakable.

Man, the thinking animal, is the filthiest, the commonest, the lowest life on earth when it comes to deviations that even animals wouldn't attempt. And this made me laugh at some of those temperate, religious and morally right fanatics who rule the morals of the world.

Yes, I'm talking about those so-called religious leaders—the pillars of society: the priests and the ministers and the parsons. They visited my establishment for the pleasures of the flesh and of so-called corruption within—they too have partaken of the devil's mass and have enjoyed themselves with the followers of de Sade!

I'll never forget the meek man who entered the Castle through the side door and, with a scarf tightly wound around his neck, asked to see the girl with the biggest breasts in the house. He paid me $100 and I immediately sent for Wilma, a new hillbilly girl from Tennessee who had a pair that was the envy of every girl in the Miami area.

The man with the scarf around his neck then accompanied Wilma upstairs and, after about ten minutes, I heard her yell downstairs. "Hey, Madam Sherry!" she cried, "come the hell up here, will you?"

I hurried upstairs and she was standing there in the doorway to the bedroom. "Come here, will you. This guy paid me a hundred bucks, didn't he? Well is that all he wanted me to do?"

"What's that?"

"He just wants to sit there and look at my tits and jerk off. See, look at him for yourself." She pointed and said in Spanish, "*Esta paa, si?*"

And there he was, the scarf that had been tightly wound around his collar, now askew, his trousers down around his ankles and he was masturbating like a fool. "Hey!" Wilma taunted, "don't you want one like a regular man?"

At that moment he completed his act and drew up his trousers with one hand, and ran out, rewinding the scarf with the other hand. "Holy Jesus, did you see his collar?" cried

179

Wilma,—*"he was a—!"* Still half naked, she stooped and picked up a small, black book which had fallen from his pocket. I found his wallet lying beside the chair where his trousers had been down around his ankles and took it downstairs, put it into an envelope and addressed it to a certain rectory in a city not too far distant from Miami.

IV

Other Suggested Tests

OTHER TESTS FOR OBSCENITY

The Supreme Court tests have not been particularly helpful in solving the dilemma of how to distinguish the obscene from the legal. Other authorities have, from time to time, endeavored to formulate criteria by which courts and lawyers could more easily detect and label obscenity. These legalistic Geiger counters are of recent vintage and have not been fully explored. Whether they will help remains to be seen.

THE AMERICAN LAW INSTITUTE
RECOMMENDATIONS

The American Law Institute is a professional association of lawyers, professors, and judges who seek to restate the law in a recommended and codified form. In certain fields, such as in the law of contracts, agency, and negligence, the organization has after years of study and consideration published books entitled "Restatements" which endeavor to codify the law. These books employ a uniform format and have behind them the weight of the most distinguished scholars in each field. They receive much consideration by all courts.

In fields where the bulk of the law is statutory, the American Law Institute submits recommended codes for adoption by legislatures. In the criminal field for many years the Institute has been working on a model penal code. In May, 1962, Judge

Herbert F. Goodrich, Director of the American Law Institute and a judge of the Third Circuit Court of Appeals in Philadelphia, Pennsylvania (since deceased), submitted the proposed official draft of the *Model Penal Code of the American Law Institute*. Under Article 251, headed Public Indecency, the Institute has presented a series of chapters on "Open lewdness," prostitution, and solicitation of "deviant sexual relations." The last section covers obscenity, and follows in full.

Section 251.4. Obscenity

(1) Obscene Defined. Material is obscene if, considered as a whole, its predominant appeal is to prurient interest, that is, a shameful or morbid interest, in nudity, sex or excretion, and if in addition it goes substantially beyond customary limits of candor in describing or representing such matters. Predominant appeal shall be judged with reference to ordinary adults unless it appears from the character of the material or the circumstances of its dissemination to be designed for children or other specially susceptible audience. Undeveloped photographs, molds, printing plates, and the like, shall be deemed obscene notwithstanding that processing or other acts may be required to make the obscenity patent or to disseminate it.

(2) *Offenses.* Subject to the affirmative defense provided in Subsection (3), a person commits a misdemeanor if he knowingly or recklessly:

(a) sells, delivers or provides, or offers or agrees to sell, deliver or provide, any obscene writing, picture, record or other representation or embodiment of the obscene; or

(b) presents or directs an obscene play, dance or performance, or participates in that portion thereof which makes it obscene; or

(c) publishes, exhibits or otherwise makes available any obscene material; or

(d) possesses any obscene material for purposes of sale or other commercial dissemination; or

(e) sells, advertises or otherwise commercially disseminates material, whether or not obscene, by representing or suggesting that it is obscene.

A person who disseminates or possesses obscene material in the course of his business is presumed to do so knowingly or recklessly.

(3) *Justifiable and Non-Commercial Private Dissemination.* It is an affirmative defense to prosecution under this Section that dissemination was restricted to:

(a) institutions or persons having scientific, educational, governmental or other similar justification for possessing obscene material; or

(b) non-commerical dissemination to personal associates of the actor.

(4) *Evidence; Adjudication of Obscenity.* In any prosecution under this Section evidence shall be admissible to show:

(a) the character of the audience for which the material was designed or to which it was directed;

(b) what the predominant appeal of the material would be for ordinary adults or any special audience to which it was directed, and what effect, if any, it would probably have on conduct of such people;

(c) artistic, literary, scientific, educational or other merits of the material;

(d) the degree of public acceptance of the material in the United States;

(e) appeal to prurient interest, or absence thereof, in advertising or other promotion of the material; and

(f) the good repute of the author, creator, publisher or other person from whom the material originated.

Expert testimony and testimony of the author, creator, publisher or other person from whom the material originated, relating to factors entering into the determination of the issue of obscenity, shall be admissible. The Court shall dismiss a prosecution for obscenity if it is satisfied that the material is not obscene.

185

PREDOMINANT APPEAL

It is, of course, important to recognize that the American Law Institute's recommendations were prepared prior to the United States Supreme Court decisions of 1964. Thus, the first important difference is the Supreme Court's theory that in order for material to be obscene it must be "utterly without redeeming social importance." If it has *any* redeeming social importance, under the Supreme Court test, it is not obscene. The American Law Institute Test on the other hand, makes the significant phrase the *predominant appeal.*

The American Law Institute modifies this test somewhat by indicating that the objectionable item not only must have a *predominant appeal* to prurient interest but also must go "substantially beyond customary limits of candor." But this again is much more limited than the Supreme Court view. The adoption by the Supreme Court of the American Law Institute theory would scarcely have caused the Illinois Supreme Court to reverse itself in a case such as the *Lenny Bruce* case.[1] This is because the supreme court could easily have said that Lenny Bruce's performance had a predominant appeal to prurient interest and went "substantially beyond customary limits of candor." However, the Illinois Supreme Court could not say that there was *no* "redeeming social importance" in the Lenny Bruce performance, because it would have been untrue. Lenny Bruce is a modern critic of society, and much that he criticizes and holds up to scorn merits critical comment. Except for choice of language, what Bruce says often ranks with modern criticism as expounded in the philosophical journals. Consequently, because of the existence of *redeeming social importance* the Lenny Bruce performance is not obscene.

NONCOMMERCIAL DISSEMINATION

The American Law Institute, in Section 3, Subsection (b) of its codification, recommends that obscenity which is distributed by an individual to his associates on a *noncommercial* basis should not be prosecuted. In technical language, the Institute states that such action becomes an "affirmative defense," that is, after the charge is made the defendant says, "Yes, I did it, but my defense is it was noncommercial." This is similar to the statement by an accused murderer, for example: "I did it in self-defense." This, too, is an affirmative defense. It is a defense which says, "I performed the act but the reason I did it and the circumstances under which it was done remove the conduct from the criminal."

In setting up this doctrine the Institute went beyond the decisions rendered in any case. Its basic theory was that private conduct in the sexual field should never be punished. For example, departing from legal tradition in the United States, the Institute voted against including private homosexuality not involving force or corruption of the young as an offense in a modern penal code. In the new Model Penal Code any form of deviate sexual intercourse is a crime *only* if it is accomplished through force or with children, etc. In the absence of force, sodomy, homosexuality, and similar practices are no longer considered offenses.

This theory was carried over into the obscenity section by eliminating noncommercial private dissemination. Translated into today's society and mores this situation exists:

If an individual invites a group of personal friends and associates to his home and shows them French stag movies, this constitutes privileged conduct. If that person does exactly the same thing but includes someone who is not a "personal associate" or makes an admission charge, then a crime has been committed.

One major difficulty with the Institute theory is its implication that if a considerable amount of obscene material is found there should be punishment unless the dissemination is on a non-commercial basis. Also, the definition of obscenity in the Institute test is too restrictive and is not a real test.

THE THEORY OF HARD-CORE PORNOGRAPHY

A number of courts follow the theory that only "hard-core pornography" can be banned; all else is cleared. These authorities feel that where a statute says that it prohibits the dissemination of "obscene pictures" then the pictures must constitute hard-core pornography. The leading disciple of this view is Justice Potter Stewart. Justice Stewart sets forth his position clearly and succinctly in his concurring opinion in the movie film case of *Jacobellis vs. Ohio*: [2]

> I have reached the conclusion, which I think is confirmed at least by negative implication in the Court's decisions since Roth and Alberts, that under the First and Fourteenth Amendments criminal laws in this area are constitutionally limited to hard-core pornography. I shall not today attempt further to define the kinds of material I understand to be embraced within that shorthand description; and perhaps I could never succeed in intelligibly doing so. But I know it when I see it, and the motion picture involved in this case is not that.

Many people seriously believe they are discriminating enough to differentiate between ordinary obscenity and "hard-core pornography." Some take the position that hard-core pornography is easily recognizable and therefore no definition is needed. In referring to hard-core pornography one writer says that such material is "readily identifiable" and needs no "legal Geiger counter . . . to apprise the viewer of the nature of hard-core materials." [3] This attitude is of very little assistance in arriving at a just decision, but it does demonstrate that hard-core pornography, like obscenity, has its gray area where people will differ.

D. H. Lawrence, an authority on the subject, while he does not mention "hard-core pornography," does appear to equate it with what he refers to as "genuine pornography." Lawrence says:

> But even I would censor genuine pornography, rigorously. It would not be very difficult. In the first place, genuine pornography is almost always underworld, it doesn't come into the open. In the second, you can recognize it by the insult it offers, invariably, to sex, and to the human spirit.
>
> Pornography is the attempt to insult sex, to do dirt on it. This is unpardonable. Take the very lowest instance, the picture post-card sold underhand, by the underworld, in most cities. What I have seen of them have been of an ugliness to make you cry. The insult to the human body, the insult to a vital human relationship! Ugly and cheap they make the human nudity, ugly and degraded, they make the sexual act, trivial and cheap and nasty.
>
> It is the same with the books they sell in the underworld. They are either so ugly they make you ill, or so fatuous you can't imagine anybody but a cretin or a moron reading them, or writing them. [4]

This, from the author of *Lady Chatterley* whose chapters concerning the sex relationship of the gamekeeper and the lady, and whose employment of four-letter words was regarded by many as the essence of hard-core pornography!

Two important students in this field are Doctors Phyllis and Eberhard Kronhausen, who wrote *Pornography and the Law* in 1959. They divided the subject into two areas. One they called "hard-core obscenity" and this they equated with "pornography" and all that is recognized as illegal. The other area they described as sexual material which is not illegal and this they called "erotic realism." Their definition follows:

In pornography (hard core obscenity) *the main purpose is to stimulate erotic response* in the reader. And that is all. *In erotic realism, truthful description of the basic realities of life, as the individual experiences it, is of the essence,* even if such portrayals (whether by reason of humor, or revulsion, or any other cause) have a decidedly anti-erotic effect. But by the same token, if, while writing realistically on the subject of sex, the author succeeds in moving his reader, this too, is erotic realism, *and it is axiomatic that the reader should respond erotically to such writing,* just as the sensitive reader will respond, perhaps by actually crying, to a sad scene, or by laughing when laughter is evoked.

This reduces the problem to one of what was the author's purpose in writing. If the author wanted to stimulate an erotic response, then it would be hard-core pornography, but if the writer simply intended to write realistically on the subject of sex and incidentally caused a response in the reader then it would constitute erotic realism.

If the Kronhausens are correct, then the test has no significance. It would be very difficult (if not impossible) in a case where a newsstand proprietor was arrested for selling a magazine or paperback book, to bring in the author and psychoanalyze him to ascertain his purpose in writing the book or article.

However, the Kronhausens do, elsewhere in their book, set forth some measure of testing in order to determine the purpose of the author. The Kronhausens' test holds that hard-core pornography involves a series of erotic scenes without interpolation of non-erotic scenes or passages. According to them, where seduction is involved, the woman is "more often than not a willing collaborator." In other words, the female characters who figure prominently in "obscene" books are generally as anxious to be seduced as the men are to seduce them. Beyond that the Kronhausens give as examples incest without guilt, profanation of that which is sacred, homosexuality, lesbianism, flagellation, and the use of taboo words. In fact, although the Kronhausens purport to have presented a scientific study, their material (while extremely interesting) is of no assistance in determining whether an item constitutes hard-core pornography or simple obscenity or something else entirely.

The famed anthropologist Margaret Mead has an often-quoted definition of hard-core pornography as "words or acts or representations that are calculated to stimulate sex feelings independent of the presence of another loved and chosen human being."[5] She adds that hard-core pornography is essentially made out of day-dreams "composed without regard for any given reader or looker, to stimulate and titillate."

Finally, Mead states:

> Pornography does not lead to laughter; it leads to deadly serious pursuit of sexual satisfaction divorced from personality and from every other meaning, . . . the difference between the music hall in which a feeble carrot waves above a bowl of cauliflower while roars of laughter shake the audience of husbands and wives on their weekly outing, and the striptease, where lonely men, driven and haunted, go alone, is the difference between the paths to heaven and hell, a difference which any society obscures to its peril.

The anthropologist's definition and distinction between hard-core pornography and simple obscenity may be very helpful to anthropologists, but it does nothing for lawyers. Under the Mead definition the burlesque and the striptease are categorized as hard-core pornography, yet the law has passed beyond that point and no longer considers them obscene.

Psychological literature makes Herculean efforts to differentiate between hard-core obscenity and simple or non-hard-core obscenity. However, it serves no real purpose. For example, one writer says hard-core pornography "is not in itself the object of an experience, esthetic or any other, but rather a stimulus to an experience not focused on it. It serves to elicit not the imaginative contemplation of an expressed substance but rather the release in fantasy of a compelling impulse."[6] This offers little practical guidance. Another writer describes any indulgence in pornography as a form of "psychic masturbation."[7] It could be argued that the endeavor to differentiate hard-core pornography from ordinary obscenity is in itself an exercise in "psychic masturbation."

In brief, careful study of all the authorities[8] who endeavor to distinguish between hard-core pornography and simple obscenity leads to the conclusion that the distinction is one which (as in many other fields) works in reverse. An item is examined and suggests the conclusion that it be banned. This is then duly described as "hard-core pornography." Another item, upon examination, appears to have less objectionable features, and this is labeled "not hard-core pornography."

THE DILEMMA OF VARIABLE OBSCENITY

For a long time a controversy has raged over whether material in the law is obscene in the abstract or whether its obscenity depends upon the usage to which it is put. *United States vs. 31 Photographs,*[9] which arose in 1957, illustrates this problem most graphically. In this case the Institute for Sex Research of Indiana University (frequently referred to and generally better known as the "Kinsey Institute") endeavored to import a quantity of photographs, books, and other items to use for scientific study and research. The United States Customs Department refused to permit the import and, acting under the procedure provided in the Tariff Act, the United States Attorney in New York filed a libel requesting the federal court to declare the material obscene and forfeit to the government for destruction.

District Judge Palmieri, with relish, attacked the problem squarely and accepted the premise posed by the United States

Attorney. He said he would assume that the material was of such nature that to the average person, applying contemporary community standards, the dominant theme taken as a whole would appeal to prurient interest.

The Kinsey Institute did not deny that the material would normally be regarded as obscene or even hard-core pornography; but maintained that the material was useful to it in scientific study. The Institute filed an affidavit by the Director of Federal Prisons to show that the Institute had made important and significant contributions to the study of sexual adjustment among prison inmates. Other affidavits indicated that the material was needed for that purpose (further study of sexual conduct).

Judge Palmieri noted that the material would ordinarily be regarded as obscene but that it was going to be used only by the scientists at the Institute and to them it would have no "appeal to their prurient interest." Therefore he ordered the material released to the Institute and denied the government's request for a confiscation order. In his relatively revolutionary concept, the judge advanced the theory that the obscenity of the material depended on for whose eyes it was intended.

Chief Justice Warren hinted at this same idea in the *Roth*[10] case (before he abandoned his liberal view) when he said:

> The line dividing the salacious or pornographic from literature or science is not straight and unwavering . . . it is manifest that the same object may have a different impact, varying according to the part of the community reached. But there is more to these cases. It is not the book that is on trial; it is a person. The conduct of the defendant is the central issue, not the obscenity of a book or picture. The nature of the materials is, of course, relevant as an attribute of the defendant's conduct, but the materials are thus placed in context from which they draw color and character. A wholly different result might be reached in a different setting.

In actual practice the law unquestionably accepts the doctrine of variable obscenity. For example, only rarely is any effort made to censor a play, basically because a play caters primarily to responsible and mature adults. The comparatively high cost of admission tends to limit the audiences to the sophisticated and educated. As a consequence, the police officers themselves hesitate to interfere.

A similar distinction exists in the hard-cover and soft-cover book field. It is rare, again, that courts or police officers attempt to interfere with the distribution of hard-cover books. These books, like the theatre, are protected by their higher cost and are therefore granted immunity on the theory that children cannot afford to buy them and the sexually immature are unlikely to encounter them. Of course, this is purely theoretical, because it is common knowledge that children and the sexually immature will in many cases save up their pennies in order to purchase such books. However, the law does not usually begin to move until the book is produced in the paperback edition at a very low price, at which time the powerful arm of law enforcement makes itself felt.

Once again in practice the law makes a distinction between forms of obscenity and proves the variability of its standards.

THE "NOTHING IS OBSCENE" POSITION

Many people of diverse interests share the view that there should be no doctrine of obscenity at all and that freedom to communicate ideas is so precious that it should be shielded from all dangers by the elimination of any form of censorship on account of obscenity. A leading protagonist of this viewpoint is the Reverend Robert W. Haney who, in *Comstockery in America*,[11] makes this major point:

> Many-sided though it is, censorship possesses the one unify-

ing emotional response of fear—of a world which would, if we faced it, threaten us with the task of becoming individual human beings. Our blushes and smirks and self-righteous denunciations of four letter words, lewd pictures, and all the other paraphernalia of obscenity and pornography are little more than the attempt to feel noble when we are really being absurd. And we pass on through generations this legacy of fear. All the muck and dirt which pornographic literature and photography can pour out into our bookstores or on to our newsstands is trivial beside the real damage to the human soul —the systematic production of frightened and inept men and women which goes under the name of censorship.

The Reverend Haney used as his basis the value of freedom and the ineffectual aspect of censorship. Another leading authority— Justice Hugo Black—took the same view, but for other reasons.

The First Amendment to the United States Constitution specifically prohibits Congress from "abridging the freedom of speech, or of the press." In 1925, the United States Supreme Court ruled that the adoption of the Fourteenth Amendment to the Constitution imposed the limitations of the First Amendment on each of the state legislatures.[12] Therefore, said Justice Black, we are faced with a constitutional prohibition which specifically states that no legislature—state or federal—may enact any law abridging freedom of speech or press. Then he took up the argument of whether freedom of speech or press can be *slightly* abridged. The Justice gives his answer:

Certainly the First Amendment's language leaves no room for inference that abridgments of speech and press can be made just because they are slight. That Amendment provides, in simple words, that "Congress shall make no law . . . abridging the freedom of speech, or of the press." I read "no law abridging" to mean "NO LAW ABRIDGING." The First Amendment, which is the supreme law of the land, has thus fixed its own value on freedom of speech and press by putting these freedoms wholly "beyond the reach of FEDERAL power to abridge." No other provision of the Constitution purports to dilute the scope of these unequivocal commands of the First Amendment. Consequently, I do not believe that any federal agencies, including Congress and this Court, have the power or authority to subordinate speech and press to what they think are "more important interests." The contrary notion is, in my judgment, court-made not Constitution-made.

If, as it seems, we are on the way to national censorship, I think it timely to suggest again that there are grave doubts in my mind as to the desirability or constitutionality of this Court's becoming a Supreme Board of Censors—reading books and viewing television performances to determine whether, if permitted, they might adversely affect the morals of the people throughout the many diversified local communities in this vast country. It is true that the ordinance here is on its face only applicable to "obscene or indecent writing." It is also true that this particular kind of censorship is considered by many to be "the obnoxious thing in its mildest and least repulsive form. . . ." But "illegitimate and unconstitutional practices get their first footing in that way. . . . It is the duty of the courts to be watchful for the constitutional rights of the citizen, and against any stealthy encroachments thereon." While it is "obscenity and indecency" before us today, the experience of mankind—both ancient and modern—shows that this type of elastic phrase can, and most likely will, be synonymous with the political, and maybe with the religious unorthodoxy of tomorrow.

Censorship is the deadly enemy of freedom and progress. The plain language of the Constitution forbids it. I protest against the judiciary giving it a foothold here.[13]

This is an extreme position but it must be said that to a considerable extent the majority of the United States Supreme Court has been moving in that direction. However, it leaves open many questions which, most properly, Justice Black has not as yet discussed and need not discuss until the problem arises.

Consider the case of the disturbed individual who satisfies his need by calling women on the telephone in order to mouth obscenities.[14] It is highly unlikely that Justice Black would regard such conduct as protected by the United States Constitution. Of course, this conduct can also be punished purely on the basis of the invasion of the right of privacy without regard to the obscene character of the language. However, most legislatures would probably want to mete out harsher punishment to the culprit who uses obscene language than to the one who simply invades privacy through the use of the telephone for commercial solicitation. At the present time such conduct would be constitutionally punishable and will probably remain so for the foreseeable future.

Many other problems arise in the wake of the uncompromising viewpoint that there may not be any censorship of any form or kind whatsoever. How, then, handle the problem of sex pictures in bad taste shown to children? Sufficient people in the United States today equate such conduct with the most heinous of crimes and it must, under present mores, be punished. Unquestionably, again, this is conduct which will be punished, unless radical changes occur in present American morality.

In fairness to Justice Black's position it must be understood that the most militant fighter in defense of civil liberties recognizes that freedom of speech, oral or printed, has its limitations. It is obvious that freedom of speech does not entitle a person to get up in a crowded theatre and yell, "Fire!" Additionally, no legal theorist has ever argued that freedom of speech allows a gangster to use his ability to communicate as a means of conspiring with others in order to commit crimes. In a sense he is using nothing more than speech, but if it is speech which leads to crime it is not permitted.

Justice Black and Reverend Haney would certainly agree with the foregoing examples. Therefore, in analyzing this theory, it must be understood that the nature of the judicial process is such that justices do not attempt to anticipate future cases in deciding the case at hand. The case which resulted in the opinion quoted above involved an adult bookseller who had been convicted under a Los Angeles ordinance for selling a book which the Los

Angeles court regarded as obscene. The majority of the court set the bookseller free on the ground that he had no knowledge of the obscene character of the book. Justice Black refused to concur in that theory because he felt it was insufficient protection under the Constitution for such an important right as freedom of speech. He wanted the bookseller set free on the basic theory that the Constitution does not permit the punishment of a bookseller for selling an ordinary book (regarded as obscene by some) to another adult. Justice Black was not purporting to write a treatise on the law of obscenity, and he did not indicate what would happen if a bookseller sold such a book to a child or if an act of a different nature was performed. This attitude leads most naturally into the next significant theory in the field of obscenity.

THE CURTIS BOK VIEW

In 1949 a brilliant Philadelphia jurist, Curtis Bok, had before him a criminal case in which the police had arrested a bookseller for selling such books as Farrell's *Studs Lonigan Trilogy*, Faulkner's *Sanctuary*, and Caldwell's *God's Little Acre*. In a masterful opinion,[15] including a detailed analysis of the history and cases in the field, Judge Bok dismissed the indictment. He pointed out a book could only be regarded as obscene if "the commission or the imminence of the commission of criminal behavior resulting from the reading of a book" could be proved. He made no effort to say what kind of books would cause the commission of crimes or the imminence of criminal behavior. He appeared not to believe that books, per se, can cause criminal behavior. This attitude is reminiscent of the bromide that no book ever raped a woman, and man is aroused to rape, not by a book, but by the presence of a woman.

However, the Bok theory is a strong one. Simply stated, Bok

198

argues that freedom of speech is of such importance and significance that it must not be inhibited except to protect against criminal behavior. Furthermore, it must be demonstrated that the
failure to prohibit this freedom will cause, or has caused, the
commission of a crime.

Today, the leading protagonist of this viewpoint is Justice William O. Douglas. In the *Roth*[16] case, Justice Douglas wrote the
following:

> If we were certain that impurity of sexual thoughts impelled
> to action, we would be on less dangerous ground in punishing
> the distributors of this sex literature. But it is by no means
> clear that obscene literature, as so defined, is a significant
> factor in influencing substantial deviations from the commun-
> ity standards.
>
> There are a number of reasons for real and substantial
> doubts as to the soundness of that hypothesis. (1) Scientific
> studies of juvenile delinquency demonstrate that those who
> get into trouble, and are the greatest concern of the advocates
> of censorship, are far less inclined to read than those who do
> not become delinquents. The delinquents are generally the
> adventurous type, who have little use for reading and other
> non-active entertainment. Thus, even assuming that reading
> sometimes has an adverse effect upon moral conduct, the effect
> is not likely to be substantial, for those who are susceptible
> seldom read. (2) Sheldon and Eleanor Glueck, who are among
> the country's leading authorities on the treatment and causes
> of juvenile delinquency, have recently published the results of
> a ten-year study of its causes. They exhaustively studied approx-
> imately 90 factors and influences that might lead to or explain
> juvenile delinquency, but the Gluecks gave no consideration
> to the type of reading material, if any, read by the delinquents.
> This is, of course, consistent with their finding that delinquents
> read very little. When those who know so much about the
> problem of delinquency among youth—the very group about
> whom the advocates of censorship are most concerned—con-
> clude that what delinquents read has so little effect upon their
> conduct that it is not worth investigating in an exhaustive
> study of causes, there is good reason for serious doubt concern-

ing the basic hypothesis on which obscenity censorship is defended. (3) The many other influences in society that stimulate sexual desire are so much more frequent in their influences and so much more potent in their effect, that the influence of reading is likely, at most, to be relatively insignificant in the composite of forces that lead an individual into conduct deviating from the community sex standards. The Kinsey studies show the minor degree to which literature serves as a potent sexual stimulant. And the studies demonstrating that sex knowledge seldom results from reading indicates the relative unimportance of literature in sex thoughts as compared with other factors in society.

The absence of dependable information on the effect of obscene literature on human conduct should make us wary. It should put us on the side of protecting society's interest in literature, except and unless it can be said that the particular publication has an impact on action that the government can control.

A SUGGESTED SOLUTION [17]

In many fields our law—the common heritage of Anglo-American law coming down through the centuries in England and the United States—has been extremely intelligent and facile in developing solutions to tough and sticky problems. For example, the problem of how to punish those who, with disregard for considerations of safety, have injured or killed others while driving automobiles or handling firearms. These cases also involved a balancing of interest: that is the right of one group of people to drive automobiles or use firearms versus the right of people going about their own business not to be injured by a recklessly driven automobile or a carelessly employed firearm.

The law ultimately solved this problem to the reasonable satisfaction of practically all lawyers, judges, and analysts. In this field it is not difficult, when advising a client in advance, to tell him what to do, what not to do, and how to insure against criminal responsibility. For instance, commercial truck clients are advised to inspect their vehicles regularly, to be careful in the selection of drivers, to use only tested and approved equipment, and the like. Heeding this advice generally protects the client from criminal prosecutions.

In the obscenity field, unfortunately, there are no guidelines, no safeguards, and little worthwhile advice except that watchword of overcautious lawyers throughout the ages,"if you want to be safe, don't do it."

Translated, this means that the conscientious lawyer must advise his clients that, if they want to be completely safe, they must avoid publication of any material which could conceivably be offensive to any policeman, district attorney, or trial court judge. This is obviously too high a price to pay for safety. If publishers had been guided by such advice throughout the years, no Dreiser, no Faulkner, no Caldwell, no Irving Wallace, not even an Albert Ellis could have enriched the American literary scene. Indeed, using this "safe" criterion, scarcely a modern writer from James Baldwin to Mary McCarthy would have written the books being published at this moment. Nevertheless, the dilemma must be resolved.

DIFFERENTIATE THE MEDIA

At the heart of any solution lies the necessity for differentiating between general circulation media and specialized media. To illustrate: Television, radio, and the daily newspaper are all prime examples of the widespread general circulation media. On the other hand, a private subscription-only magazine is a perfect example of a highly specialized medium for the communication of ideas.

The general circulation media should be subject to control,

but a private circulation item should be without censorship of any kind. There is an important reason behind this: the basic premise upon which any form of censorship today should be permitted.

In order to understand this premise, it is necessary first to comprehend fully the basic nature of the legal process. All law involves what the lawyers call a "balancing of interests." This simply means weighing the value or social utility of the conduct involved as against the harm it may cause. For example, the right to spit in the street involves a certain amount of freedom of human action. If, while walking in the street, mucous forms in the throat and no tissue or handkerchief is available, a compulsive need to discharge the accumulation may lead to expectoration on the sidewalk or in the street. But the law says that this is offensive to others; it causes the spread of virus and bacteria; it is unsightly and violates aesthetic sensibilities; tissues or a handkerchief should be available; death will not result from the retention of the mucous until a proper place becomes available for relief. When the importance of the individual's freedom to expectorate is weighed against the interests of society in banning indiscriminate expectoration, society wins hands down; and no court will today seriously entertain an argument that a law prohibiting expectoration in public places should be regarded as illegal.

At the other end of the spectrum, it is necessary to recognize that almost any law, of any kind or nature whatsoever, which would inhibit religious freedom would be voided by the courts. This is so because society has placed such a high value on an individual's freedom to pursue his own ideas of religion that interfering laws, regardless of how valuable in themselves, are regarded as not sufficiently worthy to be sustained. It is for this reason that the United States Supreme Court refused to permit prayer in the public schools. So long as the religious beliefs of any individual are offended by public prayer in the schools, the High Court holds that no prayer can be permitted.

To some extent every law governing human conduct is on the scales of justice. Examine a typical anti-obscenity law in the light of this analysis. Such a law provides that any vendor found guilty of selling printed matter regarded by an enforcement agency as obscene may be fined or imprisoned for a specified period of time. Now weigh this law on the balancing of interest scales. The conduct inhibited is the freedom of writers to employ words as they please in any combination, the freedom of publishers to print and distribute reading matter that they believe is marketable, and the freedom of a merchant, either of the pushcart or plush shop variety, to sell the material to responsible adults regardless of what may be found between the covers. These interests are formidable and weigh heavily when placed in the scales of justice. Any law which will interfere with all of these freedoms must be weighed with care, and in that weighing the social utility or value of the interfering law requires deep and thoughtful examination. Basically, the only value in the obscenity law is that it will remove a certain amount of offensiveness to those who are offended, annoyed, or irritated by possible obscene or pornographic material.

This, then, is the content in Justice's scales. On the one side is the freedom of those who communicate ideas to engage unfettered in such communication and on the other side is the interest of certain sensitive people in being free from contamination of their sensitivity by material which they regard as offensive.

In judging a simple book, certainly the freedom to write, publish, and sell outweighs the right of someone who might be offended, because those who would be offended need not read the book. It is conceivable that by accident the sensitive woman may pick up *Lady Chatterley's Lover,* Mary McCarthy's *The Group,* or a James Baldwin novel. She might begin to read it without realizing it contained material which would be offensive to her. However, upon the first encounter with a frank sexual passage or a four-letter word she is free to close the book and never open it again. This accidental temporary exposure is surely a small price to pay when it insures the freedom of writers to write and publishers to publish.

This theory does not eliminate the doctrine of obscenity *in toto*. A good illustration of where the doctrine is eliminated and where it remains is with a movie. If a movie owner frankly advertised his movie as being for adults only and as treating sex with unusual candor or as containing nude scenes, the movie owner would be free to show his movie without interference by the law. Here is a situation in which any adult likely to be offended need not attend the theatre. Non-adults would be, and should be, refused admission by the theatre owner. Thus that portion of the problem is eliminated easily.

The second phase concerns the advertising of the movie on the outside of the theatre. Assume that the theatre is in a typical urban area where the passersby may be children, as well as men and women of all types. In such a situation the theatre owner would be prohibited from showing on the exterior billboards offensive or suggestive pictures which could offend the casual passerby without his consent. Some may say: Let those who are offended not look, or let them cross the street or walk on some other street. This may be too high a price to pay, because the right to pass freely through the city streets is a very high-ranking freedom. In addition, the protection of the younger members of society is an important duty. Some people believe (and many, of course, do not) that frank and suggestive material or simple nudity can cause harm to the moral fiber of youth. Whether or not this is accurate is certainly an important subject for future scientific study. Although scientific thought has not yet made a conclusive determination, many people adhere to the view that the material will be injurious to children. Consequently, so long as these persons do firmly believe it, it is probably not too high a price to ask the theatre owner to modify his advertising material and displays in the front of the theatre. He can show nudes on the screen all day, but he would be well advised to put some clothing on the billboard portrayals outside the theatre.

A similar principle would apply to newspapers of general circulation, radio, and television. These are all media that impinge on broad segments of the community without the consent of the individual members thereof. The price that these media pay for being of general circulation is they must be selective in the material they contain so as not to give offense to the more sensitive and not to put material before youth which many regard as injurious.

DECIDE AND PROVE

For many years the law accepted the basic principle that the obscene character of a challenged item was a question of fact which a designated trier of facts ultimately would decide.[18] Normally in most trial courts a jury decided the facts and in administrative proceedings such as those involved in the Post Office Department or with the Bureau of Customs, an Administrative Examiner made the decision. During the prolonged period of time that this situation existed, subtlety had no place; and tests for obscenity had to be broad and simple, and capable of complete comprehension, application, and conclusion by the man on the street. Although influenced in great measure by the charge of a trial judge, juries were usually ready, willing, and able to find most items characterized by the district attorney as obscene to be so, both in law and in fact.

Luckily for writers, publishers, and booksellers, that day is gone. The present rule is that only the judge can make the final decision, because now obscenity is a constitutional judgment rather than a simple issue of fact.[19] To illustrate for those who have not rubbed elbows with this legal jargon: In the law a "fact" is a statement on which all reasonable men would automatically agree. For example, the statement that there is a dog walking down the street is a fact, and a jury can consider the issue and, if contested, can decide whether it was or was not in fact a dog walking down the street. On the other hand, if a witness says there was a Doberman pinscher coming down the street, it becomes an opinion rather than a fact. It is now necessary to demonstrate that the person involved is knowledgeable enough to recognize a Doberman pinscher from a Shetland sheepdog, an Airedale, or a Basset hound. Now the issue has left the realm of fact and entered the area of opinion. Finally come questions like "obscenity," which are combined issues of fact and opinion and in addition must meet constitutional standards of law.

There was a time when judges tried to duck around this problem by saying, "This is really a question of fact, and I will let the jury decide and be bound by that decision." However, in the *Roth* case, Justice Harlan said: "I do not think that reviewing courts can escape this responsibility by saying that the trier of fact, be it jury or judge, has labelled the questioned matter as 'obscene' for, if 'obscenity' is to be suppressed, the question of whether a particular work is of that character involves not really an issue of fact but a question of Constitutional judgment of a most sensitive and delicate kind."

This theory is now reasonably well accepted and the practice is for the court to decide whether an item is obscene rather than to pass it on to the jury in order to avoid the responsibility for a difficult decision.

In endeavoring to apply the test that obscenity is measured by the medium in which it appears, the judge obviously must make the ultimate decision, and the question arises: Upon what basis? For here, too, are delicate questions of constitutional judgment. For example, assume a television program in which the dress of the leading female performer is cut quite low, and the station is bombarded with protests. This could involve the station, the producer, and even the performer in an obscenity criminal case. The judge must make the final decision, but on what would he base his grounds?

At one time the sole evidence possible was the specific passage in a book or picture or other item considered obscene by the district attorney. For example, when in 1930 the Massachusetts courts banned Theodore Dreiser's *An American Tragedy*,[20] eminent counsel[21] defending the book tried to get the entire book introduced into evidence, arguing that if the jury could read the full book they would see that the isolated passages cited by the district attorney were not really obscene. The court summarily refused to permit the entire book to go into evidence, stating that it was too long to read to the jury. The court did not even consider the subsequently advocated solution of sending in enough books so that each member of the jury could have one.

Although that incident occurred thirty-five years ago (not very long as the law goes), a great change has taken place since that day. Today a judge arrives at his decision on the basis of the entire book, the reputation of the author, and all the surrounding circumstances.

However, disputes continue to arise. Only a few years ago booksellers in New York were convicted for selling two allegedly obscene books entitled *Queen Bee* and *Garden of Evil*.[22] During the trial, counsel for the defense offered in evidence similar books sold freely in adjacent bookstores "to indicate . . . the current standard in the community of literature." The court refused to admit that type of evidence, declaring "that is not the way that standards are made." At the same time the Supreme Court of California reached an opposite conclusion,[23] permitting expert testimony on the question of comparable literature sold in the community. In fact, today it is extremely likely that most courts and the United States Supreme Court will permit introduction of comparable material sold in the community.

More important, perhaps, is the question of who shall testify on these questions. It is vital, in the interests of justice, for the testimony to be from experts in the medium. In cases involving television (there are practically no such cases), writers, show producers, directors, and others who are intimately engaged on a day-to-day basis with the production of television material, should be the ones to testify. Their testimony on any question—including whether the lady singer's dress was cut too low—would be based upon comparison with the other shows currently being viewed. These experts should be shown the tape of the broadcast and then asked this question, "In the light of contemporary national community standards, do you regard the way the lady star dressed as an action offensive to such a degree that it would constitute obscenity in the present state of television art?"

In other words, it is those who know the media well who must present opinions on whether someone has overstepped the bounds of "proper" behavior or dress. This should not allow for battles of the experts. If the defendant can produce well-respected and court-accepted experts in the art or medium involved, that should suffice. This is not a place for niceties of judgment where the result may be guilt. It must be remembered at all times that the crime requires "patent offensiveness," and such cannot be proved subtly. That is not to say that any time a defendant can produce one expert he can go scot free. Ultimately it is the judge who must decide whether the defendant acted in good faith and whether the defense is *bona fide*. If so, there should be no obscenity.

In each and every case where honest disagreement exists among the experts, rather than a sham concocted by the defense, the material in question should always receive the benefit of the doubt. This is completely in keeping with the underlying function and purpose of the First Amendment—to protect constitutionally the freedom of those who communicate, to express new and novel ideas. At present sponsors and advertisers who want to offend no one exert a sufficient drag on experimentation and novelty. Courts should not add more legal restrictions. There should be no borderline cases. Some decisions even express a thought that the suppression of borderline material is in itself a violation of civil liberties.[24] That idea is good, and perhaps some-day it will be adopted by the United States Supreme Court.

JUSTIFICATION FOR OBSCENITY LAWS

If a proponent of obscenity legislation is asked, "What is the real reason you support such legislation?" he is likely to answer, "I believe that obscenity causes men to engage in criminal mis-conduct ranging from seduction to rape, and that it causes women to give in to such conduct." In other words, the chief foundation for most legislation outlawing obscenity is the theory that obscenity can produce criminal conduct. It is amazing that with the mass of society believing such a theory so little real evidence exists to support it. This belief in the criminal con-sequences of obscenity ought to have produced many scientific studies and demonstrations to prove the point, but analysis of the literature reveals a dearth of any real investigation, and what there is tends to contradict the popular belief.[25] In 1955 Haines interviewed one hundred juvenile inmates of an Illinois prison.[26] All those interviewed were between the ages of 16 and 21 and "each inmate interviewed was told that Senator Kefauver was interested in the effects of television, movies and radio on teen-agers and would like to know his reaction as to the role these mediums played in his committing an offense, or offenses, which resulted in his incarceration." The young prisoners volunteered to cooperate and were interviewed in private. Ninety-four out of the hundred reported that they had seen the small French comic type of pamphlet showing sexual acts. Thir-teen per cent admitted that they were customarily excited sexually by visual examination of such materials. Then the report continues, "Some stated that, after looking at the booklets, they sought sexual relief on the streets, through their girl friends, or through self-abuse." This authority came to the conclusion that "television, pornography, and movies play a distinct role in the creation of anti-social behaviour in susceptible teen-agers." Much more important than this conclusion is an analysis of the results themselves. Of all of the subjects examined, not one who was incarcerated for criminal sexual behavior indicated that his crime was in any way related to examining, or being subjected to, obscene or pornographic materials. All that any subject reported was the very normal answer that sexual materials excited him or her sexually. In addition, it should be noted that these subjects indicated sexual stimulation almost equally great from television, movies, and pornographic materials. In view of the fact that even Anthony Comstock could find little to regard as pornographic in today's television, a situation arises akin to the Vassar questionnaire, where certain women in response to a sexual question replied that they were stimulated more by men than anything else. Basically the Haines study indicates that, although the sex motif will stimulate sexually, it does not create criminal conduct.

An earlier study by Ramsey,[27] who interviewed 280 boys between the ages of 11 and 18, revealed that nudity, "obscene pictures" (undescribed), and "daydreaming" ranked almost equally as causes of sexual arousal. Since even the Comstocks never envisioned outlawing daydreaming, it is difficult to see how they can continue to want to prohibit qualitatively equal stimuli.

THE KINSEY ANALYSIS[28]

The Kinsey Institute made a study of what subjects create

sexual arousal and compared the effectiveness of the various stimuli. The excitants investigated included portrayal of nudes, observing genitalia, commercial movies, burlesque, the observation of sexual acts, the reading of ordinary literature, and the reading of erotic stories. The following table gives the results:

		Definite frequent	Sometimes	Never	Number
Portrayals of nudes	male	18%	36%	46%	4,191
	female	3%	9%	88%	5,698
Observing genitalia	male*	"many"	"many"	"few"	
	female	21%	27%	52%	617
Commercial films	male	6%	30%	64%	3,231
	female	9%	39%	52%	5,411
Burlesques [strip tease]	male	28%	34%	38%	3,377
	female	4%	10%	86%	2,550
Observing sex acts	male	42%	35%	23%	3,868
	female	14%	18%	68%	2,242
Reading literary materials	male	21%	38%	41%	3,952
	female	16%	44%	40%	5,699
Reading erotic stories	male	16%	31%	53%	4,202
	female	2%	12%	86%	5,523

* Percentages not reported

A study of the table reveals some interesting facts. First, a considerable difference is evident between the effect of the various stimuli upon males and females. The more direct the stimulus—for example, observation of the sex act—the more likely it is to stimulate the male with some degree of frequency.

The best conclusion that can be drawn from the Kinsey studies is that sexual material will unquestionably produce a sexual arousal. However, research reveals no indication whatsoever that exposure to such material will cause criminal conduct.

In an old study two German investigators[29] studied whether any relationship existed between reading matter selected by a prisoner and the nature of the crime he had committed. The results showed the following: Murderers indicated a marked preference for high-grade information books and adventure stories. Swindlers preferred light novels. Thieves selected books on practical culture, and sexual offenders preferred sex books. Again, there is little to go on. Although sexual offenders preferred sex books, no proof existed that the sex books created the sex offense. Perhaps the aberration which caused the offense also caused the partiality to the book.

When all the research to date has been analyzed, the only conclusion that can be reached is that there is insufficient data to decide whether pornographic material can stimulate anyone to criminal conduct. One of the best summaries of the problem appears in an opinion[30] by Judge Jerome Frank:

> To date there exist, I think, no thorough-going studies by competent persons which justify the conclusions that normal adults' reading or seeing of the "obscene" probably induces anti-social conduct. Such competent studies as have been made do conclude that so complex and numerous are the causes of sexual vice that it is impossible to assert with any assurance that "obscenity" represents a ponderable causal factor in sexually deviant adult behavior.

THE GOVERNMENT VIEW

Some years ago the United States government, in defending its power to refuse to permit the use of the mails to disseminate magazines and literature which might be regarded as obscene, presented this argument: "The distribution of obscenity causes a substantial risk of inducing immoral sexual conduct over a period of time by breaking down the concept of morality as well as moral standards." [31] The key is the phrase "over a period of time." The Justice Department in its brief to the Supreme Court did not contend that one or two magazines put in the possession of even a weak-minded individual could cause him to go out and commit a sexual crime. Rather it argued that over the years constant exposure to what it regarded as pornography corrupts the moral standards and produces sexual misconduct. At another point the Justice Department made this argument:

> The man who finds that the Government will or can do nothing to stop the distribution of pornography to his family will be less willing to abide by society's demands on him, whether it be as to gambling, distribution of narcotics, or the candor with which he fills out his income tax. Similarly, the corruption of moral standards in the realm of sexual conduct cannot help but corrupt other aspects of moral life. Morality, like morale, cannot be undercut at one point without affecting all conduct.

This line of argument is the kind that is self-assertive. It is there because it is there. Apparently it demands no proof. However, opponents of this view hold that there is no evidence, either historical or clinical, that complete freedom or license to publish material at will has caused at any time in the past, or will cause in the future, any one individual to commit a crime, or create a breakdown of moral standards of society in other fields such as narcotics or income tax—to use the government's example.[32]

THE REAL REASON WE HAVE
OBSCENITY LEGISLATION

Professor Louis Henkin of Columbia University hit the nail on the head with the following analysis:[33] The same rule bans sexually stimulating material such as nudity and copulation that prohibits scatological material. Those who oppose obscenity oppose with equal fervor the four-letter word describing sexual intercourse and the four-letter words describing excretions. A picture of a nude and a picture of a human being defecating are equally abhorrent to a Comstock. Yet the scatological could scarcely be regarded as sexually arousing. To a large number of people it is repellent. Unquestionably, many who might be on their way to being sexually aroused by some form of stimulus would find themselves chilled if suddenly faced with a vivid pictorial representation of scatological material. Yet both are barred with equal fervor.

Consequently it cannot be said that obscenity is banned solely because it may arouse sexual misconduct. The real reason is because it is offensive. Certainly today's citizenry includes a large number of individuals who, when exposed to any form of sexual or scatological material, are repelled or offended.

Another basis for obscenity legislation is its religious origin. Originally obscenity was punished only in religious courts, and the temporal courts ultimately accepted the burden because they regarded this aspect of religious discipline as part of the general law. In fact, the major cases which produced the laws of obscenity all had religious overtones. The *Hicklin* case involved a diatribe against the confessional and the *Curll* case involved a book entitled *The Nun in Her Smock*.

On this point Professor Henkin observed:

> I have suggested the need to examine, in the light of the due process clause, the power of the state to deprive a person of liberty or property for the purpose of preserving "morality" serving no social, utilitarian purpose. Contemporary constitutional doctrine may suggest yet another related difficulty about obscenity and other morality laws. For the morality that these laws would protect can trace a discernible path back to origins in religious authority. Can government, which may not establish religion, or interfere with the free exercise of religion and non-religion, enforce a morality rooted in religion? Is legislation, the sole or chief purpose of which is the

preservation of a quasi-religious morality, consistent with the separation of Church and State now recognized as the law of the Constitution?

* * * * *

The morals of a people are a present reality regardless of their sources. Whatever their roots, whatever their erstwhile function or context in religious observance, laws against incest or polygamy, for example, now reflect mores and institutions—in particular, the family—that are the fabric of our society. Moreover, many morals crimes rooted in the Bible—incest, polygamy, usury, perhaps also adultery—may find some secular rationalization or justification, some valid governmental purpose even in a secular state, some concern defined in terms of categorical imperative, of avoiding injury to others, of achieving some social aim. That other morals crimes, however, retain heavy traces of their religious origin is evidenced, in part, by the fact that they are not universally punished as crimes and cannot be credibly rationalized. What secular purpose based on injury to others, or to the group, can justify laws against private homosexuality between willing adults? Against other forms of private sodomy? Against various practices of the conjugal bed, including contraception? Against "profanity," "sacrilege," "immorality," "obscenity"? In these cases, one may argue, the religious elements are clear and predominant. Most would accept that it would be a forbidden establishment of religion, or interference with freedom of religion, if the state sought to prohibit taking the name of the Lord in vain or making graven images; why may the state constitutionally forbid homosexuality? The state could not, probably, prohibit private blasphemy or sacrilege; why may it prohibit obscenity?[34]

V

Special Problems

NIGHT CLUB ACTS AND LENNY BRUCE

Until recently night clubs produced only run-of-the-mill problems of censorship. A stripteaser took off one too many items and the show was raided. Normally everyone recognized this sport of the police as a demonstration that the gendarmes were watching the morals of the citizenry and when things got too bad they were ready to call "Halt!"

The magistrates and judges contented themselves with lecturing the participants and letting them go with token fines, warnings, or—at worst—suspended sentences.

Lenny Bruce, a new type of comedian, changed all of that. After a series of arrests for so-called pornographic night club acts, Bruce was finally arrested and convicted in Chicago and sentenced to a thousand-dollar fine and a year's imprisonment. In a typical night club or burlesque act situation, the small fine is paid and the matter is forgotten. However, when the authorities impose a substantial fine and a year's sentence, appeals must be taken and thus the *Bruce* case began its long journey through the courts of Illinois. The following are extracts of the act which annoyed the police and judges and became the subject of the trial in the Supreme Court of Illinois:

> I'll tell you who the Christian of the year is. Jimmy Hoffa. Jimmy Hoffa is sure more of a Christian than Bobby Kennedy. Why? Because Jimmy Hoffa hired ex-convicts, as Christ would have. I assume Christ would have hired ex-convicts. . . . The only medicine that's good for you is iodine, because it burns you, sinner. Douching with CN or Lysol that wasn't diluted. Ooh.

219

* * * * *

I'd like to do a flick where we have a good psychotic rapist who has been in a nut house—let Jonathan Winters do it. He's in the loony bin about, let's see, six months. He's planning to get out, he's being very good, see, and he's got the therapy.

Now we cut to a lady's nut house and we have these nymphomaniacs and they both get out at the same time. They make their break and they meet each other, which is very frustrating to Jonathan, you know.

* * * * *

Now about doing it. How do you feel about that, you people? Is that about the dirtiest thing that we could do to each other? Priests don't do it. Nuns don't do it. Puttamumsioganumba doesn't do it. Rabbis are close to celibacy. It's really not very nice, is it, doing it? I don't think you'd like me to do it to your mother or your sister.

* * * * *

. . . They hate Americans everywhere. You know why? Cause we fucked all their mothers for chocolate bars, and don't you forget that, Jim.

You don't think those kids who heard that since 1942— "You know what those Americans did to your poor mother? They lined her up, those bastards, your poor father had to throw his guts up in the kitchen while he waited out there that master sergeant shtupped your mother for their stinking coffee and their eggs and their frigging cigarettes, those Americans."

I said, Jim, that's all they've heard, those kids. Those kids now are 23 or 25 years old. The Americans—there's the guy that did it to my mother.

Will you assume this story's correct, you say, "There's the fellow who fucked my mother, oh thank you, thank you, thank you. Thank you for that and giving us candy."

* * * * *

See that moralist and purist? Is that the good, good lady? What did she do for her husband? Does that schmuck stay in his underwear yelling, "Touch it once, touch it once"? Is it bizarre that married guys have to jerk off more than anyone else cause your old ladies won't ball you and you can't chippy?

* * * * *

Now, I hang out at the gas station in between shows and get gravel in my shoes. And the conversation is really inspiring: . . . .

"You been in a lot of gas stations, right? You ever see a toilet like this?"

"Oh, it's beautiful. . . ."

"You sell many of these condoms here?"

"I don't know."

"You fill up the thing there?"

"Uhh."

"You wear condoms ever?"

"Yeah. . . ."

". . . You want to put one on? Can I put one on?"

"What, are you crazy or something?"

"No, I figure it's something to do. We'll both put a condom on, we'll take a picture."

"Naa, get the hell out of here, you nut, you."

Based upon a tape recording of the act the jury found Bruce guilty and the judge, Daniel J. Ryan, imposed the sentence of a year in the House of Correction and $1,000 fine.

The case was appealed and finally reached the Supreme Court of Illinois where, on June 18, 1964, the court in an opinion by Justice Robert C. Underwood, affirmed Bruce's conviction.[1] The Illinois Supreme Court theory was as follows:

Lenny Bruce has a constitutional right to express any idea he desires but "his means of doing so and the language thus used may bring the entire performance" within the ban of a statute against obscenity. "In such case it is not the idea which created a difficulty but only the manner in which it is presented."

221

The court then must discuss the legal argument that the Bruce act contained nothing which was sexually stimulating and, in the words of the defense brief, the listener "may be shocked, he may be offended, he may be amused, he may be bored but he will never be aroused sexually." Therefore, says counsel for the defense, since the basic significance of obscenity is its sexual arousal, nothing in the Bruce nightclub act could be regarded as obscene. The Illinois Court denies this contention, holding that it is constitutional to impose criminal penalties on someone who purveys material "which is obscene because of its revolting qualities." The court further finds that the obscenity law of Illinois is not confined to material which is "sexually stimulating" but it may also "embrace that which is repulsive and disgusting." Consequently, Judge Underwood states: "Judged by these standards we believe that the performance is characterized by its continual reference, both by word and acts indicating masturbation, to sexual intercourse or sexual organs in terms which ordinary adult individuals find thoroughly disgusting and revolting and patently offensive when contemporary community standards are applied."

Finally, the court considers the argument of counsel for the defense that, according to many authorities, a matter to be obscene must be "utterly without redeeming social importance." The Illinois Appellate Court refuses to accept this argument, stating that in Illinois the rule should be a sort of balancing formula in which the social importance of the work or act or language is weighed against the amount of obscenity. The court clearly believes that the obscenity in this case outweighs any value of the act.

On the above reasoning the Illinois Appellate Court sustained the Bruce conviction. Exactly four days later the United States Supreme Court handed down a new series of decisions on obscenity matters and immediately, in a rare and unusual maneuver, the Illinois Supreme Court on its own motion vacated its decision, saying:

> On June 18, 1964, this court adopted an opinion in this case. On June 22, 1964, the Supreme Court of the United States handed its decision in *Jacobellis v. Ohio*. The views expressed in the opinions in that case are pertinent to the problem in this case. The parties should therefore be afforded an opportunity to consider their suggestions as to the effect of the decision in the *Jacobellis* case upon the issues in this case.
>
> On the court's own motion, IT IS THEREFORE OR-DERED that the opinion filed in this case is withdrawn and the judgment heretofore entered is vacated.

Finally, in November, 1964, the Illinois court filed its new opinion, saying in effect:[2] Our original idea was that we balanced Bruce's satire and good material against the revolting and disgusting, and the latter weighed the most. Therefore we struck down the performance and found it legally obscene. Now under the *Jacobellis* rule, "we must concede that some of the topics commented on by the defendant are of social importance." The "entire performance is thereby immunized" and the defendant is discharged.

Bruce has run afoul of the law in almost every major city in the United States and has been arrested almost a score of times. Only a few times has he been fully tried. He was acquitted in San Francisco in 1962, then convicted in Chicago, and recently convicted again in Manhattan. The Chicago trial caught the press unawares, but the New York trial received full publicity. Articles appeared in publications ranging from *Newsweek* to *New Republic*. In his New York trial Bruce had the advantage of being represented by a leading obscenity trial lawyer, Ephraim London. The prosecution was handled by Assistant District Attorney Richard M. Kuh, who has to his credit more than a hundred convictions for obscenity. The trial lasted for weeks. In accordance with good procedure the defense presented an imposing array of cultural talent to testify that Bruce's act was not obscene. Richard Gilman, drama critic of the magazine *Newsweek,* gave a detailed appreciation of Bruce's comic and imaginative repertoire. The critic Nat Hentoff testified, "Bruce makes people think, he provokes his audience with absurdity and gets them to react." The defense even included an Episcopal minister, Sidney Lanier, who testified that Bruce's night club act was "in some ways helpful, and even healing."

A star witness was the newspaper columnist Dorothy Kilgallen. She described Bruce as a "brilliant and moral man" who made "valid, important comments whether or not I agree with them."

Despite this testimony, the lower court found Bruce guilty of violation of New York's famous Section 1140a of the Criminal Code, prohibiting immoral shows and exhibitions. Professor Albert Goldman, who teaches English at Columbia University, wrote in *New Republic* about the trial:

> The three judges—John M. Murtagh, a Roman Catholic; Kenneth M. Phipps, a Negro; and J. Randall Creel, a WASP —made it clear that they regarded Bruce's work with profound personal distaste, but were willing to hear or read anything that could be said in the comedian's defense. To a man, defense witnesses asserted that Bruce is a brilliant social satirist, and then struggled to prove it from the crude and unfunny "bits" mercilessly laid out in the transcript. The inflation of values was bizarre: Bruce was compared to Rabelais, Swift, Twain, Joyce, Henry Miller and Hosea. All the witnesses found the "dirty words" acceptable by "contemporary community standards" (one clergyman remarked that the only bar to the use of Bruce's language in the pulpit was custom).

*   *   *   *   *

Though the trial was good theater, it was not an honest search for truth. The defense witnesses evaded a direct confrontation with the facts. Instead of conceding Bruce's power to shock and infuriate by a public display of the ugly, the twisted, the perverse, and justifying his use of such powers by the remarkable cathartic effect he sometimes achieved, these liberal, intellectual witnesses turned the case into the conventional issue of the blameless artist versus the uncomprehending world.

The perversion of the issues apparent in the Bruce trial illuminates powerfully a cultural dilemma that is likely to become more serious in the future. Of the two obvious ways of dealing with a militant and revolutionary *avant garde,* the one—repression—succeeds only in driving it underground and thereby increasing its intensity. The steady relaxation of restraint exemplified by the Supreme Court liberalization of the definition of "obscenity" has an equally frustrating effect on those whose social contribution is relentless challenge to established values. To meet protest with ever-expanding permissiveness is to refuse to feel its bite, to translate it into "art" or "satire" or other expressions that seem comfortable, thus forcing the dissident into ever more extravagant gestures of defiance.

Elsewhere in this book it has been suggested that it is emotionalism that causes the problems in the obscenity field. Lenny Bruce is a perfect example of a performer who arouses the emotions of the censors to the nth degree. Here, verbatim, is the description of Bruce's act by the majority opinion:

1. Eleanor Roosevelt and her display of "tits."
2. Jacqueline Kennedy "hauling ass" at the moment of the late President's assassination.
3. St. Paul giving up "fucking."
4. An accident victim—who lost a foot in the accident—who made sexual advances to a nurse, while in the ambulance taking him to the hospital.
5. Uncle Willie discussing the "apples" of a twelve-year-old girl.
6. Seemingly sexual intimacy with a chicken.
7. "Pissing in the sink" and "pissing" from a building's ledge.

225

8. The verb "to come," with its obvious reference to sexual orgasm.

9. The reunited couple discussing adulteries committed during their separation, and the suggestion of a wife's denial of infidelity, even when discovered by her husband.

10. "Shoving" a funnel of hot lead "up one's ass."

11. The story dealing with the masked man, Tonto, and an unnatural sex act.

12. Mildred Babe Zaharias and the "dyke profile of 1939."

Here is a deliberate prodding of sacred cows. Picking on the most revered and untouchable people and institutions—wives of presidents, biblical personages, young girlhood—in obscene language. There is little wonder that he was arrested, tried, and convicted. How a court, without emotion, can later calmly, quietly, and judiciously recognize that the passages of *Tropic of Cancer* are not obscene—but Bruce's statements are—will be revealing. We know that the courts can do it—they can rationalize anything, but the intellectually honest judges do not like to do it and frequently balk at making distingushing decisions that have no distinction. It may be that an appellate court may say, "You can use this language in books or in a night club but if you apply it to cherished and revered people and institutions you sacrifice your privilege and it becomes obscene and therefore illegal."

In any case the final decision of the appellate court will be interesting and possibly enlightening.

NUDIES AND THE MOVIES

A Chicago juvenile court judge wrote a letter to a local newspaper bitterly condemning the movies and flatly asserting that films "cause, indirectly or directly, more juvenile crime coming into my court than all other causes combined." The year of the letter? It was written in 1905. The history of nude movies begins about 1900 in the nickelodeon, which burgeoned from a handful of storefront places of entertainment in New York to over 5,000 locations throughout the country in less than five years. The movies might have eliminated our Puritan morality if they had been permitted to follow their logical course. Consider the titles of some of the old favorites: *Old Man's Darling, Child Robbers, Beware My Husband Comes* (intended or accidental double entendre?), *The Unwritten Law, The Bigamist, College Boy's First Love, The Female Highwayman, Gaieties of Divorce.*

By 1910—in addition to the condemnation by the Chicago judge—newspapers, ministers from the pulpit, morality organizations, censorship groups, and law enforcement officers were complaining that films catered to the base passions and stimulated children and immature adults to sexual crimes and violence. In general the five-cent theatres were regarded by these authorities as hopelessly without merit and deserving banishment. The situation deteriorated to such an extent that in 1909 New York Mayor George B. McClellan closed the movies and kept them closed until a form of pre-censorship was developed. In 1911 the Commonwealth of Pennsylvania established the first state statutory censorship board. Other states quickly followed Pennsylvania's lead.

The film industry lived with state and local censorship until after World War I. In most areas the problem was more apparent than real. It merely meant that the movie producers had to have the right connections, the proper people pulling the correct wires, and adequate payoffs skillfully handled. This was not because the movies were pornographic in fact or in law, but solely because it was the way of bureaucracy of the times. The movies used "come-on" titles but delivered nothing. In spite of such titles as *Shocking Night, Luring Lips, Virgin Paradise, Scrambled Wives, Purchase Price,* and *Plaything of Broadway,* the promised sex never materialized and the films were all morality stories.

227

At the end of World War 1, movies became a major industry in the United States and the cost of submitting to censorship in more than thirty states and twenty-five cities moved the industry to attack the problem.

In 1921 the movie producers banded together and hired Will H. Hays, then Postmaster General in Harding's cabinet, to head an association to establish and maintain standards. to avoid censorship. The Hays office, working under a completely artificial code, established broad principles which kept films in line for four decades.

Even today the code is stultifying, limiting, and self-denying. Profanity is forbidden. An occasional "hell" or "damn" is permitted if required by the script, but that is the limit of profane expression. Nudity is banned unless it involves photography of natives of a foreign land in a documentary film or travelogue. Our main bugaboo "obscenity" is prohibited in "words, gesture, reference, song, joke or by suggestion."

The code goes far beyond the law or even ordinary good taste. It expressly eliminates common words such as "chippy, fairy, goose, nuts, pansy, S.O.B.," etc. In general the code emasculates American movies and defies the producers to create a strong drama or even a sexy comedy without violating it.

Enforcement is accomplished by the grant or withdrawal of a "seal of approval." By and large, the withholding of a seal of approval condemns the ordinary movie to economic strangulation. Many theatres will not accept a movie without the seal. Organizations such as the Catholic Legion of Decency will arbitrarily condemn any picture without the seal.

On some occasions a movie producer may feel so strongly about a movie that he will release it despite its lack of official sanctification and, in other cases, the producer believes the movie is so good that it can succeed in any case. In recent years the leading examples of successful releases without the "seal" involving American movies were *The Moon Is Blue* and *The*

Man with the Golden Arm, and in foreign films *Room at the Top* and *Never on Sunday.*

The present boss is Chief Censor Geoffrey M. Shurlock, who, within his imposed artificial limitations, appears to be doing a good job. Mr. Shurlock's approach is that the movies may go as far as existing public morality will permit. He tries to gauge public opinion and to permit movies to do whatever would not be offensive to the bulk of the movie-goers. Obviously, under this regimen, movies are doomed to be followers instead of the leaders they could become.

This situation existed until 1960, when a cameraman named Russ Myers sensed that the time was ripe for the baring of a woman's bosom on the screen. In the past there had been films of nudist camps which, after a struggle, had passed legal challenge, but as yet there had been no general distribution of pictures with a frank and open viewing of the exposed female breast. Myers filmed such a picture, entitled *The Immoral Mr. Teas,* in a week for less than $25,000. It was an instantaneous success and will probably gross more than a million dollars. Of course it lacked the seal of approval and could be shown only in specialized theatres which were already screening foreign films containing seduction scenes and fleeting shots of nude women.

Imitators of Myers became legion, and a specialized group of about four hundred theatres now show the nudies throughout the country. They won all legal battles with local and state censors and since they have generally kept within the bounds of good taste (simply exploiting the nude female bosom) they are usually permitted to continue without challenge.[3]

Hollywood is now straining at the leash to produce movies showing nudity despite the code. Already some producers are including nude scenes for overseas showing. Others are using tricks and devices to accomplish the result—at least for advertising purposes. For example, in *Irma La Douce* Shirley MacLaine is filmed nude in the bathtub and Jack Lemmon views her through a telescope. However, he uses the wrong end and the image on the screen is minute. There is unquestionable nudity, but a movie patron would have to bring field glasses along in order to see it. Nevertheless it provided some excellent advertising subject matter.

THE LEGAL SITUATION

Censorship of films first came before the United States Supreme Court in 1915 in the case of *Mutual Film Corp. vs. Industrial Comm'n.*[4] The case involved Ohio state censorship, and attorneys for the film argued that precensorship of films is a violation of the freedom of speech guarantees of the federal Constitution. The United States Supreme Court denied the contention and ruled that the showing of films was "a business pure and simple, originated and conducted for profit, like other spectacles, but not to be regarded . . . as organs of public opinion." In other words, the High Court decided that movies were not entitled to that same protection of freedom of speech which had already been granted to books, newspapers, and magazines. Apparently, but for some obscure reason, films were different.

It is true that this absurd opinion had some excuse. The case before the court was unfortunately ahead of its time. Taken literally, the free speech and free press section of the United States Constitution applies only to laws enacted by Congress, but the case under consideration involved a law passed by the Ohio Legislature. Until 1925 the Supreme Court, when confronted by violations of free speech and free press, differentiated between laws passed by the state legislatures and laws passed by Congress. However, in that year, in a case[5] involving seditious writing (not obscenity), the High Court for the first time decided that the adoption of the Fourteenth Amendment to the Constitution (which provided that state legislature had to observe rules of due

230

process) made those legislatures subject to the First Amendment, and obligated them to comply with the rules of freedom of speech and press.

The first indication that at last the time was ripe for a change in legal attitudes toward the movies came in 1948 in a case involving—once again not obscenity—anti-trust legislation. In *United States vs. Paramount Pictures*[6] the United States Supreme Court in a *dictum* said, "We have no doubt that moving pictures like newspapers and radio are included in the press whose freedom is guaranteed by the First Amendment."

This was not a final decision and lawyers are quick to recognize "asides" uttered by courts which may become holdings when cases arise, or which may be ignored. It is often said that the courts can always find a form of words to avoid doing what they have said they would do.

However, when the question arose squarely on point, the United States Supreme Court followed the *Paramount Picture* case. In *Joseph Burstyn vs. Wilson,*[7] involving the picture *The Miracle,* the issue was not obscenity but religion. Justice Tom Clark rendered the ruling of the court: "We hold only that under the Constitution and Amendments thereto a state may not ban a film on the basis of a censor's conclusion that it is sacrilegious." The Court established the principle that while a state may still set up a system of previewing a picture it cannot ban it except on grounds compatible with the Constitution. Over a period of years the High Court generally held unconstitutional licensing statutes and precensorship but usually based its decisions not on the rule that precensorship was unconstitutional but that the ground for precensorship was invalid. For example, the following grounds for denying a license are regarded as too vague and generally unconstitutional: "Prejudicial to the best interests of the people,"[8] "sacrilegious,"[9] "harmful,"[10] "immoral and tending to corrupt morals,"[11] and "obscene, indecent and immoral and such as tends to debase or corrupt morals."[12] In effect, the High Court says that generalities will not be permitted as the basis for a refusal to permit the showing of a film.

The real test of the issue came before the Supreme Court in 1961 in the case of *Times Film Corp. vs. Chicago*.[13] This was in effect a prearranged case, in which the producers of the film *Don Juan* requested a permit to show the film and refused to submit the film for pre-viewing. The movie was a version of the Mozart opera *Don Giovanni* and had nothing in it which might possibly lead to a refusal of permit. However, by a five-to-four decision the United States Supreme Court decided that precensorship of movies was constitutional. Chief Justice Earl Warren delivered a strong dissent, arguing that the opinion of the court "comes perilously close to holding that not only may motion pictures be censored but that a licensing scheme may be applied to newspapers, books and periodicals, radio, television, public speeches and every other medium of expression. The Court in no way explains why moving pictures should be treated differently than any other form of expression."

Warren noted that the case involving the movie *The Miracle* was in the courts for five years before it was permitted to be shown and as a consequence the film never was shown in Chicago. He adds, "This is the delay occasioned by the censor. This is the injury done to the free communication of ideas. This damage is not inflicted by the ordinary criminal penalties."

Justice Douglas submitted his own dissenting opinion in which he argued that if anything is wrong with a film it should be punished by prosecution in the criminal courts, and he added:

> If, however, government must proceed against an illegal publication in a prosecution, then the advantages are on the other side. All the protections of the Bill of Rights come into play. The presumption of innocence, the right to jury trial, proof of guilt beyond a reasonable doubt—these become barriers in the path of officials who want to impose their standard of morality on the author or producer. The advantage a censor

enjoys while working as a supreme bureaucracy disappears . . .
the First Amendment was designed to enlarge, not to limit,
freedom in literature and in arts as well as in politics, eco-
nomics, law, and other fields. . . . Its aim was to unlock all
ideas for argument, debate and dissemination. No more potent
force in defeat of that freedom could be designed than censorship. It is a weapon that no minority or majority group,
acting through government, should be allowed to wield over
any of us.

Murray Schumach, movie industry reporter for the *New York
Times,* in his recent and excellent book, *The Face on the Cutting
Room Floor,* predicts:

> Prior restraint may not squeak through the Supreme Court
> many more times. State and local censors seem to be on the
> ropes. But they may persist a long time unless the movie in-
> dustry shows the determination of such small movie companies
> as Times Film, or the dedication of such lawyers as Bilgrey,
> Ernst, Lindey, London, Nimmer. The fight against state and
> local censors is the best investment Hollywood can make. But
> it must be prepared to go all the way. It must be willing to go
> into the courts every time it thinks its freedom has been vio-
> lated. That is the only way it will carry to a logical conclusion
> the beginnings that were made by *Ulysses* and *The Miracle.*

Schumach's prediction came perilously close to realization in
two recent decisions of the Supreme Court. In *Freedman vs. Maryland,*[14] the owner of a Baltimore movie house refused to submit
a routine film, *Revenge at Daybreak,* to the Maryland Board of
Censors, as required by the law of that state. He was fined, and
appealed the decision up through the state courts to the United
States Supreme Court. The High Court, in an opinion by Mr.
Justice Brennan, reversed, and—significantly—*there were no
dissenters!*

The court did *not* rule that precensorship is illegal; it simply
declares that the Maryland statute contained insufficient consti-

tutional safeguards. Justice Brennan outlines the following criteria as basic to a proper precensorship statute.

1. The law must require prompt action on the part of the reviewing (censoring) board. [The Maryland law contained no time limit.]

2. It should have judicial participation, although a prompt judicial review might suffice. [In one Maryland case judicial review took six months, and that is definitely too long.]

3. Burden of proof must always be placed on the censor.

4. The law should not provide for *final* restraint [temporary may be satisfactory] without an *adversary* judicial review.

On March 15, 1965, in the case of *Trans Lux vs. Board of Regents* the Supreme Court struck down the New York State statute on movie censorship on exactly the same grounds.

The present state of the law appears to be that, while a state or city may have a constitutional precensorship law for movies, no legislative body has created one yet.

OBSCENITY AND THE FILMS

A considerable body of case law growing out of the censorship of films has involved the question of whether the authorities had the right to set up prelicensing schemes for films. At the present time such prelicensing appears to be constitutionally legal, but most students and scholars in the field agree with Murray Schumach that precensorship has but a short life left.[15]

The second major problem the movies face has been the question of what constitutes obscenity in films. The movie version of *Lady Chatterley's Lover,* made in France and imported by Kingsley Pictures, is a good illustration. The case originated in the State of New York, where the official censorship body denied a license to the picture on the ground that it portrayed an act of sexual immorality, namely adultery, as desirable, and as an

234

acceptable and normal pattern of behavior. All New York courts affirmed this decision.

On appeal the majority of the United States Supreme Court reversed the Court of Appeals of New York.[16] The High Court did not go into the problem of obscenity but considered the question of constitutional protection for the freedom to advocate ideas. It held that advocating adultery was an idea and that censoring the film only because it advocated this idea was unconstitutional. Mr. Justice Stewart wrote the majority opinion, which said that the New York law, as interpreted by its courts, violated the "First Amendment's basic guarantee . . . of freedom to advocate ideas . . . [and] thus struck at the very heart of constitutionally protected liberty." Justices Black and Douglas agreed, but added that they believed that the New York statute and courts were also wrong because they permitted prior censorship. Chief Justice Warren and Justice Clark rounded out the majority, although the latter only agreed with the result because he felt that the New York statute was too vague to meet basic requirements of constitutional due process.

Justices Harlan, Frankfurter, and Whittaker wrote separate opinions in which they concurred with the result but not with the rules set forth by the majority. These judges wanted to hold the New York law constitutional but wanted to reverse the New York Court of Appeals because there was nothing in the movie that could properly "be termed obscene or corruptors of the public morals by inciting the commission of adultery."

This decision aroused the Comstocks as few decisions ever had before. The Republican Congressman from Michigan, Clare E. Hoffman, castigated the court and charged that it "endorsed adultery." The *American Mercury* magazine published a series of articles condemning the decision and terming it part of a worldwide anti-Christian conspiracy inspired by Jews and Communists. Senator James O. Eastland of Mississippi introduced a constitutional amendment which would give each state the right to decide by law questions of "decency and morality." Senator Herman Talmadge of Georgia called the decision "shocking and unconscionable."

These diatribes against the court may have had some effect. As discussed earlier in this volume, in 1964 the Supreme Court decided the question of the obscenity of *Les Amants*.[17] Although the Ohio Supreme Court was reversed for approving punishment of a movie owner who exhibited this film, three judges, including the Chief Justice, dissented; and throughout the dissent runs a querulous note of protest against requiring the Supreme Court to decide questions of this nature.

As of this writing, it is possible to say with some degree of safety that practically any movie in reasonably good taste will receive constitutional protection. Complete nudity above the navel (even including the navel) should not affect a film. The subject matter, whether it be adultery, homosexuality, or religion, should not affect the result. Unquestionably restrictions do still exist. At the lower levels, a battle rages at the moment over whether movies can show scenes of sexual intercourse, even though they are photographed with subtlety and reasonably good taste. These cases have not yet reached the courts but they are being discussed in the pages of *Variety*. Sodomy and its variants are probably too far out to be proper subjects of moving pictures. But none of these questions can be predicted with any degree of accuracy.

CLASSIFICATION BY AGE[18]

The current battle in the movie field is to arrive at some system of classification. In most countries of Europe and in Great Britain, age classification is well accepted. Movies are rated as suitable for general viewing, for adults and children accompanied by adults, or for adults only.

American film producers have been bitterly fighting age classification. Economic statistics reveal that it has a severe impact on the profits from a picture. In many areas of this country, in the drive-in movies, and especially in films for television, viewing is a family affair. When children are not permitted, the adults tend not to see the film. Purely on the dollars-and-cents basis, Hollywood's pocketbook suffers. Hollywood cannot afford classification. Although opposing the classification system, officials of the industry have avoided becoming embroiled in public debate. The last significant speaker on the subject was Eric Johnston who, until his death in 1963, headed the Hollywood censorship office. On appearing before a Congressional committee, Johnston said:

> Basically, classification is one of those things that has never been fully defined. There are many kinds of classification, ranging from advisory to statutory . . . we only get on solid ground when we consider the effects of classification—any form of it. For here we see it for what it is: censorship, nothing more, nothing less. Who can dispute that classification is essentially a surrender of parental authority . . . and no system of classification could ever be devised to reflect accurately the quality of a motion picture. Doesn't classification say two things to a parent? Someone else's idea of suitability is what counts. Quality, individual taste, intellectual value, don't matter.

Stanley Kramer, a well-known producer and director, stated bluntly: "Classification means somebody classifies and that is censorship. . . . I think that any shackle on what I hold films to be, that is, an art form, is ridiculous. Some people suggest that the producer himself ought to classify his films. But I am not sure that even my censorship would be objective."

Despite Hollywood's objections to classification, a number of states and cities are considering seriously, or have already enacted, laws which require some form of age classification. Maryland has a law which provides $100 fine and thirty days in jail for any exhibitor who shows a film regarded as "obscene" to children under eighteen.[19] The exhibitor can, of course, avoid the impact of the law simply by refusing admittance to children under eighteen.

In Ohio a similar law was recently introduced with the additional proviso that anyone under eighteen attending a drive-in theatre must be accompanied by a parent or guardian. Considering that in many states drivers' licenses are granted at sixteen, it creates an interesting situation—drive, but not into the movies. The constitutionality of such a law is in doubt.

The first legal test of such statutory classifications came in *Paramount Films vs. Chicago*[20] in which, by law, the Chicago Commissioner of Police prohibited anyone under the age of 21 from viewing *Desire Under the Elms*. With unusual dispatch the local Federal District Court found the Chicago ordinance under which the Commissioner of Police had acted unconstitutional on the following grounds: (1) A 21-year age limit is unreasonable; (2) if a picture is obscene, it is obscene regardless of who views it [an absurd conclusion]; (3) the standard set up by the ordinance was "hopelessly indefinite."

The censors always want to impose the highest age limit possible. Some bluenoses would even prohibit anyone under the age of 35 from seeing certain films. On the other hand, the lower the age limit, the more likely it is that the law will be held constitutional. Probably the ideal age limit would be 16 because of the many precedents such as drivers' licenses and compulsory education which apply to a minimum age of 16. There may even be some justification for a 18 year age limit, which was the age set for military selective service. Certainly a person old enough for military service is entitled to certain freedoms. The likelihood of constitutionality of statutes with advanced age limits of 20 or 21 is extremely remote.

A look at the handling of this problem in foreign countries indicates the absurdity of the probable results. In South Africa the age restriction customarily is 12. "For Adults Only" normally means that anyone over 12 years of age may view the films. However, if the South African censors see a particulary offensive picture they issue a special certificate, limiting other age groups, and—in the case of a picture called *The Bed*— they even issued a certificate barring the film to everyone between the ages of 4 and 18.

Cuba, under Batista, had two censorship boards. The first decided either that the film was viewable by adults or not viewable at all, and the second decided whether children under 12 could see the picture.

Certainly there can be no question that the law may distinguish between children and adults and may establish the age at which a person becomes an adult for a particular purpose—provided that legislation is reasonable. There is a long record of limitations on drinking and driving for children, and in some fields such as wills and contracts the law regards children (anyone under the age of 21 for this purpose) on a par with lunatics. The age of 21 is required for voting, and age requirements for acting as jurors, running for certain elective offices, etc., are commonly accepted. The problem came before the United States Supreme Court in *Prince vs. Massachusetts*.[21]

A member of the sect of Jehovah's Witnesses was convicted under a state child labor law for permitting his daughter to sell religious magazines. The defendant argued that the law, if applied to him, abridged his freedom of religion. The court ruled that the authority of a state over activities of children is much broader than the state's jurisdiction over adults. The court held: "The state has a wide range of power for limiting parental freedom and authority in things affecting the child's welfare; this includes to some extent matters of conscience and religious conviction." This case probably laid the foundation for constitutional statutory age classification of films.

The real issue here is whether certain kinds of movies can or will cause harm to children. Unfortunately, scientific evidence on this subject is too limited for an authoritative conclusion. A study by Holady and Stoddard back in 1933[22] indicated that children are unquestionably affected by movies and will accept erroneous information as accurate if they see it in a movie. In addition, the study showed that children tend to retain at a very high level any information obtained from films. Approximately that same year another study revealed that films can disturb the sleep of children.[23] Yet another learned investigation indicated that the effects of this nightmare quality would fade in a few days.[24] In general, probably the most accurate statement at the moment is that there is a complete paucity of real evidence which could determine whether children can be or would be injured by exposure to certain kinds of films. Consequently in the absence of evidence either way, the probability is that the courts will and should uphold the legislatures if they conclude that they must protect children from the effects of certain types of films. So long as the legislatures are reasonable and specific the courts will probably uphold them. Reasonableness, however, must include the selection of a reasonable age limit. The age 20 or 21 cannot be such a limit.

One of the bugaboos of this entire subject which regularly arises to haunt public speakers and lecturers on the topic is the question: "How about all the cases where a boy goes out and rapes a girl after seeing a sexy movie?" The Hollywood office of the censors has a classic answer on file. It has a newspaper clipping about a youth who raped and murdered his teen-age date while necking in a car shortly after seeing a movie. Was this movie *Anatomy of a Murder, The Rape of Olga's Girls,* or something similar? The movie was Walt Disney's *Snow White and the Seven Dwarfs*. It must certainly be obvious even to the most opinionated that such a movie did not cause the criminal conduct. It is also highly questionable whether, even if the movie had been one of the horror or sex films, and the unfortunate criminal act had occurred, it would be right and logical to conclude, without additional evidence, that the viewing of the film caused the conduct. Police records contain many files of rapes and murders which have occurred after such simple human actions as eating a meal, having a night's sleep, and—most frequently—after a few drinks at a bar. These are human activities difficult or even impossible to legislate out of existence.

THE PROBLEM OF PRIVATE LETTERS

It is common knowledge that the federal government pressed for statutes prohibiting the use of the mails for obscene material in order to protect the morals and moral fibre of its citizenry. What happens when one private citizen sends another private citizen a letter which contains one or more dirty words? This problem recently came before the courts in the case of *United States vs. Darnell.*[25] The male defendant sent a woman a letter in which he described, as the court says, "baldly in four and three letter words" her husband's sexual relations with her and also homosexual relations with the defendant. The defendant was convicted for violation of the federal statute which bars the mailing of "any obscene, lewd, lascivious, indecent, filthy or vile" matter.[26]

One problem of this case was that the letter was only mildly obscene. The three-letter word used was "ass" to refer to the anus and the four-letter word was "cunt" to describe the vagina.

Although there are a number of cases[27] which either specifically hold or implicitly assume that the federal statute would apply to letters, there is really not enough reason for the court so to hold. A note writer in the *Stanford Law Review*[28] comments adversely concerning this decision:

241

Applying the statute to private, non-commercial letters unnecessarily restricts freedom of speech and may encourage blackmail against those who use relatively common terminology in letters. Therefore, without a clear expression of Congressional intent or an express holding by the Supreme Court, the statute should not be held applicable to such letters; and the *Darnell* court improperly assumed that it did apply.

This commentator also states:

> It is unfortunate that the *Darnell* case came to trial. The right of free private communication is as important as the right to speak and write for the public and should not be curtailed by criminal sanctions when the effect of the communication is merely to offend. The power of the Federal Government should not be exerted to prevent trivial results. . . . The *Darnell* letter might offend good taste and manners, but it does not appear to offend the statute.

It does seem a heavy-handed action for the federal government to undertake the burden of punishing someone who merely deposited in the mail a letter containing profanity. After all, the criminal sanctions of the federal government are supposed to be reserved for important items such as prevention of counterfeiting, elimination of narcotics and white slave traffic, the preservation of civil liberties and civil rights, the prevention of vote frauds, the detection of interstate kidnappers, and major crimes against the federal government. It seems demeaning for the federal authorities to be compelled to take cognizance of such a problem. However, this field provokes strong emotionalism, and many people feel that writing a letter to a woman with a word that is unseemly should receive vigorous punishment. A false chivalry, but quite common.

OFFICIAL AND UNOFFICIAL
VIGILANTE CENSORSHIP

With the United States Supreme Court and many state courts finding less and less material censorable, those who strongly mind what other people read or look at have adopted new forms of censorship. For example, we have the official or semi-official group, customarily sponsored by state law of some kind, which is prepared to render its advice (usually gratuitously) as to what literature may be offered for sale. A significant case in this direction is *Bantam Books, Inc. vs. Sullivan*[29] in which the state of Rhode Island adopted a *Commission to Encourage Morality in Youth*. The governor appointed the commission members, and it was their duty to study publications and periodicals and notify wholesalers of any that were "objectionable for sale, distribution or display for youth." Acting under this statute the commission provided local chiefs of police and distributors with the names of a series of objectionable magazines and books.

The notices were followed by "friendly" visits from the police and commission members. The local wholesaler, obviously fearful of possible official action against him, took the necessary steps to prevent all of the publications condemned by the commission from being distributed. The national publishers brought a legal suit to test the Rhode Island statute and the legal validity of the existence of the commission. In an 8 to 1 opinion the United States Supreme Court held that the Rhode Island procedure was unconstitutional, since it subjected "the distribution of publications to a system of prior administrative restraints." And, in fact, the United States Supreme Court found that Rhode Island had created an unconstitutional system of informal censorship.

This case provides a strong indication that states will not be permitted lightly to interfere with the distribution of books and periodicals.

Frequently the county prosecutors or district attorneys in various areas have set themselves up as super-censors. Sometimes these prosecutors maintain elaborate set-ups within their offices to read books and magazines and advise wholesalers or newsstand operators which ones are objectionable. In other cases the procedure is the essence of simplicity—the district attorney merely awaits complaints, at which time he looks over the material and sends to the wholesaler a list of what items he feels violate the law. Regardless of whether the district attorney follows the simple or complex procedure, it is clear that the case law on the subject holds this type of action unconstitutional.[30] A state or municipal official may not become a censor and render gratuitous advice as to what may or may not be sold. Obviously, any such action by an official carries with it the implied threat of an arrest or the withdrawal of a license[31] or some other penalty, and courts have been alert to stop this type of precensorship. A state official or district attorney may institute steps to punish or impose legal sanctions upon anyone in his jurisdiction selling an item which the official believes to be obscene. However, this is a far cry from advising in advance. When official action is taken *after* the event, an entire array of constitutional safeguards comes into play. When the action is taken prior to sale, the constitutional safeguards are precluded.

In some cases there have been spontaneous creations of organizations devoted to "cleaning up the newsstands" or "raising the reading habits of the community" or some other goal directed toward censoring the material to be sold in the community. In most cases these organizations are the outgrowth of a local group tied in to the Citizens for Decent Literature, Inc., a Cincinnati-based organization that has waged a vigorous campaign for a decade. In most cases the local vigilante groups flower in a burst of enthusiasm, are carried along by the momentum generated by the organization of the group, and then wither and die when it becomes a problem of sustained hard work. The groups appear to be most successful in small towns, and they are usually associated with a church. Once they get the support of the town newspaper, they are all set to dictate—at least temporarily—the reading habits of the community. In a typical case, the minister of the church plus a few of his favorite parishioners call an organizational meeting, either in the church or in the town high school. The meeting becomes a headline item in the local newspaper and the first one brings out a group equally divided between eminently respectable people who honestly believe that more attention should be given to censoring the literature that appears at the local newsstand and stores, and crackpots who believe that sex is the root of all evil and must be driven, like snakes, out of the community. Officers are selected and readers are appointed. The readers pass books or magazines from one to the other and collect comments. If a majority of the readers decide that a book is "objectionable," they will either circulate the objectionable nature of the book or advise the local wholesaler and retail outlets that the book is undesirable and should not be available to the local readers.

In small-town areas there is no one who has a large enough stake to fight the group. The wholesaler concentrates on selling more of *Reader's Digest* and *Saturday Evening Post,* and the individual outlets simply eschew the banned publications until the fuss blows over.

After a time the local newspaper finds other headlines and the reading becomes a chore which ends up in the hands of the fanatics. Soon almost everything becomes "pornographic" and either the national distributor steps in with a legal action or the committee gradually falls apart from lack of popular support.

Because this is a new and novel field, very few cases have gone to the appellate courts. However, there are cases in allied fields which indicate that the vigilante groups can be stopped. An important one is *Council of Defense vs. International Magazine Co.*[32] The case had nothing to do with obscenity, but the principle is the same. A New Mexico vigilante group believed the Hearst newspapers were unpatriotic in failing to support the federal government in World War I. In an effort to improve the patriotism of the Hearst publications, this group urged a boycott by both newsdealers and readers. It published an Honor Roll of dealers who had agreed not to handle Hearst publications and it provided cooperating dealers with a seal of loyalty. Uncooperative retailers were threatened with loss of patronage.

The publishers of the periodicals involved brought an action under the federal and state antitrust laws. The injunction was granted by the federal court. In its opinion the court states:

> Whatever may have been the derelictions of Hearst as an individual or in his newspapers, it is absolutely clear that complainant which was engaged solely in publishing and selling magazines, had published no objectionable matter in its magazines, and it had nothing to do with the Hearst newspapers, nor any interest in them. The declared and obvious purpose was to destroy complainant's business in New Mexico. This purpose was proceeding toward success, when halted by the injunction of the court below. The various defendants were planning and acting together to effectuate the above purpose. They were doing so without legal warrant or protection. Their acts amounted to a conspiracy to boycott or blacklist the magazines published by complainant. All of these publications came into the state through interstate commerce. The only purpose of shipping the magazines into New Mexico was for sale there; hence a movement which sought to prevent, and was succeeding in preventing, newsdealers, who were here the importers, from receiving, handling, and selling such magazines directly interfered with that commerce. We think this situation within the prohibition of the Sherman act.

The above case is accurate in its ruling and is supported by other cases.[33] However, there is a significant distinction between these cases and the problem of any Committee for Decent Literature. Most of the cases which used the antitrust laws to prevent boycotts involved profit-enterprise problems. For example, when a labor union tried to boycott a bakery for having its bread baked in another state, it violated the Sherman Act but was obviously a profit-motivated problem.[34] Although the main case already discussed the Sherman Act as prohibiting boycotts based upon ideology, this aspect has not been studied thoroughly. The *Columbia Law Review*,[35] in a note on the subject, indicated that there is some reason to believe that "the sole legitimate concern of the antitrust laws is the preservation of competition in the marketplace and that they should apply only to combination of entities engaged in business or mercantile activity seeking to protect or obtain a competitive advantage. The history of their applications has, by and large, exhibited little deviation from this economic context." If this view is followed, then the legal defeat of the vigilante group must rest not upon the antitrust statute, but upon the common law.

Under the common law no person may meddle in the contractual affairs of another without a privilege so to do. The vigilante groups obviously interfere with the sales of books, magazines, and newspapers and in doing so interfere also with contractual relationships between the retailer and the wholesaler. One early case[36] considered this specific problem. Here a vigilante group organized to stop publications which they deemed to be objectionable. The national publisher brought an injunction action to prohibit their interference. The Massachusetts Federal Court set forth the issue clearly when it said:

> May an unofficial organization, actuated by a sincere desire to benefit the public and to strengthen the administration of the law, carry out its purpose by threatening with criminal prosecution those who deal in magazines which it regards as illegal; the effect being, as a practical matter, to exclude such magazines from sale through ordinary channels, and thereby to inflict loss upon their proprietors?

The court analyzed this specific question and concluded that the organization was acting illegally:

> The defendants have the right to express their views as to the propriety or legality of a publication. But the defendants have not the right to enforce their views by organized threats, either open or covert, to the distributing trade to prosecute persons who disagree with them. The principles at law involved which are interesting and might be much elaborated, are analogous to those under which secondary boycotts are illegal. . . .

This case is of great importance because it was cited with approval by the United States Supreme Court in the *Bantam Books* case[37] and it was referred to in such a way as to indicate that the United States Supreme Court approved of the principle. For example, in the *Bantam Books* case the problem was whether an *official* state commission could regulate the reading habits of the public. The United States Supreme Court analyzed this question and concluded that, if in the Rhode Island case there had been no official state tribunal, then the action by the group "would present a claim, plainly justifiable, of unlawful interference in advantageous business relations." And then the court cited the *American Mercury* case. Thus the court made it clear that a vigilante group may not threaten boycotts or criminal prosecution of those who will not observe its views as to what constitutes proper reading habits.

There are a series of cases which apparently permit certain people to dictate under threat of boycott or actual boycott. However, a careful reading of these reveals that they involve ministers who tell their flock what to do or teachers or school boards who tell the students what to do. Such action has always been legally protected. A typical case[38] of this nature was one in which the bishops of the Roman Catholic Church had issued a pastoral letter forbidding parishioners to read plaintiff's newspaper. The owner of the newspaper brought an action for an injunction, which the court refused. The court implied the result might have been different if the bishops had "attempted to forbid social or business intercourse with the plaintiff . . . [which] could not affect the faith of the members." In another case[39] a religious sect objected to certain broadcasts on the radio and, to prevent them, they threatened to boycott a department store. This induced the department store to terminate a contract for religious broadcasts with the radio station. The court refused to interfere with this action, stating that the church could protect itself against an attack upon it. These cases define the limit of the privilege.

A school or church may take vigorous action to protect itself, and this action may include requesting *its own members* not to patronize a particular economic unit. However, it is submitted that this privilege is restricted in two ways. In the first place, the goal or objective must be a laudable one from the viewpoint of the courts, and secondly the requested nonpatronage or boycott must be limited to those to which the requester has a relationship. This means that a church can ask its *own* members not to do something, and a school can ask *its* students not to do something. However, if either goes beyond these boundaries and addresses the general public it is questionable whether the privilege still exists.

In considering the goals, the Negro objective cases merit consideration. They start with the cases back in the thirties when Negroes picketed stores to force them to hire a percentage of Negroes. Such picketing was generally enjoined.[40] More recently, in the sixties, a new twist to an old effort appears. Negroes formed the Economic Action Committee which wanted stores to deal with Negro salesmen primarily. The court enjoined the picketing on the ground that it was for the specific purpose of creating "discriminatory racial practices."[41] This is an example of an objective which the courts do not regard as laudable.

The latter is particulary appropriate in the vigilante obscenity cases because these are situations in which individuals, frequently untutored and unlettered, attempt to decide what the community should read.

In a not atypical case[42] recently, the chairman of a small town Committee for Decent Literature, who directed all its affairs and supervised the approved reading list, admitted on cross-examination that he had never completed high school; he was a welder with a night school certificate; he rarely read books; he was quite interested in World War II and read a lot about it but could not remember the name of a single book on the subject! But he had strong ideas on what should be permitted to be sold within the boundaries of his town.

If the selection of books and magazines is left to these self-appointed literary policemen, newsstands and bookstores will be well stocked with religious, children's, and garden and cook books, and magazines, but with little else.

THE LAW HELPS THE RAIDERS

During the 1950's and on into the early years of the following decade, a customary vote-getting maneuver by city administrations was the raiding of newspaper stands to grab headline space. The front pages of metropolitan dailies abounded with such examples of the headline writer's art as "Police Engage in Smut Raid," or "Detectives Grab Smut Pile," or even "Smut Raiders Grab Thousand Books." A statistical correlation of the raids with elections showed an alarming increase of raids shortly before any contest. The thinking was simple: The newsboys might vote for others, but the church groups and the bluenoses would love the crusaders for "clean literature."

In some cases the local distributors stepped in and began legal action to contest the validity of the raid, or simply tried to stop interference with the regular course of business. Such actions frequently met success, indicating that the random and haphazard raid based upon a whim of a district attorney or a police officer was not valid exercise in constitutional power. The decisions, although not uniform, tended generally to condemn such actions; some courts did refuse to interfere, but they were in the minority.[43]

Because of persistent court interference, the police associations and district-attorney groups began to lobby through the state legislatures special laws designed to assist them in their search and seizure practices. Since these laws created planned chaos in the book and magazine field, it was inevitable that they would ultimately be tested by the United States Supreme Court. The first test involved a Missouri statute which provided that a police officer could go before a judge and get a blanket search warrant authorizing him and his assistants to go in and grab "pornographic material." The United States Supreme Court[44] easily invalidated the statute, calling it censorship of the worst kind without any form of advance judicial determination that the material was obscene. The court held that states may not prevent circulation of non-obscene literature and therefore suppression of any literature must be based upon a satisfactory and constitutional determination of obscenity.

The state of Rhode Island tried another method when it appointed a Commission to Encourage Morality in Youth. This Commission listed publications and advised distributors and dealers of those publications it regarded as potentially corruptive of youth. Although theoretically the commission was primarily concerned with the effect of this type of literature on youth, the net effect—after a few police visits—was to suppress the circulation of books even to adults.

This too came before the United States Supreme Court when Bantam Books, Inc., a national distributor, brought an action in Rhode Island to have the law declared unconstitutional. Mr. Justice Brennan, with Justice Harlan dissenting, wrote the ma-

251

jority opinion, condemning the Rhode Island statute.[45] The majority opinion sheds considerable light on what is regarded as the proper judicial process in the obscenity field. First, the opinion described the operation of the statute, noting that a majority vote of the commission lists a book as objectionable and publicizes that decision. It continues:

> Herein lies the vice of the system. The Commission's operation is a form of effective state regulation superimposed upon the State's criminal regulation of obscenity and making such regulation largely unnecessary. In thus obviating the need to employ criminal sanctions, the State has at the same time eliminated the safeguards of the criminal process. Criminal sanctions may be applied only after a determination of obscenity has been made in a criminal trial hedged about with the procedural safeguards of the criminal process. The commission's practice is in striking contrast, in that it provides no safeguards whatever against the suppression of non-obscene, and therefore constitutionally protected, matter. It is a form of regulation that creates hazards to protected freedoms markedly greater than those that attend reliance upon the criminal law.

Justice Clark concurred but indicated that he did so on a very limited basis and that if the Commission had better standards the law, in his opinion, might be constitutional. Justice Harlan dissented, squarely accepting the Rhode Island procedure.

The Clark concurring opinion and the dissent by Harlan created some confusion until 1964, when a similar case[46] came before the Supreme Court.

This case involved a Kansas statute which provided that a county attorney or an attorney general could go before a judge and set forth a signed and verified document of the existence of a "lewd, lascivious or obscene book, magazine, newspaper, writing, etc." in the county, at which time the judge would issue his search warrant directing the sheriff or some other peace officer to bring before him the prohibited items.

Under the statute all interested parties were advised of a hearing to be held not less than ten days after the seizure. At the hearing the judge determined whether the items were obscene and, if so, he would order them destroyed "by burning or otherwise." If they were found not obscene they would be returned.

The attorney general of the state of Kansas, armed with the authority of this statute, obtained an order from the District Court of Gary County directing the sheriff to seize all copies of certain paperback novels at the distributor's place of business in Junction City, Kansas. A hearing was held before a judge, who directed the sheriff to destroy 1,715 copies of thirty-one seized novels.

The United States Supreme Court reversed the Kansas Supreme Court on the ground that the procedures relating to the seizure of the novels "were constitutionally insufficient because they did not adequately safeguard against the suppression of non-obscene books." Justice Brennan rendered this opinion, in which concurred Chief Justice Warren, Justice White, and Justice Goldberg. The basic theory of the Supreme Court is that no official, with or without authority of a statute, may *seize* any book (this would cover magazines, movies, etc.) without a prior judicial *adversary* determination that the item was obscene.

The decision on the Kansas statute has been somewhat misinterpreted in some areas. Some enforcement officials have reached the conclusion that they may not prosecute any person for violation of an obscenity statute without a prior *adversary* determination that the material is obscene. This is erroneous. The decision of the High Court deals only with the legality of a seizure and does not concern itself with the legality of a criminal prosecution. Thus, if a newsstand proprietor sells an item which the district attorney believes to be obscene he may send out a detective to purchase a copy of the item (in the vernacular "make a buy") and thereafter prosecute upon evidence that the newsstand proprietor sold this item. The decision does indicate that under no circumstances may the police seize one or more of the purportedly obscene items either with or without a search warrant.

The Supreme Court indicates that the proper procedure is to obtain legally some of the allegedly obscene material and take it before a judge, thus giving the opposing side an opportunity to be heard, and then to obtain a search and seizure warrant or other document.

The emphasis here is on the *adversary* nature of the procedure. The court is eliminating the *ex parte* or one-sided affairs where the district attorney brings a batch of material to a judge and says, "I think this is obscene, your honor, and please give me a warrant to search this man's premises." Now the district attorney must serve notice to the possessor of the material and let him have his day in court *before* his material is seized.

The case does create an interesting procedural problem for the police where the material involved is sold only in the grey or black market. For example, in most metropolitan areas there are vendors who will sell—to persons known to them not to be police officials or stool pigeons—material generally recognized as pornographic. This may include stag films, French postcards, and comic books portraying sexual deviations and perversions. The police may be tipped off that this commercial traffic is going on in a particular store, but how can they obtain the evidence necessary to carry on criminal or other procedures? Before the Kansas case the police simply went to any judge or magistrate, executed an affidavit of probability, obtained a search warrant, and proceeded to search the premises and seize the material. The Kansas case says that this cannot be done unless that judge or magistrate makes a prior *adversary* determination that the material is obscene. The police now have the much more difficult job of obtaining the evidence through normal legal methods. Perhaps a complaining customer will give them a copy; perhaps an undercover operator may be able to buy some of the material.

Finally, there is one other avenue which must be tested. The police may be able to obtain a search warrant, examine the material, take pictures of it, but not seize the actual items. The seizure is clearly prohibited by the Supreme Court decisions. Then, based solely on the pictures that the police have taken, they may be able to get a valid search and seizure warrant from a judge after an *adversary* proceeding. Obviously this is a lengthy and roundabout procedure, and it is even possible that long before a judicial determination of obscenity is obtained, the questionable material may have disappeared. Nevertheless, the police still have available to them standard criminal procedures. If they can prove that a crime has been committed, they can make an arrest, without actually seizing the objectionable items. The seizures that used to occur before the Supreme Court stopped them were too frequently substitutes for criminal action, designed only to apply economic sanctions against the vendor of the material in question. It is certainly good to stop such indiscriminate action. On the other hand, if a vendor of admittedly obscene material is so careful that he sells only to adults who buy willingly, quietly, and who refuse cooperation with the police, the inability to prosecute does not appear to be catastrophic either to morality or to law enforcement in general.

VI

Law of Obscenity -- 1965

CONFUSION CONFOUNDED

There are many fields of law which a lawyer or a student could categorize with complete accuracy as being confused. However, nowhere is confusion so confounded as in the law of obscenity. The basic field does not really lend itself to the body of decisions and precedents which are commonly regarded as law. In a rare flash of intellectual honesty a former general counsel of the Post Office Department, Roy C. Frank, in testifying before a congressional committee,[1] admitted that, in endeavoring to decide what matters were obscene and should be denied the use of the Post Office facilities, he might give an item to five different people and could easily receive five different opinions. This was in 1952. There has been no change to date. Here is an excellent example of precisely the same situation that currently exists.

In 1960 there appeared on the scene a rash of cheaply made (but comparatively highly priced) paperback books frankly designed to capture the actual and perpetual adolescent trade— an imprint known as Nightstand Books. These books came more from a baker's mold than from an author and an editor. They all had exactly 192 pages, a sexual theme, vivid descriptions of sexual acts without the use of the taboo four-letter words, and they always had a sexual title. Wherever possible, the title included the word "sin." Since the books were cleverly prepared to attain a maximum amount of sexuality without running afoul of the law, they did not become involved in many legal cases. However, they did come before the United States Supreme Court in a case involving the legality of a seizure. There follow the names of some of the books that appear in that case: *Born for Sin, Sin Girls, Sin Camp, Isle of Sin, Sin Cruise, The Sinful Ones, No Longer a Virgin, Lover, Trailer Trollop, Sex Spy,* etc.

The publisher thought so little of the books that he did not even copyright them by submission to the Library of Congress, although they did have imprinted in them "Copyright 1961, Nightstand Books." This appears to be simply an attempt to acquire a copyright without spending the few dollars and the time necessary to fill out the copyright form and file it with the Library of Congress.

I have evaluated all of the books involved in the Kansas case and many others, also, and have selected the following as probably the most "far out" example giving a true representation of the type of book involved. The book is entitled *Lover* and is subtitled "A Professional Stud in the Big City Lust Jungle." The cover shows the nose and eyes of a male and in each eye is reflected a nude woman. It is the story of Johnny Wells, a 19-year-old boy, who discovers that in various ways he could make a good thing sensually and monetarily out of being a male prostitute and catering to wealthy women. The book takes Johnny through a series of episodes, each going a little further than the last until the following, which is his last adventure:

LOVER

He sipped his cognac and waited for something to happen. In the days when he was hustling he didn't wait for things to happen. He spotted a likely prospect and worked for his money.

Now he didn't care enough to try too hard. Besides, he was drinking a little bit more than usual and the cognac was beginning to reach him. He was content to simply sit and drink until something came his way. And if nothing did come his way, well, that was all right too. He didn't really care that much. He wasn't going to starve to death. He could afford to bide his time.

He felt very old and very tired. Often he tried to remind himself that he was all of eighteen years old but he could never really believe it. Or was he eighteen? It seemed to him that he'd hit another birthday somewhere along the way, that he was in fact nineteen, but he had trouble keeping track.

It didn't really matter. As far as he could tell, he was neither eighteen nor nineteen. He felt at least forty, sometimes older. In eighteen or nineteen years — did it matter which? — he had done more living than most men did in a lifetime. And it was beginning to show.

He finished his cognac and signaled for a refill. It was funny, he thought. He'd originally switched to cognac as a steady drink for three reasons. One — he liked the taste. Two — it was something a gentleman could drink. And three — he could nurse a drink for an hour and never get drunk.

Funny.

Nowadays he drank his cognac without really tasting it. And the gentleman bit certainly didn't matter — he had other more important things to worry about than his boyish concept of what a gentleman was and what a gentleman did and all nonsensical manure like that.

And the third reason certainly didn't apply. He didn't nurse his drinks any more. He drank them right down, and he got drunk on them.

Funny.

He decided he wanted a cigarette. He reached in

his pocket and pulled out a cigarette case, reached in again and got his silver lighter. He took a cigarette from the case and put it to his lips, then flicked the lighter. It lit on the first try, as it always did, and he took the light and drew smoke into his lungs. It tasted foul. Everything did lately.

"Want to hold the light, sweetie?"

He turned and looked at her.

She wasn't bad, was in fact better than he was used to. She was in her thirties but that was to be expected — girls in their twenties got all the romance they wanted without paying for it. This one was holding up well. She had jet black hair swept back into a bun and her skin was firm and pinkish. She still had a shape, too — a nice pair of boobs, unless they were phonies, and a trim waist. He couldn't see her legs and didn't know whether they were good or not.

He lit her cigarette.

"Thanks," she said. "Nice night, huh?"

"Very nice."

"The night is nice and so are you. Busy tonight, honey? Or can we get together?"

Most of them didn't talk like this one. Most of them were subtle as all hell, while this one had half the subtlety of an atomic weapon. He started to resent her, then changed his mind. In a way her bluntness was refreshing. Hell, she knew the score and so did he. Why not call a shovel a shovel?

"Sure," he said. "I guess we can get together."

"It has to be tonight," she went on. "There's a very special party tonight."

There was always a very special party.

"A highly unusual party," she went on. "You've

probably never been to one like it."

"I've been to lots of parties," he said.

"Ever been to an orgy?"

That one stopped him. He stared at her, and his expression must have been a riot, because she burst out into hysterical laughter. "Oh, come on," she said. "Let's get out of this inverted whorehouse. I'll tell you about it outside. I think you may kind of like it."

They went out onto the street. It was cold out and he caught them a cab. They got into the back seat. She gave the driver an address on Park Avenue in the Nineties and curled into his arms. He played his role properly, taking her in his arms, kissing her, holding her close.

Suddenly she took one of his hands and placed it under her skirt. "That's right," she said, "that's where I like to be held."

They rode three blocks in silence while she made appropriate purring noises to indicate her approval.

"A wild group of people," she explained. "All of us rich and all of us bored, like it says in the peepshow magazines. Every once in a while we have a meeting and show some movies. Ever seen a movie?"

"I see lots of movies."

"I mean stag movies."

"No," he said. "I've never seen one."

"They're fun," she told him. "Not as much fun as doing it yourself. of course That's the most fun of all. Nothing quite like it. But the pictures are fun themselves. They sort of set the stage, get a person in the mood."

"You feel as though you re in the mood already," he said to her.

"Really?"

"Uh-huh."

"I was born that way. But to get back to the picture. This one guy has a brownstone uptown, where we're going. There'll be four couples there. Another woman like me — Park Avenue matrons with time on our hands and money to burn is the way the magazines would put it. And two guys, the guy who owns the house and another like him. There'll be a nice little call girl for each of the guys and another gigolo for the other gal and you for me. Eight all told."

"I got a question," he said.

"Go on."

"Why don't you and the two guys go to it and save money?"

"Because they're our husbands. We need a little variety once in a while, sweetie."

That shut him up. She went on to explain the set-up — there were four love seats in the living room, and each couple had a love seat, and they sat on them during the movie. *Sat* was a euphemism — they did whatever they wanted to do.

Then, when the movie ended, they paired off and went somewhere or simply stayed in the living room and kept at it. It didn't make too much difference.

"Sound okay?"

"I suppose so," he said.

"Any questions?"

"Yeah. One."

"Go on."

"What's in it for me?"

"A lot of fun," she said. "The joy of having me

a few dozen times. Need more?"

"Yeah."

"Mercenary," she said. "There's also a quick five hundred bucks in it for you. Good enough?"

"Fine," he said.

The living room took up most of the first floor of the brownstone town house. The other "couples" were all on hand when Johnny arrived with the woman, whose name turned out to be Sheila Chase. Her husband, Harvey Chase, owned the brownstone. He had a little trollop on his arm with curly brown hair and mammoth mammaries. Another man, introduced as Max Turner, was escorting a light-skinned Negro prostitute with breasts just as large as those of the little trollop on Chase's arm.

Turner's wife Gloria was standing beside a young man whom Johnny had no trouble identifying as a comrade-in-arms. The kid's name was Lance and he worked the same bars as Johnny.

It was a weird scene if ever there was one. First Max Turner made a little speech, and then every-. body took off his or her clothes and stood around naked and unashamed. It gave Johnny a good chance to have a long look at the body of the woman he was going to be with.

She wasn't bad at all. Happily, her boobs were all hers. They had a slight sag to them but nothing any man in his right mind would complain about. And her legs were very good indeed. She had stretch marks on her abdomen that were a sign that she had borne children at one time or other. That sort of bothered Johnny. He couldn't quite see her as the perfect mother. The picture didn't fit.

But he wasn't complaining. Five hundred dollars was more than adequate for one night's work. And the work might even turn out to be enjoyable. There was no way to say for sure one way or the other, but it might be interesting.

He had never seen a stag movie before. Vicarious sex never particularly appealed to him, perhaps because he had had so much first-hand experience along those lines. The only thing similar to watching a stag movie in his experience was when he had watched the lesbian make love to Moira in the hotel room in Las Vegas.

And that hadn't excited him. Instead it had nauseated him, and he had had to throw up as soon as it was over.

Sure. But maybe this would be different. He would have to wait and find out.

Sheila Chase sat down on one of the velvet love seats and he took his seat beside her. The lights went out. A silver screen rolled down from the ceiling and he stared hard at it, waiting for something to happen. He heard Sheila's ragged breathing at his side; it wasn't at all hard to see that she found such movies extremely exciting.

Well, maybe he'd get a kick too. The cognac was still working in his head and he felt almost drunk but not too drunk to function properly. He dropped an arm over her shoulder and let his hand cup her breast. It was very large and he liked the feel of it against his palm. He held it and watched the screen.

The picture began.

Title Card: HOT STUFF.

The motion picture is set in the great outdoors. It opens with a long shot of a scene somewhere out in the country, possibly shot in upper New York State, possibly in some part of California where most movies and starlets are made The rural scene pans over a stretch of open field to the shore of a small lake.

Long shot of a girl walking across the field to the lakeshore. She is wearing a man's flannel shirt open at the neck and a pair of tight levis. The camera follows her to the water's edge, concentrating on her buttocks. They are plump, and she is walking in a burlesque of the typical trollop's strut.

At the edge of the water she stops and turns to face the camera. She smiles.

Subtitle: I'M HOT. I THINK I'LL TAKE A SWIM.

This said, the girl begins to undress. She opens the buttons on the shirt one at a time to reveal breasts which the loose shirt had kept well hidden up to this point. The camera dollies in for a close-up of her breasts. She drops the shirt to the ground.

Her hands play with her breasts. The camera watches.

Subtitle: I WISH SOMEBODY WOULD DO THIS FOR ME.

The camera moves back. The star of this epic now undoes the belt of her denim slacks, then unzips them and peels them off. She pirhouettes for the camera in order to expose all her charms to its omniscient eye.

The camera focuses on her buttocks. She turns again. The camera pans her body from her feet to her waist.

Then the girl plunges into the water. She begins to swim lazily about as the camera watches from the shore.

Now a man comes into view.

He does not notice the girl, nor does he take any note of the girl's clothing. Instead he simply walks to the lakeshore, then turns as the girl did to face the camera. He is a tall, dark, good-looking man with long and neatly-combed black hair. He smiles at the camera.

Subtitle: HO HUM. THINK I'LL TAKE A SWIM.

The man begins to undress. He is wearing a skin-tight tee shirt which he peels off over his head and throws to the ground. He has a good suntan, as if he is in the habit of swimming like this every day of the week. His chest is hard and taut, his arms well-muscled.

The camera moves to one side and the man again faces it, so that his side is to the water.

Shot of the girl's face. She is crouching in the water so that only her face is visible. She is smiling hugely, her eyes wide. It is obvious that she sees the man and likes what she is looking at.

Shot of the man as he strips quickly.

Shot of the man's face.

Subtitle: WISH I HAD A WOMAN

The girl swims in toward shore. She reaches the shore and climbs up on the bank, smiling at the man.

Shot of the man. He is obviously very pleased that the girl has arrived.
Shot of girl's face again.
Subtitle: DO YOU LIKE ME?"
Shot of man, nodding his head YES.
Shot of girl. The camera pans her body. She touches herself, walks toward the man. He reaches out and places his hands on her breasts. He begins to fondle her and the camera closes in.

Johnny was perspiring.

He hadn't expected this. Viewed from a distance, the picture was crude and stupid. It shouldn't be exciting, not to a man who'd literally had more women than he could count. It should be boring from start to finish.

It wasn't.

On the contrary. He wasn't sure why this was possible.

It certainly wasn't that the woman was pretty She wasn't bad, but he had a better-looking woman on the couch next to him. And he'd made love to many better-looking women in his time.

He guessed that it must be the idea of watching something forbidden. Something like that, maybe. It was hard to tell. but that was his guess.

Sheila moved beside him.

He saw her face in the half-light. Her mouth was tense with desire and beads of perspiration dotted her forehead. He could smell her as well. She used a great quantity of a very expensive perfume but that wasn't all he smelled.

He smelled *her*.

"Johnny — "

"Come here, baby."

She came to him and he drew her down, pressed his face between her breasts. For a moment it was as if there were two Johnny Wells, one of them on the couch with Sheila Chase and the other standing off at a distance watching and snickering at him. The standing-off one had plenty to snicker at, he had to admit.

Here he was, an experienced guy, a guy who'd been around plenty. Here he was lying on a love seat with another man's wife while the other man was with a cuddly little call girl. Here he was watching a picture of two people making it and getting interested himself.

Well, what of it?

He didn't care about a lot of things now. He didn't care who or what Sheila Chase happened to be. He cared only that she also happened to be a woman, and that at the moment he needed a woman, and that she was handy.

That was plenty.

So he bit her and heard her cry with pain and passion both at once.

"Johnny — "

He looked at her.

"The line from the picture," she moaned. "The line the girl says to him right before they do it."

He waited.

She quoted the line. It had been strange to see those words in print on the screen, and it was even stranger to hear them come tumbling from her lips.

He gave her just what she asked for.

On the screen, the man and the woman finished their first bout of lovemaking. The man is lying flat on his back, scratching himself with one hand. The woman is lying on her side, looking down at him.

Subtitle: LET'S DO IT AGAIN.

They both stand up. The camera moves for a side angle as the woman bends down, finally crouching on her hands and knees.

The man moves behind her.

Shot of woman's face, passionate.

Subtitle: NOW!

Shot of the man's face, smiling hugely.

The man does it to her.

Finally the man and woman finish.

"I'm ready again," Sheila said.

"You're always ready "

"I'm burning up. But it's the damnedest thing I don't want to stop watching the picture."

"Neither do I."

She was grinning. "I told you it was exciting," she said. "You didn't think it would be. But it is. It's exciting as all hell."

"I know what you mean."

"You too?"

"Uh-huh."

She sighed. "And now I want to make love. I want to keep watching the picture, but I also want to make love. Two drives, each in a different direction. Profound, huh?"

"Sure."

He knew what she meant. He had thought that one session on the love seat with her would take his mind off sex for a while, but the picture was having too great an effect upon him. Once again he was caught up with desire for her. And the picture was still exciting. He didn't want to take his eyes off it if he could help it.

"I have an idea," she said.

"Yeah?"

"I want to watch the picture," she said, "and I want to make love."

"How?"

"You won't be able to see the picture," she told him. "I will, but you won't. I guess that's the price you pay in return for the five hundred dollars. See what I mean?"

He saw what she meant.

"It won't be too great a sacrifice," she said. "You've seen most of the movie already. Now I want you to kiss me while I watch the rest of it."

"I get it."

"You know what I want you to do?"

"Uh-huh."

"And it's fair, isn't it? I don't want you to miss the show but there's no help for it. I'm paying you, after all. Lots of money. Five hundred dollars."

"I understand."

The man and the woman had finished, and they were now both cavorting in the water. The camera examined them in the distance but there was not much to see.

Then a young girl came into camera range. Now the young girl is undressing and the camera is watching her. She is a very lovely young girl and seems to be very young. She wears no makeup and her breasts are small.

She is nude now and the camera is busy examining her body.

Shot of the faces of the man and the woman. They are looking at the girl and they seem interested.

Shot of man's face alone.

Subtitle: SHE'S A PRETTY ONE.

Shot of woman's face.

Subtitle: WE COULD HAVE FUN WITH HER.

The two of them swim madly for shore. They clamber up on the bank and run for her.

Shot of the girl. She does not seem to know what to do. The expression on her face says that she is frightened but she makes no move to run away.

Shot of man's face.

Subtitle: NOW WE'VE GOT YOU!

The man grabs the girl from behind and holds her around the waist. She struggles but cannot get away. The woman moves in front of the girl and takes the girl's breasts in her hands.

Shot of woman's face.

Subtitle: I'M GOING TO HAVE FUN WITH HER.

The woman suits her actions to her words.

The camera has a good time watching this most unusual display.

Shot of man's face.

Subtitle: IT'S MY TURN NOW.

The man and the woman succeed in getting the unwilling girl down upon the ground.

The man falls upon the girl and begins to make love to her.

The camera watches.

He was walking.

It was night, a very black night, and he was walking. Five fresh hundred dollar bills were in his wallet. They had not been there before.

They were his to keep. They were his in reward for having participated in the most sickening display of promiscuity he had ever heard about, not to say had anything to do with. They were his, and he had worked hard for them.

He wanted a drink.

The movie ended, and that was just a signal for the rest of the festivities to begin. The festivities had been odd ones. Someone had given him something to drink, something which contained a powerful stimulant, and the stimulant had gotten him through the evening in one piece.

In the course of the evening he had made love, not just to Sheila, but to every woman around at least once. He had made love in manners not even *he* had had any familiarity with. He had made love in ways that were sickening and disgusting, but he had done everything they had wanted him to do.

Now he was exhausted

These books have been involved in sporadic cases but never actually analyzed as thoroughly as they were when Attorney General William M. Ferguson of the state of Kansas brought an action against 59 similar objectionable books and asked that they be destroyed in accordance with Kansas law. The case went to the Supreme Court of Kansas where Judge Schuyler W. Jackson found that the significant point was whether the books were in fact "obscene." The court stated that *if* the books were obscene they could be treated as contraband and burned just as narcotics, dangerous weapons and poisoned food would be treated. Judge Jackson's opinion of the books was that they were unquestionably obscene and carried pornography to the last possible extreme.

Before this problem could reach the United States Supreme Court two unquestionable authorities wrote a detailed analysis of the entire field, including a careful study of this decision and the Nightstand Books. The scholars were M. C. Slough, who is a graduate of Columbia University, has a law degree from Indiana University, and was former dean of the University of Kansas Law School, and P. D. McAnany, who is an A.B. of Rockhurst College, an M.A. at St. Louis University, and has a law degree from Harvard University Law School. These two scholars say the following about the Nightstand Books:[2]

> The authors have examined and read several of the books listed as objectionable. They are unqualifiedly pornographic and just as obviously "thrown together" for a "quick sale." Lacking literary merit, they neither shock nor offend because they are so blatant and blunt. Written in a dull and slimy style, they are void of subtlety and spare nothing for the imagination. Among the books examined are: *Born for Sin* (story of a nymphomaniac who works her way from small town truck stops to big city and back peddling her body); *Lesbian Love* (following seduction by female school teacher heroine tries heterosexual love but returns to lesbianism);

Lover[3] (story of a nineteen-year old male whore who pro-
gresses from Bowery to Fifth Avenue); *Orgy Town* (central
character visits teenage vice dens and takes part in orgies on
the beach, in the bushes, and in the bedroom); *Sex Spy* (story
of a female spy in a Latin American setting—lesbianism, sadism, and rape); *Trailer Trollop* (theme includes abuse of
prostitute by men which forces her to try lesbianism, but
virtue triumphs in the end and she returns to illicit hetero-
sexual activities.)

These analysts believe that there is no question that the books
meet the obscenity test of the United States Supreme Court, and
in addition they consider laughingly the specific contentions of
Stanley Fleishman, counsel for the appellants. In response to Mr.
Fleishman's contentions that the Kansas procedure is unconstiti-
tutional, these two authorities say "this nonsense."

In other words, at this point there exists the definitive analysis
of the Supreme Court of Kansas, and the authoritative study of
two learned scholars, that the *Nightstand Books,* under the law as
it existed in early 1964, were unquestionably legally and constitutionally "obscene" and both could be and should be destroyed by
burning as provided in the Kansas statute.

The case went to the United States Supreme Court with the
same parties and same attorneys involved. Attorney General
William M. Ferguson appeared and argued for the state of Kansas, and Stanley Fleishman, of Hollywood, California, appeared
and argued for the book owners. The United States Supreme
Court reversed the Kansas court, primarily on the basis of procedure, stating that unless books are found to be obscene in a
contested proceeding, they could not be seized at all. Most of the
members of the court did not go into the question of whether
the books were obscene. However, Justice Potter Stewart based
his entire decision on the question of obscenity. This justice is
one who accepts the theory of "hard-core pornography." He
pointed out that if this case involved hard-core pornography he
would vote to uphold the Kansas statute. But then, referring to

the *Nightstand Books*, he said: "But the books here involved were not hard-core pornography." Here we have diametrically opposed opinions on the same books!

Even if these decisions and these learned authorities are meticulously studied, no real conclusion can be reached as to whether a Nightstand Book is or is not constitutionally obscene. At the moment there is not even a final decision of the United States Supreme Court on the subject. One justice of the United States Supreme Court does not believe the Nightstand Book to be obscene. Justices Black and Douglas do not believe in holding any books obscene. Thus there are three out of the six judges who will unquestionably vote, where the specific problem is presented, to hold Nightstand Books and their counterparts *not* constitutionally obscene. On the other hand Justices Harlan and Clark in the Kansas case indicate that since a state judicial tribunal found that these books "treat with sex in a fundamentally offensive manner" they can be held constitutionally obscene. Since both Justices Clark and Harlan frequently find material obscene these two judges in a straight obscenity proceeding involving a Nightstand or similar book would probably vote to hold them obscene.

The Chief Justice in his latest decisions wants to take the Supreme Court out of the censorship business. He wants some judicial rules which will make the problem go away. Unless he changes his mind it can be safely predicted that, if a responsible Court in a straight obscenity proceeding carefully and reasonably concludes that a Nightstand Book is obscene, he will vote to uphold that decision.

Justice William J. Brennan, Jr., has never in the Supreme Court voted to find *any* item obscene. He was there throughout the major cases and has been a stalwart in action, if not in express language, in favor of eliminating censorship. It is likely that Justice Brennan would go along with Justices Stewart, Black, and Douglas.

277

Justice Byron R. White was involved in only two cases: the *Jacobellis* case involving the innocuous movie *Les Amants* and the *Tropic of Cancer* case. In the movie case he voted with the majority to upset the Ohio criminal conviction. This means that he will agree to independent review by the High Court and will not accept the decision of the highest state court as sacrosanct. However, he does regard *Tropic* and *Pleasure Was My Business* as obscene. The likelihood is that he would go along with Justices Clark and Harlan and the Chief Justice in holding Nightstand Books obscene.

This leaves us with a four to four line up in rough cases. Consequently, the deciding vote, until the complexion of the Court again changes, will be that of the latest appointee to the High Bench—Abe Fortas. The new Justice is known to be a liberal and a progessive and, based upon probabilities, is likely to vote along with Black and Douglas against all forms of censorship. Fortas' record in government and as a civil liberties lawyer, supports this view. However, upset and surprise has been the keynote over the years as Supreme Court Justices have voted contrary to the handicapper's form sheet.

At this time predicting what the United States Supreme Court will do in an obscenity case involves prophesying which position Justice Abe Fortas will take. Beyond that, other questions arise. For example, Justice Hugo Lafayette Black, the prime stalwart against censorship, was born in 1886. One large unknown is how long Black will continue on the Court. After nearly thirty years of service this great man must be growing weary.

BORDERLINE CASES

Almost a century ago Chief Justice Morrison R. Waite of the United States Supreme Court said: "Every man should be able to know with certainty when he is committing a crime."[4] But to-day in the obscenity field in a close case one cannot possibly tell. Even after a specific United States Supreme Court decision no one can predict what will happen with a specific item. For instance: On June 22, 1964, the United States Supreme Court decided by a five to four decision that the book *Tropic of Cancer* could *not* be held constitutionally obscene. It is true that the court did not write a lengthy opinion, but each justice gave his reasons why he reversed. Those who did not want to reverse did not give reasons but those who did reverse indicated clearly that the reason was that they believed that the book was entitled to constitutional protection. Normally, following such a decision, the book *Tropic of Cancer* could be circulated freely throughout any of the fifty states without fear of arrest. Nevertheless, five months later John Hastings and Samuel Sokolove were arrested for selling *Tropic of Cancer*—not in the bible belt of Kentucky or Arkansas and not in a small town where decisions of the Supreme Court frequently do not penetrate for years, but in the fourth largest city in the United States, the City of Brotherly Love—Philadelphia.[5] Not only were these men arrested but they were brought before a trial judge—an experienced, veteran judge —one who held there was prima facie evidence for prosecution.

Most lawyers would agree that this sort of thing can happen but that if the case is carried to the United States Supreme Court it will unquestionably be reversed. In the field of obscenity even this is subject to doubt. A case in point: The well-known attorney, O. John Rogge, formerly Assistant United States Attorney General, has been one of the leading lawyers in the field of obscenity and has specialized in representing nudists in their fight to be permitted to publish magazines depicting natural nudity. It was Rogge who fought the many-year battle to get the United States Supreme Court specifically to find nudist pictures constitutionally protected against criminal prosecutions for obscenity. He accomplished this result in a definitive decision involving the

Post Office in 1958.[6] In 1960 this same attorney represented a mail seller of nude photographs. There was practically no difference between the photographs involved in this case and those involved in the Supreme Court decision, except possibly that in the latter case the photographs were more artistic and less blunt. After trial, the jury convicted the defendant and Rogge appealed through the Circuit Court and on to the United States Supreme Court. For some reason the United States Supreme Court denied certiorari—thus refusing to look at the case![7]

THE JUDGES REFUSE TO BE CONVINCED

Another major difficulty with this field of obscenity is that the judges refuse to accept the decisions. The *Oakley* case just cited is an example, but perhaps even more apt are three recent decisions. In a 1964 case a district judge in a federal court in Philadelphia had before him a package of nudist magazines, which it seemed reasonable to conclude were all under the protection of the United States Supreme Court, granted in the *Summerfield* case. However, the District Judge found the magazines obscene.[8] At approximately the same time the Supreme Court of Nebraska found similar, if not identical, magazines to be legally obscene.[9] The defense attorney in the Nebraska case, in a letter to the author, says, "To be very frank about it, the Supreme Court of Nebraska decision has badly shaken up my faith in the judicial system here. I had been a prosecutor for eight years, and never in my life had I seen a record which in my opinion, contained so many errors."

Most of these same magazines were also before Judge David L. Ullman in a criminal case, also in 1964. Judge Ullman took the case away from the jury with a little speech in which he made these points:

opinion is accepted literally, then that magazine could not be regarded as legally obscene. After all, fifty percent of the magazine has content of "social importance" and, even though the balance meets all of the standard tests for obscenity, one may *not* be weighed against the other.

It is extremely dubious whether the United States Supreme Court meant to reach the above conclusion. The full explanation of the Supreme Court opinion must be as follows: No work can be prohibited if, taken as whole in its unified and related condition, it has social importance. However, if there is unrelated and unnecessary material which in itself would normally be regarded as obscene, the probability is that the court would sustain a finding of obscenity.

NOW—THE LAW

With all the foregoing as precautionary remarks, the following should indicate the probable course of the law as it will be interpreted by the major courts in the middle of the seventh decade of the twentieth century:

Nudity

No nudity, in reasonably good taste, confined to voluntary viewing adults, will be held obscene. This includes nudity in magazines, in films, and even in person on the stage or in a nightclub. It includes complete nudity—pubic hair, genitalia, and nipples showing. It should be emphasized that to some extent this involves the consideration of certain factors: (1) *The nudity must be in reasonably good taste.* Exaggeration of the genitalia or other portrayals which might be regarded as in bad taste will take the representation out of its legal protection; (2) *It should be related to its setting.* A "girlie" magazine intended for adults, a film, or any scientific or artistic work, can have unlimited nudity. However, an unusually candid nude on a highway bill-

285

board or in a family newspaper would probably still run afoul of the law.

Books

No novel or ordinary nonfiction work should be held obscene if it is a serious work and was not recently written solely for the purpose of titillating pubescent and perennially adolescent minds. If the courts can find a form of outlawing the writings contrived to titillate without interfering with the serious works, there is a reasonable chance that they may do so. Today a score of publishers print and distribute hundreds of books designed solely to capitalize on the newly liberated sexual motif. Here are the names of some of these books: *Playtime Books, Bedside Books, Ham Books, All Star Novels, Midnight Readers, Boudoir Books, Spicy Books, Connoisseur Books, Nightstand Books, Night-Books, Night Time Books,* and many others. These have not been tested and it is a fifty-fifty shot—a toss-up—whether they will be permitted or prohibited. Books like Henry Miller's *Tropic of Cancer* and Madame Sherry's *Pleasure Was My Business* are not really precedents because either can qualify as a serious book with a significant sexual theme and containing much that is of social importance and value.

Magazines

The standard girlie type magazines exemplified best by *Playboy,* will unquestionably be constitutionally protected. These will include *Gent, Nugget, Escapade,* and the hundred other imitators. However, a series of magazines has sprung up recently which endeavors, in following the standard format, to add an extra fillip by catering to or emphasizing some form of fetishism. One magazine will emphasize garters; another, women's high heels; and others, simply nudity in an exaggerated, unrelated form. Some of these magazines are *Black Nylons, High Heels,*

Garter, Masher, Nylon Nude, Taboo, Dazzle, Buxom, Flip, Frenchy, Gypsy, Wildcat, etc. Many of these are in for trouble and may not be protected at this time. Especially is this true of the magazines which cater to flagellation, and other forms of sadism and masochism. There are a number of these—mostly sold under the counter—which specialize in scenes showing whipping, cruelty to sexual portions of the anatomy, breast pinching, etc. These will probably be denied constitutional protection.

Films

Any film in reasonably good taste will probably receive constitutional protection, so long as it confines its viewers to voluntary adults and announces frankly the nature of its subject matter. But here, too, some subject matter will not be permitted. Unless very much related to the nature of the film, a graphic representation of sexual intercourse would probably be outlawed. However, suppose a film is made on the subject of *Sexual Intercourse Throughout the Ages and Throughout the World?* The subject matter would include various positions used in different times, and various approaches including the foreplay, and all the other accouterments of intercourse. If made in good taste, even such a movie might receive its share of constitutional protection. On the other hand, if used simply as an excuse to present film clips of sex acts and a sex circus, it probably would be banned.

Records

In a recent case the Supreme Court of Nebraska[18] held a set of records obscene. Party records with sex motifs have recently become popular and are sold freely in most major cities of the country. If confined to sales to responsible adults, there is every reason to believe that these will be given constitutional protection by most courts and especially the United States Supreme

Court. It is extremely difficult to discriminate between a book and a record. Each is subject to the rule that if the reader or listener doesn't like it he or she can close the book or turn off the record. This in itself should be the major protection of any book or record.

Live Performances

Under normal standards live performances of either strippers or night club comedians should receive the full protection of the law. Both are within the framework of the doctrine that if the viewer is not amused, or is embarrassed, he can easily get up and walk out. In addition, the likelihood is that in both instances the viewer knows in advance what to expect from the performance. Occasionally, isolated instances may occur of a sensitive woman staying on in a night club to listen to Lenny Bruce, for example, and then being literally overwhelmed by the sexual bluntness of his patter and too embarrassed and fearful of possible public comment to rise and leave. However, this would be relatively rare and should not be sufficient to stop the act.

Live dramatic performances on the stage will probably receive constitutional protection from now on regardless of what they include. This is an area where the courts may leave the stopping of a show to the critics and the patrons. Unless the show is independently good, it is unlikely to last regardless of its portrayal of sexual or scatological material.

Miscellaneous

Sculpture, paintings, cartoons, objects of art, and similar items receive blanket protection. Most of these items are quite expensive, have obvious social utility to the connoisseur, and are not likely to become the aphrodisiacs of teenagers. Few of these have reached the courts, and it is unlikely that even the more prudish police and blue-nosed prosecuting attorneys will want to tangle with the art world. The Post Office Department had one bout with an attempt to ban an advertising piece containing a reproduction of *The Naked Maja,* and the artistic backlash is still stinging.

There are minor items of a novelty nature which may create some trouble: a bathmat made out of foam rubber simulating women's breasts, a penis holder to aid an older man encountering difficulty, ball point pens which, turned upside down, reveal copulating couples, etc. However, whichever way the courts rule, the decisions will probably be *sui generis* and will not establish principles. The social utility of the item, the method of distribution, and the advertising will all influence the final decision.

CONCLUSION

It must now be obvious to any reader who has even skimmed this book that the law of obscenity is a quicksand of conflicting and emotional decisions. It is based almost entirely on the completely unproved premise that obscene material can be harmful. Cases are decided, in the main, by most judges (from ground level justices of the peace and magistrates to United States Supreme Court Justices) on the basis of how the material strikes them personally and with total disregard of principle or precedent.

This cannot continue in an enlightened day and age. The pendulum has swung from "almost anything is obscene if indicted" in the 1930's and 1940's to "practically nothing is obscene if you fight hard enough." Neither position states a principle or a precedent. The Supreme Court of the United States cannot for long sit as the High Censorship Board of our country. History has demonstrated that the High Court grows weary of specific fields and ultimately finds a mechanism for eliminating the flow of cases. For example, once almost every public utility rate decision went to the Nine Men in Washington. The fatigue factor set in and they threw the problem out with a principle and a guide. This result is inevitable in the obscenity field. The only difficulty is that in obscenity emotions run so high that the justices cannot agree on a principle. However, eventually they will disregard emotionalism and grapple with the problem of creating a real guide—not a loose combination of words (such as, "appeals to prurient interest") that means nothing.

In establishing the criteria the court must be practical. It can say—"nothing is obscene." This would solve the problem. It cannot say, as the Chief Justice appears to desire, "We'll leave the problem to the state courts and, if reasonable, we'll support their decisions." The *Tropic of Cancer* cases should prove that this procedure won't work—the result is inevitably conflicting decisions that have to be solved by the Supreme Court.

The best proof we have of this, if proof be needed, is the conflict over *Fanny Hill.* Following in the wake of *Tropic of Cancer,* most lawyers believed that John Cleland's now classic memoirs of a prostitute would not be found obscene. But although Cleland used no four-letter words and wrote with the utmost circumlocution, the book was recently held obscene by Judge Morris Pashman[19] of the Superior Court of New Jersey and caused the New York Court of Appeals to split four to three with a bitter dissenting opinion. The majority, in an opinion[20] written by Judge Bergan, finds that because the book has "slight literary value" it cannot be constitutionally banned. However Chief Justice Desmond has a rough dissenting opinion in which he says among other things: "I refuse to believe that all this can continue to be the law. I predict that the law will turn and the pendulum swing back. Sometime and somehow we will return to this historical meaning of 'freedom of the press.' " Judge Scileppi also dissents vigorously saying, "It is inconceivable that judicial thinking can become so beclouded by unwarranted fears and spurious cries of censorship so as to result in giving constitutional protection to *Fanny Hill.* It is one of the foulest,

290

sexually immoral, debasing, lewd and obscene books ever published either in this country or abroad." He also adds, "If this
classic example of pornography is not obscene, then I doubt if
any written matter can be found to be obscene."

The Supreme Court must realize that every book, every movie
—in fact, every item allegedly obscene—contains just enough
differences that the decision on one need not necessarily be a
binding precedent on another. It is well known that *Tropic of
Cancer* and *Pleasure Was My Business* (the story of Madam
Sherry's brothel) are both entitled to constitutional protection.
Between the two we have every four-letter-word and most sexual
acts and perversions. Yet the courts are approaching *Fanny Hill*
as a new item—never really considered.

Here follows an excerpt from *Fanny Hill* to compare with
other selections:

The 16-year-old Fanny Hill meets Mr. H--- in a bar. He takes
her to his room and into his bed. Pleased with her sexual prowess,
he installs her in his home as his mistress. Inadvertently Fanny
sees him making love to a maid and revenges herself with a
virgin servant boy.

I was then lying at length upon that very couch, the scene of Mr. H . . .'s polite joys, in an undress which was with all the art of negligence flowing loose, and in a most tempting disorder: no stays, no hoop . . . no incumbrance whatever. On the other hand, he stood at a little distance, that gave me a full view of a fine featur'd, shapely, healthy country lad, breathing the sweets of fresh blooming youth; his hair, which was of a perfect shining black, play'd to his face in natural side-curls, and was set out with a smart tuck-up behind; new buckskin breeches, that, 'clipping close, shew'd the shape of a plump, well made thigh; white stockings, garter-lac'd livery, shoulder knot, altogether compos'd a figure in which the beauties of pure flesh and blood appeared under no disgrace from the lowness of a dress, to which a certain spruce neatness seems peculiarly fitted.

I bid him come towards me and give me his letter, at the same time throwing down, carelessly, a book I had in my hands. He colour'd, and came within reach of delivering me the letter, which he held out, aukwardly enough, for me to take, with his eyes riveted on my bosom, which was, through the design'd disorder of my handkerchief, sufficiently bare, and rather shaded than hid.

I, smiling in his face, took the letter, and immediately catching gently hold of his shirt sleeve, drew him towards me, blushing, and almost trembling; for surely his extreme bashfulness, and utter inexperience, call'd for, at least, all the advances to encourage him: his body was now conveniently inclin'd towards me, and just softly chucking his smooth beardless chin, I asked him if he was afraid

.. ..ady? . . . , and with that took, and carrying his hand to my breasts, I prest it tenderly to them. They were now finely furnish'd, and rais'd in flesh, so that, panting with desire, they rose and fell, in quick heaves, under his touch: at this, the boy's eyes began to lighten with all the fires of inflam'd nature, and his cheeks flush'd with a deep scarlet: tongue-tied with joy, rapture, and bashful-ness, he could not speak, but then his looks, his emotion, sufficiently satisfy'd me that my train had taken, and that I had no disappointment to fear.

My lips, which I threw in his way, so as that he could not escape kissing them, fix'd, fired, and embolden'd him: and now, glancing my eyes towards that part of his dress which cover'd the essential object of enjoyment, I plainly discover'd the swell and commotion there; and as I was now too far advanc'd to stop in so fair a way, and was indeed no longer able to contain myself, or wait the slower progress of his maiden bashfulness (for such it seem'd, and really was), I stole my hand upon his thighs, down one of which I could both see and feel a stiff hard body, confin'd by his breeches, that my fingers could dis-cover no end to. Curious then, and eager to unfold so alarming a mystery, playing, as it were, with his buttons, which were bursting ripe from the active force within, those of his waistband and fore-flap flew open at a touch, when out IT started; and now, disengag'd from the shirt, I saw, with wonder and surprise, what? not the play-thing of a boy, not the weapon of a man, but a maypole of so enormous a standard, that had proportions been observ'd, it must have belong'd to a young giant. Its prodigious size made me shrink again; yet I could not, without pleasure, behold, and even ventur'd to feel, such a length, such a breadth of animated ivory! perfectly well turn'd and fashion'd, the proud stiffness of which distended its skin, whose smooth polish and velvet softness might vie with that of the most delicate of our sex, and whose exquisite whiteness was not a little set off by a sprout of black curling hair round the root, through the jetty sprigs of which the fair skin shew'd as in a fine evening you may have remark'd the clear light æther through the branchwork of distant trees over-topping the summit of a hill: then the broad and blueish-casted incarnate of the head, and blue serpentines of its veins, altogether compos'd the most striking assemblage of figure and colours in nature. In short, it stood an object of terror and delight.

But what was yet more surprising, the owner of this natural curiosity, through the want of occasions in the strictness of his home-breeding, and the little time he had been in town not having afforded him one, was hitherto an absolute stranger, in practice at least, to the use of all that manhood he was so nobly stock'd with; and it now fell to my lot to stand his first trial of it, if I could resolve to run the risks of its disproportion to that tender part of me, which such an oversiz'd machine was very fit to lay in ruins.

But it was now of the latest to deliberate; for, by this time, the young fellow, overheated with the present objects, and too high mettled to be longer curb'd in by that modesty and awe which had hitherto restrain'd him, ventur'd, under the stronger impulse and instructive promptership of nature alone, to slip his hands, trembling with eager impetuous desires, under my petticoats; and seeing, I suppose, nothing extremely severe in my looks to stop or dash him, he feels out, and seizes, gently, the center-spot of his ardours. Oh then! the fiery touch of his fingers determines me, and my fears melting away before the glowing intolerable heat, my thighs disclose of themselves, and yield all liberty to his hand: and now, a favourable movement giving my petticoats a toss, the avenue lay too fair, too open to be miss'd. He is now upon me: I had placed myself with a jet under him, as commodious and open as possible to his attempts, which were untoward enough, for his machine, meeting with no inlet, bore and batter'd stiffly against me in random pushes, now above, now below, now beside his point; till, burning with impatience from its irritating touches, I guided gently, with my hand, this furious engine to where my young novice was now to be taught his first lesson of pleasure. Thus he nick'd, at length, the warm and insufficient orifice; but he was made to find no breach impracticable, and mine, tho' so often enter'd, was still far from wide enough to take him easily in.

By my direction, however, the head of his unwieldy machine was so critically pointed that, feeling him fore-right against the tender opening, a favourable motion from me met his timely thrust, by which the lips of it, strenuously dilated, gave way to his thus assisted impetuosity, so that we might both feel that he had gain'd a lodgment. Pursuing then his point, he soon, by violent, and, to me, most painful piercing thrusts, wedges himself at length so far in, as to be now tolerably secure of his entrance: here he stuck, and I now felt such a mixture of pleasure and pain, as there is no giving a definition of. I dreaded alike his splitting me farther up, or his withdrawing; I could not bear either to keep or part with him. The sense of pain however prevailing, from his prodigious size and stiffness, acting upon me in those continued rapid thrusts, with which he furiously pursu'd his penetration, made me cry out gently: "Oh! my dear, you hurt me!" This was enough to check the tender respectful boy even in his mid-career; and he immediately drew out the sweet cause of my complaint, whilst his eyes eloquently express'd, at once, his grief for hurting me, and his reluctance at dislodging from quarters of which the warmth and closeness had given him a gust of pleasure that he was now desire-mad to satisfy, and yet too much a novice not to be afraid of my withholding his relief, on account of the pain he had put me to.

But I was, myself, far from being pleas'd with his having too much regarded my tender exclaims; for now, more and more fired with the object before me, as it still stood with the fiercest erection, unbonnetted, and displaying its broad vermilion head, I first gave the youth a re-encouraging kiss, which he repaid me with a fervour that seem'd at once to thank me, and bribe my farther compliance; and soon replac'd myself in a posture to receive, at all risks, the renew'd invasion, which he did not delay an instant: for, being presently remounted, I once more felt the smooth hard gristle forcing an entrance, which he achiev'd rather easier than before. Pain'd, however, as I was, with his efforts of gaining a complete admission, which he was so regardful as to manage by gentle degrees, I took care not to complain. In the meantime, the soft strait passage gradually loosens, yields, and, stretch'd to its utmost bearing, by the stiff, thick, indriven engine, sensible, at once, to the ravishing pleasure of the *feel* and the pain of the distension, let him in about half way, when all the most nervous activity he now exerted, to further his penetration, gain'd him not an inch of his purpose: for, whilst he hesitated there, the crisis of pleasure overtook him, and the close compressure of the warm surrounding fold drew from him the extatic gush, even before mine was ready to meet it, kept up by the pain I had endur'd in the course of the engagement, from the insufferable size of his weapon, tho' it was not as yet in above half its length.

I expected then, but without wishing it, that he would draw, but was pleasantly disappointed: for he was not to be let off so. The well breath'd youth, hot-mettled, and flush with genial juices, was now fairly in for making me know my driver. As soon, then, as he had made a short pause, waking, as it were, out of the trance of pleasure (in which every sense seem'd lost for a while, whilst, with his eyes shut, and short quick breathing, he had yielded down his maiden tribute), he still kept his post, yet un-sated with enjoyment, and solacing in these so new de-lights; till his stiffness, which had scarce perceptibly remitted, being thoroughly recovered to him, who had not once unsheath'd, he proceeded afresh to cleave and open to himself an entire entry into me, which was not a little made easy to him by the balsamic injection with which he had just plentifully moisten'd the whole in-ternals of the passage. Redoubling, then, the active energy of his thrusts, favoured by the fervid appetite of my motions, the soft oiled wards can no longer stand so effectual a picklock, but yield, and open him an entrance. And now, with conspiring nature, and my industry, strong to aid him, he pierces, penetrates, and at length, winning his way inch by inch, gets entirely in, and finally mighty thrust sheaths it up to the guard; on the information of which, from the close jointure of our bodies (insomuch that the hair on both sides perfectly interweav'd and incircl'd together), the eyes of the transported youth sparkl'd with more joyous fires, and all his looks and motions acknowledged excess of pleasure, which I now began to share, for I felt him in my very vitals! I was quite sick with delight! stir'd beyond bearing with its furious agitations within me, and gorged and cramm'd, even to surfeit. Thus I lay gasping, panting under him, till his broken breathings, faltering accents, eyes twinkling with humid fires, lunges more furious, and an increased stiffness, gave me to hail the approaches of the second period: it came . . . and the sweet youth, overpower'd with the extasy, died away in my arms, melting in a flood that shot in genial warmth into the innermost recesses of my body; every conduit of which, dedicated to that pleasure, was on flow to mix with it. Thus we continued for some instants, lost, breathless, senseless of every thing, and in every part but those favourite ones of nature, in which all that we enjoyed of life and sensation was now totally concentre'd.

When our mutual trance was a little over, and the young fellow had withdrawn that delicious stretcher, with which he had most plentifully drowned all thoughts of revenge in the sense of actual pleasure, the widen'd wounded passage refunded a stream of pearly liquids, which flowed down my thighs, mixed with streaks of blood, the marks of the ravage of that monstrous machine of his, which had now triumph'd over a kind of second maidenhead. I stole, however, my handkerchief to those parts, and wip'd them as dry as I could, whilst he was re-adjusting and buttoning up.

I made him now sit down by me, and as he had gather'd courage from such extreme intimacy, he gave me an aftercourse of pleasure, in a natural burst of tender gratitude and joy, at the new scenes of bliss I had opened to him: scenes positively new, as he had never before had the least acquaintance with that mysterious mark, the cloven stamp of female distinction, tho' nobody better qualify'd than he to penetrate into its deepest recesses, or do it nobler justice. But when, by certain motions, certain unquietnesses of his hands, that wandered not without design, I found he languish'd for satisfying a curiosity, natural enough, to view and handle those parts which attract and concentre the warmest force of imagination, charmed as I was to have any occasion of obliging and humouring his young desires, I suffer'd him to proceed as he pleased, without check or control, to the satisfaction of them.

Easily, then, reading in my eyes the full permission of myself to all his wishes, he scarce pleased himself more than me when, having insinuated his hand under my petticoat and shift, he presently removed those bars to the sight by slyly lifting them upwards, under favour of a thousand kisses, which he thought, perhaps, necessary to divert my attention from what he was about. All my drapery being now roll'd up to my waist, I threw myself into such a posture upon the couch, as gave up to him, in full view, the whole region of delight, and all the luxurious landscape round it. The transported youth devour'd every thing with his eyes, and try'd, with his fingers, to lay more open to his sight the secrets of that dark and

delicious deep: he opens the folding lips, the softness of
which, yielding entry to any thing of a hard body, close
round it, and oppose the sight: and feeling further, meets
with, and wonders at, a soft fleshy excrescence, which,
limber and relaxed after the late enjoyment, now grew,
under the touch and examination of his fiery fingers,
more and more stiff and considerable, till the titillating
ardours of that so sensible part made me sigh, as if he
had hurt me; on which he withdrew his curious probing
fingers, asking me pardon, as it were, in a kiss that rather
increased the flame *there*.

Novelty ever makes the strongest impressions, and in
pleasures, especially; no wonder, then, that he was swal-
lowed up in raptures of admiration of things so interesting by their nature, and now seen and handled for the
first time. On my part, I was richly overpaid for the
pleasure I gave him, in that of examining the power of
those objects thus abandon'd to him, naked and free to
his loosest wish, over the artless, natural stripling: his
eyes streaming fire, his cheeks glowing with a florid red,
his fervid frequent sighs, whilst his hands convulsively
squeez'd, opened, pressed together again the lips and sides
of that deep flesh wound, or gently twitched the over-
growing moss; and all proclaimed the excess, the riot of
joys, in having his wantonness thus humour'd. But he
did not long abuse my patience, for the objects before
him had now put him by all his, and, coming out with
that formidable machine of his, he lets the fury loose, and
pointing it directly to the pouting-lipt mouth, that bid
him sweet defiance in dumb-shew, squeezes in the head,
and, driving with refreshed rage, breaks in, and plugs up
the whole passage of that soft pleasure-conduit, where he

makes all shake again, and put, once more, all within me into such an uproar, as nothing could still but a fresh inundation from the very engine of those flames, as well as from all the springs with which nature floats that reservoir of joy, when risen to its flood-mark.

I was now so bruised, so batter'd, so spent with this over-match, that I could hardly stir, or raise myself, but lay palpitating, till the ferment of my sense subsiding by degrees, and the hour striking at which I was oblig'd to dispatch my young man, I tenderly advised him of the necessity there was for parting; which I felt as much displeasure at as he could do, who seemed eagerly disposed to keep the field, and to enter on a fresh action. But the danger was too great, and after some hearty kisses of leave, and recommendations of secrecy and discretion, I forc'd myself to send him away, not without assurances of seeing him again, to the same purpose, as soon as possible, and thrust a guinea into his hands: not more, lest, being too flush of money, a suspicion or discovery might arise from thence, having everything to fear from the dangerous indiscretion of that age in which young fellows would be too irresistible, too charming, if we had not that terrible fault to guard against.

And, amusingly enough from an observer's view, or damnably from a seller's or publisher's view, the decision on *Fanny Hill* will not end the matter. For example, in Pennsylvania, following *Tropic* and *Pleasure* the district attorneys and police accepted *Fanny Hill* as reasonably covered by the earlier decisions. But in January of 1965 the paperback editions of *Candy* arrived on the newsstands. Immediately, the District Attorney of Philadelphia instituted action[21] to have it declared obscene and to enjoin its distribution and sale. A few days later the District Attorney of Delaware County, Pennsylvania, announced that he had advised the newsstand dealers in his jurisdiction that *Candy* was obscene and they should not sell it.[22]

The book was originally published in Paris in 1958, credited to the pseudonym "Maxwell Kenton," although written by Terry Southern and Mason Hoffenberg, two brilliant American writers. Intended as a spoof of pornography, it won instant acclaim. The following sample is typical of the book.

(Candy's boy friend, Grindle, who has been teaching her yoga, is about to give her the next lesson. They have walked alone to a quiet pool in the woods.)

"It's good that you wear that simple shift," he said, matter-of-factly, "it will expedite the next lesson considerably."

"Are we really to have another mystical lesson now!" exclaimed Candy in sheer delight, actually giving a little jump of joy; it was all *too* perfect already! And now another mystical lesson as well! She sat down eagerly on the fluffy bed of moss, arranged her skirt primly, tucking it under her precious knees, getting comfortable and making her mind ready and alert, just the way she had always done in the interesting courses at school. She had a momentary regret that she didn't have her notebook and pencil along, but she quickly dismissed this thought for the infinitely more preferable notion of Arcadia, with the students sitting around under the trees, listening to the master talk, and *not* taking notes but absorbing everything, everything. That's the *pure* way and the *true way*, thought Candy and was extremely pleased.

"First," said Grindle, sitting down beside her, "we'll want to get out of this worldly apparel." And he began taking off his wet shoes. Then he started undoing his trousers.

"Do we *have* to?" asked the girl uneasily; she hadn't anticipated this and was somehow put off by the idea.

" 'Put your house in order,' " quoted Grindle, " 'that is the *first* step.' Certainly we must divest ourselves of all material concern—in both spirit and body."

"Right!" said Candy firmly, in an effort to dispel the great warm reservoir of feminine modesty she felt glowing up inside her and finally flushing her pretty face, as she slipped out of the simple garment.

"There!" she said pertly, and in an abrupt little movement that spoke well of her bravery, she put aside the simple shift, which was all she was wearing, and gave a little sigh of relief that she had actually been able to do it; and yet, even as she was sensing a certain pride and accomplishment in the feat, her sweet face flushed maidenly rose as, under Grindle's gaze, she felt her smart little nipples tauten and distend, as though they, alerted now, had a life quite their own.

"Good!" said Grindle. "Now then, lace your fingers together, in the yoga manner, and place them behind your head. Yes, just so. Now then, lie back on the mossy bed."

"Oh gosh," said Candy, feeling apprehensive, and as she obediently lay back, she raised one of her handsome thighs slightly, turning it inward, pressed against the other, in a charmingly coy effort to conceal her marvelous little spice-box.

"No, no," said Grindle, coming forward to make adjustments, "legs well apart."

At his touch, the darling girl started in fright and dif-
fidence, but Grindle was quick to reassure her.

"I'm a doctor of the soul," he said coldly; "I am certainly not interested in that silly little body of yours—it is
the *spirit* that concerns us here. Now is that understood?"

"Yes," answered the girl meekly, lying very still now
and allowing him to adjust her limbs, just so, well apart,
and turned out slightly.

"Eyes closed," said Grindle firmly, and when Candy
had obeyed, he sat back and surveyed the whole.

"Good!" he said at last. "Now then. This lesson will be
devoted to the transcendence of the bodily senses. Under
my guidance you shall achieve the ability to master all
bodily feeling. Is that clear?"

"Yes," whispered the closed-eyed girl. She was greatly
reassured by Grindle's tone, which was like that of an
instructor in logic, but she was still flushing and somewhat
annoyed with the way her pert little nips kept pulsing and
pouting. Those bad little smart alecks! she thought crossly
to herself.

Great Grindle leaned forward with outstretched fingers
and allowed them to play idly across the golden melon of
the girl's budding tummy. She moved a bit and even gave
a little nervous laugh.

"Now, now," said Grindle sharply, "you're not a child!
Try to be serious! The mystic path is not an easy one—
many take it, few arrive."

Under this admonishment the girl sobered quickly
enough and tried to order her thoughts.

"Now this is a so-called 'erogenous zone,'" explained

Grindle, gingerly taking one of the perfect little nipples which did so seem to be begging for attention between his thumb and forefinger, turning it gently back and forth.

"*I'll* say," the girl agreed, squirming despite her efforts to be serious.

"Yes," said Grindle, nodding sagely, "and this too, of course," taking the other one now, giving it a series of fondling tweaks, while the girl stirred uneasily.

"Now then," said Grindle, abandoning the nipples for the moment, leaving them there, like two tiny heads, craning up eagerly, and allowing his hands to caress slowly down the wondrous arch of Candy's delightful body, down the sides, along the hips and over the inner thighs to converge in the golden down, beneath which the fabulous lamb-pit was sweetening itself.

"Oh gosh," the girl murmured, as Grindle carefully turned back the rose-petal labes and revealed, in all its tiny splendor, the magnificent little jewel, the pink pearl clit, shimmering, it seemed, in absurdly delicious readiness.

"This is *another* of these so-called 'erogenous zones,' " announced Grindle contemptuously, addressing the perfect thing with his finger, giving it several gentle flicks.

"*And how,*" Candy was quick to agree, fidgeting now in spite of her attempts at control.

Great Grindle applied himself to massaging the clit adroitly.

"Goodness . . ." said the girl in soft fretfulness, ". . . I didn't know it was going to be like *this*."

"Yes, you must master these feelings," said Grindle easily. "One who is not master of his feelings is not master of his house—he is like the reed, tossed on the waves of chance. Tell me, how does it feel now?"

The lovely girl's great eyelids were fluttering.

"Oh, it's all tingling and everything," she admitted despairingly.

"First," said Grindle, continuing the massage, "you will learn *transcendence* of the senses, and in that way will you soar above all sensory concern; next you will learn *control* of the senses, whereby you may come at will—instantaneous orgasm, untouched, at my command."

He stopped the massage and raised himself to his knees.

"Open your eyes," he said. "I will show you an example of such control. You will notice that I have caused my member to become stout and rigid—as though it were in the so-called state of 'erection.' "

It was true, as the girl saw soon enough—Grindle close at hand displaying his taut member, and she flushed terribly and averted her eyes.

"No, no," said Grindle, raising her demure chin with his hand, "do not allow vulgar sexual or material associations to bear upon the matter—it is a demonstration of perfect sensory control. I have merely willed the member to become stout and rigid. It resembles the so-called *erection,* does it not? In the sixth stage, one masters *all* such muscular control, even that which is most involuntary— thus can one, by the will of the advanced intellect, achieve what was theretofore a secret of nature. Regard how I have willed my member: no base or material desire is connected with it, yet it resembles the so-called sexual erection. Does it not?"

The sweet girl nodded shyly, scarcely able to look.

"Yes. Touch it," said Grindle, "you will see for yourself."

He took her hand and encouraged it forward, and she touched it lightly. Being able to regard it now, impersonally, not as an object of lust but as a demonstration of spiritual advancement, made it a thing of interest to the young girl and she examined it curiously, touching it here and there, still with a certain reserve because of her past fearful associations—which she knew though, to be sure, were her own fault.

"You can squeeze it if you like," prompted Grindle, ". . . yes, do."

Candy squeezed the swollen member interestedly in her delicate grasp, and what appeared to be a drop of semen formed on the end.

"There!" said Grindle, in a manner of triumph. "See that drop—that's an example of *glandular* mastery as well! It is extremely rare. The late Rama Krishna approximated it, but did not fully achieve it in the end. I have willed the intricate chemistry and secretion of the fluid."

"Gosh," said Candy, raising her beautiful eyes to the great man, her face radiant now in frank reverence.

"Now resume the basic yoga position," said Grindle, "and I will continue with the instruction."

Candy lay back again with a sigh, closed-eyed, hands joined behind her head, and Grindle resumed his fondling of her sweet-dripping little fur-pie.

"Does the tingling sensation you referred to before continue and increase?" he asked after a moment or so.

". . . I'm afraid so," said the girl sadly, panting a little.

"And do you experience feelings of creamy warmth and a great yielding sensation?" demanded Grindle.

"Yes," Candy sighed, thinking he was surely psychic.

"Now I'm going to put this member into you," said Grindle judiciously, "and in that way can the sensation of the so-called 'sexual act' be approximated and surveyed to advantage."

"Oh gosh," said Candy in real disquiet, unable, despite her efforts, to shake off all the old associations it had for her, ". . . do we really *have* to?" And, almost in reflex, she drew her marvelous thighs a bit closer together.

"Never mind your crass and absurdly cheap philistine materialist associations with it," said Grindle crossly, as he adjusted her legs again and ranged himself just above her. "Put those from your mind—concentrate on your *Exercise Number Four,* for always remember that we must bring *all* our mystical knowledge to converge on the issue at hand— even as does the tiger his strength, cunning, and speed."

"Now I am inserting the member," he explained, as he parted the tender quavering lips of the pink honeypot and allowed his stout member to be drawn slowly into the seething thermal pudding of the darling girl.

"Oh my goodness," said Candy, squirming her lithe and supple body slightly, though remaining obediently closed-eyed and with her hands clasped tightly behind her head.

"Now I shall remove the member," said Grindle, ". . . not all the way, but just so, there, and in again. You see? And again so, I will repeat this, several times—while you do your Exercise Number Four."

"Gosh," said Candy, swallowing nervously, ". . . I don't think I can concentrate on it now."

"Oh yes," said Grindle, encouraging her hips with his hands, setting them into the motion of the Cosmic Rhythm Exercise she had practiced earlier in the rec-tent. And when she had satisfactorily achieved the motion, Grindle said: "Now this, you see, approximates the so-called 'sexual act.' "

"I *know* it," said Candy fretfully, greatly distracted by the thought.

"I shall presently demonstrate still another mastery of glandular functions," claimed great Grindle, "that of the so-called *orgasm*, or *ejaculation*."

"Oh please," said the adorable girl, actually alarmed, "not . . . not *inside* me . . . I . . . I . . ."

"Don't be absurd," said Grindle, breathing heavily, "naturally, in willing the chemistry of the semen, I would eliminate the impregnating agent, spermatozoa, as a constituent—for it would be of no use to our purposes here you see."

"Now then," he continued after a moment, "tell me if this does not almost exactly resemble the philistine 'orgasm'?"

". . . Oh gosh," murmured the darling closed-eyed girl, biting her lip as the burning member began to throb and spurt inside her, in a hot, ravaging flood of her precious little honey-cloister whose bleating pink-sugar walls cloyed and writhed as though alive with a thousand tiny insatiable tongues, ". . . *and how!*"

After reading the extracts of *Tropic of Cancer, Pleasure Was My Business, Fanny Hill,* and *Candy* can the reader make an intelligent differentiation? It seems apparent that the intellectually honest analyst must conclude that the differences among these books—if differences there be, pornographically speaking—are without distinction. And even if they are all cleared, interested parties are not out of the woods yet. In the field of classics is de Sade's *120 Days of Sodom* and—with respect to modern writings—*The Housewife's Handbook on Selective Promiscuity* and *Sex Life of a Cop.*

No publisher has had the temerity to produce de Sade's fanciful flight into pornography. But *The Housewife's Handbook* earned a publisher five years in prison and a $28,000 fine[23] and the novel about a policeman's sexual experiences resulted in sentences of 25 and 15 years and $69,000 in fines![24] This is truly an emotional field. Both cases are on their way to the Supreme Court and when that court rules we may learn some more about the subject. But will we have a solution to this never ending problem? Probably not. The *ad hoc* system of deciding each item without particular regard to any other will not end the dilemma.

Some intermediate solution must be found. Perhaps Curtis Bok's view—"Show me that the item is about to cause a crime to be committed"—may be resurrected. If so, it will be very close to the theory that nothing is obscene. Possibly the author's theory of differentiating between general-circulation media, such as television, and limited material like books will be accepted. Stranger events have occurred!

Epilogue

This book took several years to prepare. Of course, a considerable amount of time was consumed in trying to locate specific items like the October, 1954 issue of *One—The Homosexual Magazine* and other similar items. As I sit here reviewing the page proof, checking some of the cases, and looking at the material in broad perspective, I cannot help but compare the law and the factual situation today with what it was several years ago when I began to gather these materials. During this period we have had many decisions and a large number of court opinions from the lowest *nisi prius* courts up to the solemn pronouncements of the United States Supreme Court. We have probably had more decisions and opinions in the past three years than we had before in three centuries. Has this literal flood of court opinions helped clarify the confused legal situation? Looking backward and trying to achieve an astronaut's viewpoint of the field, I must conclude that the spate of judicial decisions has not helped to bring order out of the obscenity chaos but rather has served to compound the confusion.

For example, in 1961 the highest court of New York, then a reasonably conservative court, undertook to decide whether the magazine *Gent* could be regarded as obscene because, as the judge said, "The contents, like the cover, exhibit the same attempt to pander to and commercialize upon man's taste for the bawdy and the ribald behind the bad disguise of aesthetic respectability." In addition, the judge points out that the magazine contained "'artistic' photographs, salacious cartoons and short stories of sexual seduction." A very fine judge, Stanley Fuld, wrote a cogent opinion rejecting the obscenity contention. Later courts throughout the country tended to follow this decision. In the next several years I believe that most attorneys were prepared to render legal opinions that the routine and average girlie magazine was not legally obscene and would not be prohibited. Only a few weeks ago the Supreme Court of Arkansas issued a startling decision in which it found a series of girlie magazines, including *Gent, Swank, Modern Man, Bachelor, Cavalcade, Gentlemen, Ace,* and *Sir* all obscene and not legally able to be distributed in that state. The Arkansas opinion is by Chief Justice Carleton and states that even though there are articles in these magazines which could not be considered obscene, nevertheless "their dominant theme appeals only to the coarse and base in man's nature and any literary merit is entirely coincidental."

The Arkansas Chief Justice also makes two additional points:

1. A careful study of all of the United States Supreme Court decisions in this field indicates that there is no guide line and no criteria for deciding what is and what is not obscene and therefore each state must make up its own law.

2. Despite Mr. Justice Brennan's opinion that the standards of decency are national standards, insufficient Supreme Court Justices agreed with this opinion, so the Arkansas court would reach its own decision, and would reject the existence of a national standard. In Arkansas girlie magazines are illegal!

By itself the opinion of the Arkansas Supreme Court would be regarded as an amusing sport or freak. However, when placed into appropriate juxtaposition with the entire fabric of magazine publishing it ceases to be humorous, or amusing. We can safely assume that if the decision stands there will be other bible belt states that will reach a similar conclusion. If this be so it must have the severest impact on magazine publishing. Magazine publishing and distribution being what it is, few magazines can

314

survive without universal distribution. It takes an enormous amount of unusual and expensive handling to publish a magazine and then tell the national and local distributors that they must keep it out of Arkansas. In addition, if much of the market is taken away from a magazine it can no longer survive economically. Indeed, it is hard to believe that the United States Supreme Court will sustain a decision of this kind.

In the field of books we have the unusual and perverse situation in which recently the Supreme Judicial Court of Massachusetts (highest court) found *Fanny Hill* obscene and not distributable in that state. This is a real twist. Massachusetts, together with Wisconsin and California, upheld *Tropic of Cancer* and found it not obscene. The Massachusetts view was sustained by the United States Supreme Court. At the same time the Court rejected a state court's ban on *Pleasure Was My Business,* a simple narrative of life in and the operation of a brothel. There is basically no distinguishable difference between *Pleasure Was My Business* and *Fanny Hill.* Under normal circumstances anyone would expect the Supreme Judicial Court of Massachusetts to be pleased at its own perspicacious discernment in being on the right side in *Tropic* and, adding that to the United States Supreme Court view in *Pleasure,* would reach the conclusion that *Fanny Hill* (already cleared of obscenity in New York state) was not prohibitable under the obscenity doctrines. But this is a frustrating field in which the courts refuse to follow logic. It is an emotional field and with a change in personnel and the retirement of one judge and the appointment of another, a former minority becomes a majority and adopts a new view, whether it be accurate or not!

The total confusion is not even confined to books and magazines, although it is certainly widespread in that field. Until recently most attorneys would have expressed the opinion that a work of sculpture was completely immune from legal attack under the obscenity doctrine, unless the sculpture was in complete bad taste *and in addition* was exhibited to children, or a captive audience that did not want to see it. Certainly, the sculptor was free to develop his own art forms if he exhibited them privately or in an art gallery. Following this theory of our law we have the sculpture of Ron Boise, a 32 year old Colorado sculptor who fashions figures out of the remains of junked automobiles. Recently Boise exhibited eleven sculptures from his *Kama Sutra* theme at the San Francisco Vorpal Gallery. The police, unable to countenance the exhibition, arrested the gallery owner and a salesman and confiscated all the sculptures. There followed a nine-day trial which, as far as I know, is the first time in modern history that sculpture was ever on trial under the obscenity theory. The jury of seven men and five women acquitted the defendants and the impounded statuary was returned.

It is true that the sculpture of Ron Boise is "way out." Boise is probably to sculpture what Henry Miller is to novels—an iconoclast breaking all the rules of sexual inhibition. (See examples following.) However, this is not material that can get into the hands of a child, or that will arouse a teenager—this is adult stuff that appeals only to aesthetic and artistic sophisticates who can scarcely be harmed by it. Nevertheless, our American police feel called upon to invoke the heavyhanded processes of the criminal law in order to stop it! Truly, this is an emotional field!

However, despite all of the drag exerted by the police and the courts we are unquestionably moving forward toward greater freedom in art, literature, and even daily living. In California the topless bathing suit has become acceptable not only at the swimming pool but even in the nightclub as approved attire for waitresses. Courts are still holding magazines obscene because of semi-nude pictures, while juries are acquitting defendants making the same portrayal in the flesh. In general, we are in a confused situation but sometimes all law confuses greatest just before clarification, just as frequently the storm hits its greatest intensity shortly before clearing. The United States Supreme Court has some important cases before it and there is always the possibility that the Court will perceive the befuddled state of the law and the justices will come to agreement on creating some order out of the chaos. Unfortunately, since the judges are only human, they are of many different shades of opinions and they may find it difficult to arrive at a common solution.

I did not at any point in the text discuss Thurman Arnold's suggestion made in a brief filed with the Supreme Court of Vermont. This stalwart of the American Bar advocated the thesis that the Supreme Court of the United States should *not* try to define what was obscene and the Court's eschewal of the opportunity to set up definitive rules of law describing and delimiting obscenity was "exceedingly wise," because "no one can reason why anything is or is not obscene. . . . The Court," Arnold points out, "evidently concluded that its actions must speak for themselves in this field. This may be an unconventional way of making law, but in the field of pornography it is certainly sound judicial common sense."

Until recently Arnold's praise of the Court's refusal to set up guidelines on this subject was not overly significant so long as he was a solitary voice in the loud and raucous babble that we call obscenity law, but with the elevation of his partner, Abe Fortas, to the High Court, this unusual approach could acquire new significance.

Finally, there has just come to hand the latest publication of the Institute of Sex Research, Inc., popularly known as the Kinsey Institute. This volume, entitled *Sex Offenders,* is a study in depth of what makes the sex criminal tick.

The book furnishes little comfort to the censorious who have contended for many years that pornography is a definite cause of the commission of sexual crimes by many (if not all) such offenders. On the contrary this new study of more than 2,000

317

sex offenses (1,685 offenders) makes the following significant points:

1. "When one reads in a newspaper that obscene or pornographic materials were found in an individual's possession, one should interpret this information to mean that (1) the individual was probably a male of an age between puberty and senility, and (2) that he probably derived pleasure from thinking about sex. No further inferences are warranted." (Page 404)

2. "Summing up the evidence, it would appear that the possession of pornography does not differentiate sex offenders from non-sex offenders." (Page 678)

3. Study of the pornography men collect may show something of the men but it is the men who are what they are *before* collecting the pornography. "Men made the collections, collections do not make the men." (Page 678)

4. The response to the stimulus of pornography is in direct ratio to the subject's education, sensitivity, imaginativeness, etc. Since the majority of sex offenders are not well endowed with these qualities, "their responsiveness to pornography is correspondingly less and cannot be a consequential factor in their sex offenses unless one is prepared to argue that the inability to respond to erotica in general precludes gaining some vicarious stimulation and satisfaction and thereby causes the individual to behave overtly which, in turn, renders him more liable to arrest and conviction." (Page 673) As to the latter I comment that the argument at best indicates that it is the individual's *inability* to respond to pornography that would be the cause of the crime, *not* the pornography.

Those judges, regardless of their position in the obscenity law dispute, who have the intellectual honesty to accept the scientific value of the Kinsey Study on sex offenders must conclude that the old bromide about a causal relationship between sexual transgression and pornography is false. If so, these judges will no longer be able to punish writers, publishers and movie exhibitors except on the only remaining foundation for the prohibition of obscenity, namely, its offensiveness.

Once the courts accept this thesis, punishment must be reserved for those who actually offend—e.g., the man who addresses "dirty words" to a sensitive woman or who shows stag films to pubescents. But the writer, publisher and seller of a book—any book—who confines his dealings to the mature—will be immune from attack from any quarter. In effect, the law will be adopting the doctrine espoused by Chief Justice Earl Warren (albeit not presently being observed by him) who said in the *Kingsley Book* case, " It is the manner of use that should determine obscenity. It is the conduct of the individual that should be judged, not the quality of art or literature. To do otherwise is to . . . violate the Constitution."

Paraphrasing the Chief Justice I conclude with the plea: Let us punish people, not things. In the abstract no book, movie, play, sculpture or drawing can possibly be obscene. Examine what the defendant does with it. If an adult male reads De Sade to a *Lolita* (without parental consent) few tears will be shed if he is punished—the conduct has little, if any, social utility. But the publisher or bookseller of the same book who confines sales to willing-to-buy adults should not be criticized, let alone punished.

Ron Boise's Sculptures

FOOTNOTES

PART I

1. The Supreme Court decision is discussed in a later section. However, the statement in the text is not entirely correct. In November' 1964, upon order from a trial court judge, the District Attorney of Philadelphia arrested two booksellers for selling *Tropic of Cancer.* The judge, sitting as a committing magistrate, ruled (in effect) that the book was still obscene and he held the men for action of the grand jury. Thus, technically and temporarily, this book is *obscene* in Philadelphia. Commonwealth v. John Hastings and Samuel Sokolove, Q. Sess. Ct., Nov. Term, 1964, Nos. 1583 and 1584.

2. See Lockhart and McClure, *Literature, the Law of Obscenity, and the Constitution,* 38 MINN. L. REV. 295 (1954) and Fischer, *The Harm Good People Do,* HARPER'S, Oct., 1956, p. 14. Answered by Murray, *The Bad Arguments Intelligent Man Makes,* AMERICA, Nov. 3, 1956, p. 120.

3. Kingsley Books, Inc. v. Brown, 354 U.S. 436 (1957) .

4. A special statute, Section 22a of the Criminal Procedure Code, to permit injunctions *after* publication.

5. Times Film Corp. v. Chicago, 355 U.S. 35 (1958) .

6. ERNST and SCHWARTZ, CENSORSHIP: THE SEARCH for the OBSCENE (1964) 150.

7. Jacobellis v. Ohio, 378 U.S. 184 (1964).

8. People v. Larsen, 5 N.Y.S. 2nd 55 (Bronx Crim. Ct. 1938).

9. People v. Birch, 40 Misc. 2nd 626, 343 N.Y.S. 2nd 525 (1963).

10. Sept. 25, 1963, p. 55.

11. Sept. 2, 1963.

12. Sept. 2, 1963.

13. 2 S. & R. 91 (Pa. Sup. Ct. 1815) .

14. 335 U.S. 848 (1948).

15. See COLEMAN, OBSCENITY BLASPHEMY SEDITION (Censorship in Australia) (Brisbane, The Jacaronda Press) .

16. Koyama v. State, 11 J. Sup. Ct. Crim. 987 (1957), (1959) 75 L. Q. Rev. 103. See Tokikumi, *Obscenity and the Japanese Constitution,* 51 KY. L. J. 703 (1963).

17. IVERSEN, THE PIOUS PORNOGRAPHERS (1964) 69.

18. Affidavit of Barney Rosset, principal editor of Grove Press, Inc., in Grove Press, Inc. v. Calissi, 208 F. Supp. 580 (D.N.J. 1962).

19. Commonwealth v. Robin, No. 3177, C.P. Phila., 1962.

20. People v. Smith, App. Dep't, Super. Ct. 1962, *cert. granted,* 373 U.S. 901 (1963).

21. Heiman v. Morris, No. 61, S. 19718, Super. Ct. Cook County, Ill. 1962.

22. Attorney-General v. "Tropic of Cancer," 345 Mass. 11, 184 N.E. 2nd 328 (1962).

23. McCauley v. Tropic of Cancer, 20 Wis. 2d 134, 121 N.W. 2d 545 (1963).

24. Zeitlin v. Arnebergh, 383 P. 2d 152, 31 Cal. Rptr. 800 (Sup. Ct. 1963).

25. 13 N.Y. 2d 119, 192 N.E. 2d 713, 243 N.Y.S. 2d 1 (1963).

26. Grove Press, Inc. v. Gerstein, 84 Sup. Ct. 1909 (1964), rev'g, 156 S. 2d 537 (Fla. App. 1963).

PART II

1. See Alpert, *Judicial Censorship of Obscene Literature,* 52 HARV. L. REV. 40 (1938).

2. LeRoy v. Sr. Charles Sedley, Keble 620 (K.B. 1663).

3. In earlier treatises on allied topics we get no reference to obscenity or even "obscene libel" as it became known. For example see Coke's *De Lipellis Famosis* (1606). "From 1640 until 1727, all obscenity offenses were relegated to the jurisdiction of the ecclesiastical courts." Slough and McAnany, *Obscenity and Constitutional Freedom*—I, 8 ST. LOUIS L. REV. 279, 281 n. 9 (1964).

4. Fortescue 98, 92 Eng. Rep. 777 (K.B. 1708).

5. Rex v. Curll 2 Strange 788, 93 Eng. Rep. 849 (K.B. 1727). For additional details consult Straus, *The Unspeakable Curll* (1927).

6. See POSTGATE, THAT DEVIL WILKES (1956) and BLEAKLY, LIFE OF JOHN WILKES (1917).

7. POSTGATE, pp. 24-25.

8. For an interesting description of the original printing and some explanation of the cryptic references in the poem, see SCOTT, INTO WHOSE HANDS (Waron Press Ed. 1961) p. 88.

9. Murray v. Benbow, Jac. 474 n. (Ch. 1822).

10. Lord Byron v. Dugdale, 1 L.J. Ch. 239 (1823).

11. Alpert, *Supr,* note 1, p. 50.

12. 2 Townsend's Mod. St. Trials 356. See also 146 HANSARD, PARLIAMENTARY DEBATES (1857) 1357-61.

13. L.R. 3 Q.B. 360 (1868).

14. These are references to a number of theological authorities of the period.

15. A Catholic college for the priesthood.

16. Commonwealth v. Friede, 271 Mass. 318, 171 N.E. 472 (1930).

17. 2 S. & R. 91 (Pa. Sup. Ct. 1815).

18. JOHNSON, HOD-CARRIER (1964) 67.

19. Commonwealth v. Holmes, 17 Mass. 336 (1821).

20. BROUN AND LEECH, ANTHONY COMSTOCK: ROUNDSMAN OF THE LORD (1927); TRUMBULL, ANTHONY COMSTOCK, FIGHTER (1913) (an approved-by-Comstock biography).

21. 18 U.S.C. Sec. 1461 (1948).

22. 11 Blatch. 346 (S.D.N.Y. 1873).

23. 96 U.S. 727 (1878).

24. 24 Fed. Cas. 1093 (No. 14571) (C.C.S.D.N.Y. 1879).

25. United States v. Clarke, 38 Fed. 500 (E.D. Mo. 1889).

26. United States v. Rosen, 161 U.S. 29 (1896).

27. 209 Fed. 119 (S.D.N.Y. 1913).

28. Commonwealth v. Friede, 271 Mass. 318, 171 N.E. 472 (1930).

29. See Grant and Angoff, *Massachusetts and Censorship* (1930) 10 B.U.L. REV. 36.

30. United States v. Dennett, 39 F. 2d 564 (2d Cir. 1930).

31. ERNST AND SCHWARTZ, CENSORSHIP: THE SEARCH FOR THE OBSCENE (1964) 94-95.

32. United States v. One Book Called "Ulysses," 5 F. Supp. 182 (S.D.N.Y. 1933), *aff'd,* 72 F. 2d 705 (2d Cir. 1934).

33. People v. Viking Press, 147 Misc. 813, 264 N.Y. Supp. 534 (Mag. Ct. 1933).

34. 326 Mass. 281, 93 N.E. 2d 819 (1949).

35. Chicago v. Kirkland, 79 F. 2d 963 (7th Cir. 1935).

36. 66 Pa. D. & C. 101 (Phila. 1949).

PART III

1. Doubleday & Co. v. New York, 335 U.S. 848 (1948).
2. 99 F. Supp. 760 (N.D. Calif. 1951), aff'd, 208 F. 2d 142 (9th Cir. 1953).
3. State v. Becker, 364 Mo. 1079, 272 S.W. 2d 283 (1954).
4. Hadley v. State, 205 Ark. 1027, 172 S.W. 2d 237 (1943).
5. King v. Commonwealth, 313 Ky. 741, 233 S.W. 2d 522 (1950).
6. See Commonwealth v. Donaducy, 167 Pa. Super. 611, 76 A. 2d 440 (1950). See also Burstein v. United States, 178 F. 2d 665 (9th Cir. 1949).
7. 352 U.S. 380 (1957).
8. For the background of the Detroit situation see MURPHY, CENSORSHIP: GOVERNMENT AND OBSCENITY 53 (1963); Lockhart and McClure, *The Law of Obscenity*, 38 MINN. L. REV. 295, 306, 314 (1954).
9. May 5, 1955, p. 16. col. 1.
10. 187 F. Supp. 241 (E.D. La. 1960).
11. Lockhart and McClure, *Censorship of Obscenity: The Developing Constitutional Standards*, 45 MINN. L. REV. 5, 19 (1960). This article contains a superb analysis of the 1957 to 1960 period.
12. 62 Stat. 768 (1948), 18 U.S.C. Sec. 1461 provides that any one who deposits (knowingly) in the mails non-mailable material shall be fined (up to $5,000) or imprisoned (up to five years) or both.
13. United States v. Roth, 237 F. 2d 796 (2d Cir. 1956).
14. Roth v. United States, 354 U.S. 476 (1957).
15. 354 U.S. 436 (1957).
16. Adams Newark Theater Co. v. Newark, 354 U.S. 931 (1957).
17. Times Film Corp. v. Chicago, 244 F. 2d 432 (7th Cir. 1957).
18. 355 U.S. 35 (1958).
19. Mounce v. United States, 355 U.S. 180, rev'g 247 F. 2d 148 (9th Cir. 1957).
20. 355 U.S. 371 (1958).
21. 355 U.S. 372 (1958), rev'g 249 F. 2d 114 (D.C. Cir. 1957).
22. Ibid.
23. Kingsley Int'l Pictures Corp. v. Regents, 360 U.S. 684 (1959). See Kalven, *The Metaphysics of the Law of Obscenity*, THE SUPREME COURT REVIEW 1 (1960).
24. 4 App. Div. 2d 348, 165 N.Y. 2d 681 (1957).
25. 361 U.S. 147 (1959).

26. For comments see Breig, *The Court and Smith,* 86 CATH. U. BULL., Jan. 15, 1960, pp. 2 and 4.
27. Grove Press, Inc. v. Christenberry, 175 F. Supp. 488 (S.D.N.Y. 1959).
28. 276 F. 2d 433 (2d Cir. 1960).
29. 370 U.S. 478 (1962).
30. Jacobellis v. Ohio, 378 U.S. 184 (1964).
31. 84 Sup. Ct. 1909 (1964), *rev'g* 156 So. 2d 537 (Fla. App. 1963).
32. 84 Sup. Ct. 1903 (1964), *rev'g,* 151 So. 2d 19 (Fla. App. 1963).

PART IV

1. People v. Bruce, 202 N.E. 2d 497 (Ill. Sup. Ct. Nov. 24, 1964).
2. 84 Sup. Ct. 1676 (1964)
3. Bromberg, *Five Tests for Obscenity,* 41 CHI. B. RECORD 416, 418 (1960).
4. LAWRENCE, PORNOGRAPHY AND OBSCENITY (1953) 74.
5. MEAD, SEX AND CENSORSHIP IN CONTEMPORARY SOCIETY, NEW WORLD WRITINGS 7 (Third Mentor Selection 1953).
6. Kaplan, *Obscenity as an Esthetic Category,* 20 LAW & CONTEMP. PROB. 544, 548 (1955).
7. KARPMAN, THE SEXUAL OFFENDER 360 (1954).
8. Some other suggested references: Cairns, *Freedom of Expression in Literature,* 200 ANNALS 76-85 (1938); Abse, *Psychodynamic Aspects of the Problem of Definition of Obscenity,* 20 LAW & CONTEMP. PROB. 572 (1955) ; Eliasberg, *Art: Immoral or Immortal,* 45 J. CRIM. L. 274 (1954).
9. 156 F. Supp. 350 (S.D.N.Y. 1957). See Note, 34 Ind. L. J. 426 (1959).
10. Roth v. United States, 354 U.S. 476 (1957).
11. Published in 1960. An excellent analysis. See also ROGGE, THE FIRST AND THE FIFTH (1960), p. 106. One of the most recent protagonists of the nonobscenity doctrine is Reverend Howard Moody, Minister of the Judson Memorial Church of New York. Reverend Moody writes in CHRISTIANITY IN CRISIS (Jan. 25, 1965) that obscenity consists of that which degrades or dehumanizes. He says the normal sexual words are not obscene but the word "nigger" uttered by a bigot is one of the dirtiest words in the English language.
12. Gitlow v. New York, 268 U.S. 652 (1925).

13. Smith v. California, 361 U.S. 147 (1959).

14. Duncan v. United States, 48 F. 2d 128 (9th Cir. 1931); Commonwealth v. Lewis, 30 D. & C. 2d 133 (Q.S. Ct. Pa. 1962).

15. Commonwealth v. Gordon, 66 Pa. D. & C. 101 (Q.S. Ct. Phila. 1949).

16. Roth v. United States, 354 U.S. 476 (1957).

17. See in detail, Gerber, *A Suggested Solution for the Riddle of Obscenity*, 112 U. OF PA. L. REV. 834 (1964).

18. See People v. Williamson. 24 Cal. Rptr. 734 (Dist. Ct. App. 1962).

19. People v. Richmond County News, 9 N. Y. 2d 578, 175 N.E. 2d 681, 216 N.Y.S. 2d 369 (1961).

20. Commonwealth v. Friede, 271 Mass. 318, 171 N.E. 472 (1930).

21. Arthur Garfield Hayes.

22. People v. Finkelstein, 229 N.Y.S. 2d 367, 11 N.Y. 2d 300, 183 N.E. 2d 611, *cert. denied*, 371 U.S. 863 (1962).

23. In re Harris, 56 Cal. 2d 879, 16 Cal. Reps. 889, 366 P. 2d 305 (1961).

24. In re Louisiana News Co., 187 F. Supp. 241 (E.D. La. 1960).

25. The best summary of material to date appears in Cairns, Paul, and Wishner, *Sex Censorship: The Assumptions of Anti-Obscenity Laws and the Empirical Evidence*, 46 MINN. L. REV. 1009 (1962). This is an analysis by a law professor and two psychologists.

26. Haines, *Juvenile Delinquency*, 1 J. SOCIAL THERAPY (1955).

27. Ramsey, *The Sexual Development of Boys*, 56 AMER. J. PSYCHOLOGY 217 (1943).

28. This material taken from KINSEY, POMEROY, AND MARTIN, SEXUAL BEHAVIOR IN THE HUMAN MALE (1948).

29. Van Bracken and Schafers, *Ueber die Haltung von Strafgefangenen zur Literature*, 49 ZEITSCHRIFT FUR ANGEWANDTE PSYCHOLOGIE 169 (1935).

30. United States v. Roth, 237 F. 2d 796 (2d Cir. 1956).

31. Brief of United States in Roth v. United States, pp. 59 to 65.

32. For censorship and limitation see Schmidt, *A Justification of Statutes Barring Pornography From the Mails*, 26 FORDHAM L. REV. 70 (1957); Elias, *Obscenity: the Law, a Dissenting Voice*, 51 KY. L. J. 610 (1963); Hayes (in the periodical erroneously listed as Levy), *A Position on the Control of Obscenity*, 51 KY. L. J. 641 (1963). Against, see Gordias, *More Heat Than Light* in TO CORRUPT AND DEPRAVE, 125 (Chandoz ed. 1962); Hyman, *In Defence of Pornography*, NEW LEADER, Sept. 2, 1963.

33. Henkin, *Morals and the Constitution,* 63 COL. L. REV. 391 (1963).

34. An interesting parallel is found in the Wolfenden Report—a special study made in England by a blue-ribbon committee. An American edition entitled *The Wolfenden Report* was published by Lancer Books, 1964.

PART V

1. People v. Bruce, Ill. Sup. Ct., June 18, 1964 (opinion vacated).
2. People v. Bruce, 202 N.E. 2d 497 (Ill. Sup. Ct. Nov. 24, 1964).
3. Fanfare Films v. Motion Picture Censor Board, 234 Md. 10, 197 A. 2d 839 (1964). For earlier decisions see Excelsior Pictures Corp. v. Chicago, 182 F. Supp. 400 (N.D. Ill. 1960); Commonwealth v. Moniz, 338 Mass. 442, 155 N.E. 2d 762 (1959). Compare the American Law Institute's Model Penal Code Sec. 207.10, comment 8 (Tent. Draft. No. 6, 1957).
4. 236 U.S. 230 (1915).
5. Gitlow v. New York, 268 U.S. 652 (1925).
6. 334 U.S. 131 (1948).
7. 343 U.S. 495 (1952).
8. Gelling v. Texas, 343 U.S. 960 (1952).
9. Joseph Burstyn, *supra.*
10. Superior Films v. Dep't of Education, 346 U.S. 587 (1954).
11. Commercial Pictures Corp. v. Regents, 346 U.S. 587 (1954).
12. Holmby Products v. Vaughn, 350 U.S. 870 (1955).
13. 365 U.S. 43 (1961).
14. Freedman v. Maryland, 13 L. Ed. 649 (1965).
15. Two states have declared their censorship boards illegal. R.K.O. Radio Pictures v. Dep't of Education, 162 Ohio St. 263, 122 N.E. 2d 769 (1954) and Wm. Goldman Theatres v. Dana, 405 Pa. 83, 173 A. 2d 59 (1961). At present on a statewide basis there are prior censorship boards only in Kansas, Maryland, New York, and Virginia, although a number of cities still maintain such boards. Probably the most active is the Chicago Board. See Chi. Mun. Code, ch. 155.
16. Kingsley Int'l Pictures Corp, v. Regents, 360 U.S. 684 (1959).
17. Jacobellis v. Ohio, 84 Sup. Ct. 1676 (1964).
18. See *The Constitutionality of Government Film Censorship by Age Classification* (1959) 69 YALE L.J. 141.

19. Md. Ann. Code Art. 27, Sec. 418A (Supp. 1959).

20. 172 F. Supp. 69 (N.D. Ill. 1959).

21. 321 U.S. 158 (1944).

22. GETTING IDEAS FROM MOVIES (1937) 7-11.

23. RENSHAW, MILLER, AND MARQUIS, CHILDREN'S SLEEP (1938) 17-24.

24. BLUMER, MOVIES AND CONDUCT (1933) 75, 83.

25. 316 F. 2d 813 (2d Cir.), cert. denied, 375 U.S. 916 (1963). See *Recent Developments* (1964) 16 STANFORD L. REV. 463.

26. 18 U.S.C. Sec. 1461 (1958). The first federal law dates back to 1865. The statute was amended from time to time and included "letters" specifically in 1888. In 1955 the present wording was adopted. The word "letter" was omitted but the law was interpreted to include *all* "obscene" *matter*. See Thomas v. United States, 262 F. 2d 844 (6th Cir. 1959).

27. For example, United States v. Limehouse, 285 U.S. 424 (1932); Dysart v. United States, 272 U.S. 655 (1926); Verner v. United States, 183 F. 2d 184 (9th Cir. 1950).

28. 16 STANFORD L. REV. 463 (1964).

29. 372 U.S. 58 (1963).

30. Magtab Publishing Corp. v. Howard, 169 F. Supp. 65 (W.D. La. 1959); HMH Publishing Co. v. Garrett, 151 F. Supp. 903 (N.D. Ind. 1957); New American Library v. Allen, 114 F. Supp. 823 (N.D. Ohio 1953); Bantam Books, Inc. v. Melko, 25 N. J. Super. 292, 96 A. 2d 47 (Ch. 1953), *modified on appeal in* 14 N. J. 524, 103 A. 2d 256 (1954).

31. In the movie field, see Joseph Burstyn, Inc. v. McCaffrey, 198 Misc. 884, 101 N.Y.S. 2d 892 (Sup. Ct. 1951); Hygienic Prods., Inc. v. Keenan, 1 N. J. Super. 461, 62 A. 2d 150 (Ch. 1948).

32. 267 Fed. 390 (8th Cir. 1926).

33. Paramount Pictures v. United Motion Picture Theatre Owners, 93 F. 2nd 714 (3rd Cir. 1937) (theatre owners tried to boycott Paramount movies); People v. Masiello, 177 Misc. 608, 31 N.Y.S. 2nd 512 (Sup. Ct. 1941), *aff'd*, 271 App. Div. 875, 66 N.Y.S. 2nd 641 (1st Dep't 1946) (newspaper sellers' union tried to boycott several newspapers).

34. Fehr Baking Co. v. Bakers Union, 20 F. Supp. 691 (W.D. La. 1937).

35. *Legal Responsibility for Extra-Legal Censure* (1962) 62 COL. L. REV. 475.

36. American Mercury v. Chase, 13 F. 2nd 224 (D. Mass. 1926).

37. 372 U.S. 58 (1963).

38. Kuryer Publishing Co. v. Messmer, 162 Wis. 565, 156 N.W. 948 (1916).

39. Watch Tower Bible and Tract Soc'y v. Dougherty, 337 Pa. 286, 11 A. 2nd 147 (1940).

40. Beck Shoe Corp. v. Johnson, 153 Misc. 363, 274 N. Y. Supp. 946 (Sup. Ct. 1934) ; Green v. Samuelson, 168 Md. 421, 178 Atl. 109 (1935).

41. Levine v. Dempsey, 45 N.Y.L.J. 14 (Sup. Ct. 1961). See also Legion Salesmen's Union v. Metropolitan Package Store, 143 N.Y.L.J. 13 (Sup. Ct. 1960) (prohibits proprietors from discriminating against plaintiffs because of race or color).

42. United News Company v. Wright, C.A. No. 41-64 (D.N.J. 1964).

43. See Note (1962) 62 Col. L. Rev. 475, 494.

44. Marcus v. Search Warrant, 367 U.S. 717 (1961).

45. Bantam Books, Inc., v. Sullivan, 372 U.S. 58 (1963).

46. A Quantity of Copies of Books v. Kansas, 84 Sup. Ct. 1723 (1964).

PART VI

1. *Report of Select Committee on Pornographic Materials,* H. R. Rep. No. 2510, 82nd Cong., 2d Sess. (1952).

2. *Obscenity and Constitutional Freedom—Part I,* 8 St. Louis Univ. L. J. 279, 331, n. 189.

3. This is the book selected for example above.

4. United States v. Reese, 92 U.S. 214, 220 (1875).

5. Commonwealth v. John Hastings and Samuel Sokolove, Q. Sess. Ct., Nov. Term, 1964, Nos. 1583 and 1584.

6. Sunshine Book Co. v. Summerfield, 355 U.S. 372 (1958).

7. United States v. Oakley, 290 F. 2d 517 (6th Cir. 1960), *cert. denied,* 368 U.S. 888 (1961).

8. Dale Book Co. v. Leary, C.A. No. 34466 (E.D. Pa., Aug. 12, 1964).

9. Nebraska v. Jungclaus, 126 N.W. 2d 858 (Sup. Ct. 1964).

10. See note *8 supra.* The judge limits his opinion somewhat by an indication that an isolated nudist magazine may not be obscene but

BIBLIOGRAPHY

Abse, *Psychodynamic Aspects of the Problem of Definition of Obscenity,* 20 LAW & CONTEMP. PROB. 572 (1955).

Alfange, *The Balancing of Interests in Free Speech Cases,* 2 LAW IN TRANS. 35 (1965).

Alpert, *Judicial Censorship of Obscene Literature,* 52 HARV. L. REV. 40 (1938).

American Law Institute, MODEL PENAL CODE, Proposed Official Draft (May 4, 1962) Sec. 251.4 (1) and Tentative Draft No. 6 (May 6, 1957).

AMERICAN LIBRARY ASS'N, THE FIRST FREEDOM (Downs ed. 1960).

ATKINSON, OBSCENE LITERATURE IN LAW AND PRACTICE (1937).

Black, *The Bill of Rights,* 35 N.Y.U. L. REV. 865 (1960).

BLEAKLY, LIFE OF JOHN WILKES (1917).

BLUMER, MOVIES AND CONDUCT (1933).

Bourke, *Moral Problems Related to Censoring the Media of Mass Communications,* 40 MARQ. L. REV. 57 (1956).

Breig, *The Court and Smith,* 86 CATH. U. BULL. Jan. 15, 1960.

Bromberg, *Five Tests for Obscenity,* 41 CHI. B. RECORD 416.

BROUN & LEECH, ANTHONY COMSTOCK: ROUNDSMAN OF THE LORD (1927).

Cairns, *Freedom of Expression in Literature,* 200 ANNALS 76 (1938).

Cairns, Paul, & Wishner, *Sex Censorship: The Assumptions of Anti-Obscenity Laws and the Empirical Evidence,* 46 MINN. L. REV. 1009 (1962).

CHAFEE, GOVERNMENT AND MASS COMMUNICATIONS (1947).

Clift, *Enduring Rights,* 28 WILSON LIBRARY BULL. 853 (1954).

COLEMAN, OBSCENITY, BLASPHEMY, SEDITION (Brisbane, The Jacaronda Press).

Constitutionality of Government Film Censorship by Age Classification (1959) 69 YALE L. J. 141.

333

CRAIG, SUPPRESSED BOOKS (1963).

DENNETT, WHO'S OBSCENE (1930).

DOUGLAS, THE RIGHT OF THE PEOPLE (1958).

EHRLICH, HOWL OF THE CENSOR (1961).

Elias, *Obscenity: the Law, a Dissenting Voice,* 51 KY. L. J. 610 (1963).

Eliasberg, *Art: Immoral or Immortal,* 45 J. CRIM. L. 274 (1954).

ERNST & SCHWARTZ, CENSORSHIP: THE SEARCH FOR THE OBSCENE (1964).

ERNST & SEAGLE, TO THE PURE . . . (1928).

Fischer, *The Harm Good People Do,* HARPER'S, Oct., 1956, p. 14.

Fleishman, *Obscenity: The Exquisitely Vague Crime,* 2 LAW IN TRANS. 97 (1965).

GARDINER, CATHOLIC VIEWPOINT ON CENSORSHIP (1961).

GEBHARD, GAGNON, POMEROY AND CHRISTENSON, SEX OFFENDERS (1965).

GELLHORN, INDIVIDUAL FREEDOM AND GOVERNMENTAL RESTRAINTS (1956).

Gerber, *A Suggested Solution for the Riddle of Obscenity,* 112 U. OF PA. L. REV. 834 (1964).

Gertz, *The Illinois Battle over "Tropic of Cancer,"* 46 CHICAGO BAR RECORD 161 (Jan. 1965).

Gillotti, *Book Censorship in Massachusetts,* 42 BOSTON LAW. REV. 476.

Gordias, *More Heat Than Light,* in TO CORRUPT AND DEPRAVE, 125 (Chandoz ed. 1962).

Grant & Angoff, *Massachusetts and Censorship* (1930) 10 B.U.L. REV. 36, 147. 173-76.

HAIGHT, BANNED BOOKS (1955).

146 HANSARD, PARLIAMENTARY DEBATES (1857).

Haines, *Juvenile Delinquency,* 1 J. SOCIAL THERAPY (1955).

HALLLIS, THE LAW AND OBSCENITY (1932).

Hayes, *A Position on the Control of Obscenity,* 51 KY. L.J. 641 (1963) (Hayes is erroneously listed as "Levy").

Hearings on Obscene Matter Sent Through the Mail Before the Subcommittee on Postal Operations of the House Committee on Post Office and Civil Service, 87th Cong., 1st Sess. *(passim)* (1962).

Henkin, *Morals and the Constitution,* 63 COL. L. REV. 391 (1963).

Hofstadter & Levittan, *"No Glory, No Beauty, No Stars—Just Mud,"* 37 N.Y. St. B.J. 38, 116 (1965).

Hook, *Pornography and the Censor,* New York Times Book Review, April 12, 1964.

HUXLEY, VULGARITY IN LITERATURE (1930).

Hyman, *In Defence of Pornography,* NEW LEADER, Sept. 2, 1963.

IVERSEN, THE PIOUS PORNOGRAPHERS (1964).

JACKSON, THE FEAR OF BOOKS (1932).

Kalven, *The Metaphysics of the Law of Obscenity,* THE SUPREME COURT REVIEW 1 (1960).

Kalven, *The New York Times Case,* SUPREME COURT REVIEW 191 (1964).

Kaplan, *Obscenity as an Esthetic Category,* 20 LAW & CONTEMP. PROB. 544 (1955).

KARPMAN, THE SEXUAL OFFENDER (1954).

KAUPER, CIVIL LIBERTIES AND THE CONSTITUTION III (1962).

KILPATRICK, THE SMUT PEDDLERS (1960).

KINSEY, POMEROY, & MARTIN, SEXUAL BEHAVIOR IN THE HUMAN MALE (1948).

KRONHAUSEN, PORNOGRAPHY AND THE LAW (1959).

Larrabee, *The Cultural Context of Sex Censorship,* 20 LAW & CONTEMP. PROB. 672 (1955).

LAWRENCE, PORNOGRAPHY AND OBSCENITY (1953).

Legal Responsibility for Extra-Legal Censure (1962), 62 COL. L. REV. 475.

LEVY, LEGACY OF SUPPRESSION, (1960).

Lockhart & McClure, *Censorship of Obscenity: The Developing Constitutional Standards,* 45 MINN. L. REV. 5 (1960).

Lockhart & McClure, *Literature, the Law of Obscenity, and the Constitution,* 38 MINN. L. Rev. 295 (1954).

Lockhart & McClure, *Obscenity Censorship: The Constitutional Issue, What is Obscene,* 7 UTAH L. REV. 289.

McAnany, *Motion Picture Censorship and Constitutional Freedom,* 50 KY. L. J. 427 (1962).

McKEON, MERTON & GELLHORN, THE FREEDOM TO READ (1957).

MAKRIS, THE SILENT INVESTIGATORS (1959).

Mead, *Sex and Censorship in Contemporary Society,* NEW WORLD WRITINGS 7 (Third Mentor Selection 1953).

Meiklejohn, *The First Amendment Is an Absolute,* 1961 SUPREME COURT REVIEW 245.

MOODY, REV. HOWARD, CHRISTIANITY IN CRISIS (Jan. 25, 1965).

Mulroy, *Obscenity, Pornography and Censorship,* 49 A.B.A.J. 869 (1963).

MURPHY, CENSORSHIP: GOVERNMENT AND OBSCENITY (1963).

Murray, *The Bad Arguments Intelligent Men Make,* AMERICA, Nov. 3, 1956, p. 120.

Note, For Adults Only: The Constitutionality of Governmental Film Censorship by Age Classification, 69 YALE L. J. 141 (1959).

PAUL & SCHWARTZ, FEDERAL CENSORSHIP (1961).

Paul, *The Post Office and Non-Mailability of Obscenity: An Historical Note,* 8 U.C.L.A. L. REV. 44 (1961).

POSTGATE, THAT DEVIL WILKES (1956).

Ramsey, *The Sexual Development of Boys,* 56 AMER. J. PSYCHOLOGY 217 (1943).

Recent Developments (1964) 16 STANFORD L. REV. 463.

RENSHAW, MILLER & MARQUIS, CHILDREN'S SLEEP (1938).

Report of Select Committee on Pornographic Materials, H. R. Rep. No. 2510, 82nd Congress, 2d Sess. (1952).

ROGGE, THE FIRST AND THE FIFTH (1960).

Rorty, *Harassed Pocket-Book Publishers,* 15 ANTIOCH REV. 411 (1956).

Schmidt, *A Justification of Statutes Barring Pornography From the Mails,* 26 FORDHAM L. REV. 70 (1957).

Schwartz, *Criminal Obscenity Law: Portents from Recent Supreme Court Decisions and Proposals of the American Law Institute in the Model Penal Code,* 29 PA. BAR ASS'N. Q. 8 (Oct. 1957).

Schwartz, *Moral Offenses and The Model Penal Code,* 63 COLUM. L. REV. 669 (1963).

Schwartz, *Obscenity in the Mails: A Comment on Some Problems of Federal Censorship,* 106 U. OF PA. L. REV. 214 (1957).

SCOTT, INTO WHOSE HANDS (1961).

Slough & McAnany, *Obscenity and Constitutional Freedom I,* 8 ST. LOUIS L. REV. 279 and 449 (1964).

ST. JOHN-STEVAS, OBSCENITY AND THE LAW (1956).

TO CORRUPT AND DEPRAVE (Chandoz ed. 1962).

Tokikumi, *Obscenity and the Japanese Constitution,* 51 KY. L. J. 703 (1963).

TRUMBULL, ANTHONY COMSTOCK, FIGHTER (1913).

WOLFENDEN REPORT (The) (Lancer Books) (1964).

TABLE OF CASES

ADDITIONAL CASES

(Cases of interest not discussed in the text)

Alexander v. United States, 271 F. 2d 140 (8th Cir. 1959) (judicial control).

Bunis v. Conway, 17 App. Div. 2d 207, 234 N.Y.S. 2d 435 (1962) (threats of prosecution).

Capitol Enterprises, Inc. v. City of Chicago, 260 F. 2d 670 (7th Cir. 1958) (motion picture *Mom and Dad*) (court or jury).

City of Aurora v. Warner Bros. Pictures Dist. Corp., 16 Ill. App. 273, 147 N.E. 2d 694 (1958) (motion picture *Baby Doll* prima facie obscene).

City of Cincinnati v. Walton, 145 N.E. 2d 407 (Cincinnati Munic. Ct. 1957) (nudist and girlie magazines, sado-masochistic publications, and enormous cundrum marked "For the self-made man"; only two stories in Dude magazine and the sado-masochistic publications ruled obscene).

Commonwealth v. Blumenstein, 396 Pa. 417, 153 A. 2d 227 (1959) (movie censorship).

Commonwealth v. Havens, 6 Pa. County Ct. 545 (Allegheny County 1889) (*National Police Gazette*).

Commonwealth v. Isenstadt, 318 Mass. 543, 62 N.E. 2d 840 (1945) (Smith, *Strange Fruit*).

Dreiser v. John Lane Co., 183 App. Div. 773 (1918) (Dreiser, *Sister Carrie* in a civil suit).

Excelsior Pictures Corp. v. Regents of the Univ. of N.Y., 3 N.Y. 2d 237, 144 N.E. 2d, 31 (1957) (nude movies)

Flying Eagle Publications, Inc. v. United States, 273 F. 2d 799 (1st Cir. 1960) (short stories in magazine *Manhunt*)

Glanzman v. Christenberry, 175 F. Supp. 485 (S.D.N.Y. 1958) (photographs of nude and semi-nude women)

Grimm v. United States, 156 U.S. 604 (1895) (letter).

Hadley v. State, 205 Ark. 1027, 172 S.W. 2d 237 (1943) (nudist publication).

In re Harris, 56 Cal. 2d 879, 366 P. 2d 305 (1961) (other matter found not obscene, admitted).

Kingsley Int'l Pictures Corp. v. Blanc, 396 Pa. 448, 153 A. 2d 243 (1959) (impounding a film).

Klaw v. Schaffer, 151 F. Supp. 534 (S.D.N.Y. 1957), aff'd 251 F. 2d 615 (2d Cir. 1958) (bondage photographs).

Parmalee v. United States, 113 F. 2d 729 (D.C. Cir. 1940) (nudes).

People v. Brooklyn News Co., 12 Misc. 2d 768, 174 N.Y.S. 2d 813 (Kings County Ct. 1958) (Gent Magazine).

People v. Friede, 135 Misc. 611, 233 N.Y. Supp. 565 (1929) (Hall, *Well of Lonliness*).

People v. Schenkman, 20 Misc. 2d 1093, 195 N.Y.S. 2d 570 (Ct. Spec. Sess. 1960) (scienter).

People v. Silberglitt, 15 Misc. 2d 847, 182 N.Y.S. 2d 536 (Sup. Ct. 1958) (art model magazines).

People v. Wepplo, 78 Cal. App. 2d 959, 178 F. 2d 853 (1947) (Wilson, *Memoirs of Hecate County*).

State v. Clein, 93 So. 2d 876 (Fla. 1957) (court or jury).

State v. Hudson County News, 78 N.J. Super. 327, 188 A. 2d 444 (1963) (magazines with nudes, sadism and masochism).

State v. Miller, 112 S.E. 2d 472 (W. Va. 1960) (scienter).

Swearingen v. United States, 161 U.S. 446 (1896) (profanity).

Sunshine Book Co. v. McCaffrey, 8 Misc. 2d 327, 112 N.Y.S. 2d 476 (Sup. Ct. N.Y. County 1952) (nudist publication).

United States v. Chesman, 19 Fed. 497 (C.C.E.D. Mo. 1887) (medical tract).

United States v. 4200 Copies International Journal, 134 F. Supp. 490 (E.D.N.D. 1955) (nudist publication).

United States v. Keller, 259 F. 2d 54 (3d Cir. 1958) (personal post cards) (judicial review).

United States v. Levine, 83 F. 2d 156 (2d Cir. 1936) (*Secret Museum of Anthropology, Crossways of Sex, Black Lust*).

United States v. Peisner, 311 F. 2d 94 (4th Cir. 1962) (search and seizure case).

Womack v. United States, 294 F. 2d 204 (D.C. Cir) (1961), cert. denied, 365 U.S. 859 (1962) (comparison evidence rejected).

Yudkin v. State, 229 Md. 223, 182 A. 2d 798 (1962) (Miller, *Tropic of Cancer*).

Zenith Int'l Film Corp. v. City of Chicago, 183 F. Supp. 623 (N.D. Ill. 1960) (motion picture, *The Lovers*).

INDEX

345